"In a book as wise and refreshing as it ... ... vith the certain demise of Churches of Christ as we kⁿ... .ting account, Reese shows that the very virtues that shaped Churches of C... .night give them life again if they have the courage to claim them."

— **Richard T. Hughes, PhD**
author of *Myths America Lives By:*
White Supremacy and the Stories That Give Us Meaning

"Some White ministers speak about the Black experience from a distance. Jack Reese has lived it—in the neighborhoods of South Dallas and within the church I lead. *At the Blue Hole* is a witness to that experience. In this moving, personal account, Jack expresses the struggle of all Christians to tell the truth about themselves, to see the pain of others, and to both receive and extend God's extravagant outpouring of grace."

— **Dr. Kenneth R. Greene**
senior pastor at Metro Christ's Church, Dallas, Texas

"Jack Reese draws readers into this compelling narrative like a good mystery. Only in this case the story moves relentlessly toward the sources of new life—to the wellsprings that originally quickened Churches of Christ. In these recent years of accelerating decline, this journey is especially urgent."

— **C. Leonard Allen, PhD**
dean of the College of Bible and Ministry, Lipscomb University
author of *Distant Voices: Discovering a Forgotten Past for a Changing Church*

"Jack Reese weaves a series of engaging tales to identify resources in the Stone-Campbell story for the rebirth of dying congregations. Anyone who cares about the future of any of these churches would do well to read this book."

— **D. Newell Williams, PhD**
president of Brite Divinity School
author of *Barton Stone: A Spiritual Autobiography*

"At a time when the tectonic plates are shifting beneath us as a church and as a culture, Reese's diagnosis and prescriptions are spot on. The timing is critical.

Jack is right. We are standing at a crossroads. Decisions churches make now will profoundly shape their future."

— **Monte Cox, PhD**
dean at Harding University's College of Bible and Ministry

"By skillful narrative filled with theological insight, *At the Blue Hole* looks to possibilities that believers from all backgrounds would do well to consider. A masterful piece of work!"

— **Rubel Shelly, PhD**
professor of philosophy and ethics at Lipscomb University and
bioethics at VanderBilt University
author of *I Knew Jesus Before He Was a Christian . . .
And I Liked Him Better Then*

"In this eloquent account, Jack Reese weaves a tapestry of inspiring and frustrating characters, showing how Churches of Christ have been formed and how they might be formed now. Readers from all streams of the faith will find in this beautifully crafted narrative a stirring call to faithfulness."

— **Douglas A. Foster, PhD**
author of *A Life of Alexander Campbell*

"Jack Reese uses vivid historical narrative and spiritual and theological reflection to create a unique and innovative story. As an outsider to the Stone-Campbell tradition who has walked with different strains of that heritage, I believe *At the Blue Hole* will be of great interest to a wide readership and to scholars."

— **Patrick R. Keifert, PhD**
founder and president of Church Innovations
author of *We Are Here Now: A New Missional Era*

"*At the Blue Hole* will orient the reader in the valuable lessons of the history of Churches of Christ. More importantly, it will help all of us to see our present bearings in a clearer way and enable us to chart a solid future for the church."

— **Royce L. Money, PhD**
chancellor of Abilene Christian University

"With masterful storytelling that uniquely weaves past and present, Jack Reese implores all churches to explore the rich resources of their heritage, not just for inspiration but in the forming of their very identity. A treasure trove of resources."

— James Gorman, PhD
professor of history at Johnson University
author of *Among the Early Evangelicals:
The Transatlantic Origins of the Stone-Campbell Movement*

"For decades I wished there was a resource I could give church leaders so they could know the grit and glory of how Churches of Christ came to be. I wanted a word about the past that could shape a preferred future. Jack Reese's *At the Blue Hole* is the work I needed. If you want your church to blossom in our changing world, this is the book you and your church need."

— Sean Palmer
teaching pastor at Ecclesia Houston
author of *Unarmed Empire: In Search of Beloved Community*

"Writing as both minister and scholar, Jack Reese has given us an engaging and thoughtful book. Easy to read and hard to put down, this book will richly reward any reader interested in the impact of history upon current church life and practice."

— Rick R. Marrs, PhD
provost and professor of religion at Pepperdine University

"With impeccable scholarship and vivid storytelling, this book is a kind of wistful love song to a heritage that the author plainly loves and a call to a future fashioned by our better angels."

— Randy Harris
spiritual director at the Siburt Institute for Church Ministry,
Abilene Christian University
author of *Life Work: Confessions of an Everyday Disciple*

"With striking discernment, Jack Reese offers a guide to both the setbacks and the successes of Churches of Christ. But there is much hope here. With great insight and extraordinary creativity, Reese reveals surprising resources and gives practical advice for the future. I was glued to every page."

— Thomas H. Olbricht, PhD
author of *Staying the Course: Fifteen Leaders Survey Their Past and Envision the Future of Churches of Christ*

"With his gift for creative storytelling, Jack leads us on an enlightening journey through the past history of Churches of Christ. On this road, he discovers life-giving sources of renewal and hope for the future."

— Jerry Rushford, PhD
director of the Churches of Christ Heritage Center at Pepperdine University

"With the voice of a prophet, the mind of a historian, and the heart of a pastor, Jack Reese leads readers on a compelling journey, calling the church to face its death and seize its future. For those looking for a theologically grounded yet practical proposal to address the current brokenness in churches, this is the book to read."

— Ken Cukrowski, PhD
dean at Abilene Christian University's College of Biblical Studies and Graduate School of Theology

"Jack Reese's vivid storytelling coupled with candid and, at times, painful critique is refreshing and challenging, a clear and essential call to a forgotten history wherein lie the resources for renewal and a future."

— Grady D. King
president of Hope Network

"Because of Reese's captivating—and at times chilling—storytelling that comes only through compassion and the fire of experience, *At the Blue Hole* is a must-read for all those seeking a hopeful future."

— Charles M. Rix, PhD
dean of humanities and Bible at Oklahoma Christian University

"With the skill of a master storyteller and the bluntness of an Old Testament prophet, Jack Reese walks with members of his own church family to the place where their story began. He shines a light on the daunting challenges facing

Churches of Christ in the twenty-first century and offers a hopeful and redeeming path forward."

"A masterful storyteller, Jack Reese has rendered a great blessing for his fellowship of churches as well as other faith traditions."

"*At the Blue Hole* contains rich stories and anecdotes about Churches of Christ in America. If we are silent about our story, we may well miss some of these incredible riches that could help us step into a future of hope."

"With the touch of an artist, the ear of a poet, the mind of a professor, the heart of a pastor, and the eye of a prophet, Jack Reese provides a hopeful prescription for Churches of Christ. Anyone can benefit from his careful diagnosis and compassionate remedies."

"With a historian's insight and a storyteller's imagination, Jack Reese offers a marvelous invitation to consider the current decline in congregational life and an openness to see God's desired future. Anyone who seeks renewal in Churches of Christ or any church will find resources to fuel the imaginative work needed for new beginnings."

At the
BLUE
HOLE

Elegy for a Church on the Edge

Jack R. Reese

WILLIAM B. EERDMANS PUBLISHING COMPANY
GRAND RAPIDS, MICHIGAN

Wm. B. Eerdmans Publishing Co.
4035 Park East Court SE, Grand Rapids, Michigan 49546
www.eerdmans.com

Published 2021
Printed in the United States of America

27 26 25 24 23 22 21   1 2 3 4 5 6 7

ISBN 978-0-8028-7952-3

Library of Congress Cataloging-in-Publication Data

Names: Reese, Jack Roger, author.
Title: At the blue hole : elegy for a church on the edge / Jack R. Reese.
Description: Grand Rapids, Michigan : Wm. B. Eerdmans Publishing Co., [2021]
    | Includes bibliographical references and index.
Identifiers: LCCN 2021015387 | ISBN 9780802879523
Subjects: LCSH: Churches of Christ—United States—History.
Classification: LCC BX7075 .R44 2021 | DDC 286.6/330973—dc23
LC record available at https://lccn.loc.gov/2021015387

Scripture quotations are taken from the New Revised Standard Version unless
otherwise noted.

To Lynn and Carolyn Anderson—
courageous servants, visionary leaders,
passionate teachers, generous friends,
healers of wounded souls,
proclaimers of good news

Contents

List of Reflections   xii

Foreword by Wesley Granberg-Michaelson   xiii

Key Characters and Events   xvii

Prologue: The Blue Hole   1

1. Peace, Death, Storm, and Fire:
   Churches of Christ on the Edge   4

2. The Peacemaker and the Pallbearer:
   Choices and Consequences   36

3. Pray More, Dispute Less:
   The Road to Christian Unity   70

4. Freedom and Conformity:
   The Quest to Restore the Golden Age   111

5. Resources from the Blue Hole:
   There Is Life beneath Us Still   176

   Epilogue: Cloudburst of Grace   218

   Acknowledgments   223

   Notes   229

   Key Resources   233

   Index   239

Reflections

Culture's Clothing   41

Civil War and Churches of Christ   51

Timshel   61

Takeaways from Chapter 2: Patterns and Meaning   64

What Happened to the Holy Spirit   78

Jubilee   81

Seceder Churches Today   88

The Edge of a Rope   93

Stone's Voice   99

Takeaways from Chapter 3: Unity Matters   104

Being Wrong   121

Truth and Truthiness   130

Persistence   141

From Five Fingers to Five Steps   152

Societies and Organs, Region and Division   159

Takeaways from Chapter 4: True Restoration   170

Foreword

By best estimates, about 350,000 congregations are found in the United States. A majority are not thriving. Some experts say that in the next three decades between 30 percent and 40 percent are likely to close—around 100,000 congregations. The average age of those attending congregations has increased and the average size has decreased, with a majority dipping below one hundred members. These trends now show no theological discrimination: liberal and conservative, evangelical and mainline show similar patterns.

Of course, there are inspiring exceptions, which also frame the story. Multicultural congregations are growing, now comprising about 20 percent of all congregations in the United States. Further, pockets of growth in denominations are often driven today by people of color. Were it not for immigration, for instance, the Catholic Church in the United States would be in freefall. And those Pentecostal denominations showing growth are recipients of increasing participation from non-White members. But overall, a stark reality looms large: American Christianity—and particularly White American Christianity—is in serious, steady decline.

Churches of Christ form part of this portrait of contemporary US congregational life. And truthfully, they are a larger part of the picture than I had previously known. Until I went fly fishing in Yellowstone National Park with Jack Reese, the author of this book, accompanied by others committed to a movement of forming missional churches in today's ecclesial landscape, I didn't know much about Churches of Christ. Yet, as a fellowship of congregations, they comprise the thirteenth largest group in the United States, with about one million members in 12,000 local churches. Their relative isolation, geographically and ecumenically, has kept them off the radar.

Their own researchers, however, project a precipitous decline for this historic fellowship, reduced to as few as 250,000 members and 2,800 congregations in the next thirty years. Like many parts of American Christianity, Churches of Christ are facing a precarious and almost desolate future when the numbers and trends are analyzed with objectivity. What makes the story conveyed in these pages so compelling and valuable for those who may have barely heard of Churches of Christ is its courageous honesty about the plight of the church. Moreover, for any US congregation, these pages contain sources of hope more reliant on unpredictable grace than on faddish techniques bolstered by shallow spiritual pep talks.

Jack Reese understands that the church in the United States is in a life-and-death struggle. That's really what we're facing. Getting this starting point right is essential in any process hoping for transformational change and renewal in congregational life. It is said that history is not simply about *what was*; it is also about *what is*. The historical forces that have shaped the state of US congregations are embedded deeply in their present life. Reese reveals this reality in Churches of Christ and the whole Stone-Campbell Movement. But these lessons apply far beyond this particular story.

At the Blue Hole relates the fascinating stories of the personalities and issues that shaped the tumultuous course of Churches of Christ. But all this is framed, first, by a compelling, generic description of US congregations today, mostly trapped by stagnation and spiritual entropy through their denial of death. Then the concluding section excavates basic lessons and gifts of this ecclesial tribe's story that can offer portals for all congregations seeking God's promised and preferred future.

Reese has the courage to describe reality. "Our churches are dying. This is a hard truth," Jack writes. "That our particular church is dying may not play well in the 'News and Notes' section of this week's church bulletin, but it is true, nonetheless." In my years of work with congregations and my own denomination, I have searched to understand why so many congregations are facing death, either imminently or in a longer, yet fairly certain, horizon. Some reasons, I think, might be these:

> *Demography*. Many congregations are simply aging out. One statistic among many summarizes this. In the United States, 20 percent of the population is between the ages of eighteen and thirty-four. Only one in ten congregations reflects this demographic reality.

"Nones." The fastest-growing religious group in the United States is composed of those who answer "none" when asked to identify their religious affiliation, now about 23 percent of the population, slightly more than evangelicals. Among those under thirty, 35 percent are "nones."

Inward focus. Faced with threats of decline, many congregations become preoccupied with their internal life, struggling to attract more people through the doors in any way possible. A focus on joining God's missional work outside those doors is neglected and often lost, which nearly always leads toward death.

Impotent witness. Culture wars have mobilized a faction of largely White Christians, becoming wedded to idolatrous nationalism, judgmental exclusivism, and implicit cultural superiority. The reputational credibility of American Christianity has suffered enormously, and congregations not taking a clear stand for simple truths are dismissed by the spiritually curious as hypocritical.

Shallow spiritual formation. Our culture's addiction to instant gratification infects congregations, where members seek easy answers and spiritual highs without any depth of faith formation for the long haul. Lacking roots, commitment withers.

Such challenges, and others, go to the core. These harbingers of congregational death are not overcome by better doctrine, or more efficient organization, or crafty strategic planning. They require, first, humility, acknowledging that life-and-death issues are at stake, with no easy answers. But some pathways may open God's possibilities.

For example, the stories and traditions of a congregation, or of a denomination, should be faced with uncompromising honesty. While they contain wounds and mistakes of unfaithfulness, they also hold the resources, insights, and voices that provide seeds of renewal. Further, an honest relinquishment of our prideful confidence to predict and control the future can open space for the discovery of God's unpredictable grace to sustain our way forward.

Then we can embrace a commitment to focus on God's preferred and promised future, making participation in God's ongoing mission essential to our identity, rather than succumbing to anxious efforts riveted on institutional survival. That moves us toward spiritual transformation, which takes root within ourselves and can lead to the discovery of renewal and new life within our congregations and in the wider structures of denominational life that serve them. That is how we can face the threat of death and hold on to promises of new life. That is how we can turn, step by step, through metanoia—repentance—which changes our direction, and rediscover the living streams of God's grace, flowing into our future.

In this artful and honest story of his own tribe, Churches of Christ, Jack Reese offers wisdom for all congregations and wider fellowships living within present American society. The pathways for us all may not hold the certainties we crave, but they are marked by the sustaining grace we need. The stories on these pages are a gift to illumine our journey.

Wesley Granberg-Michaelson

Key Characters and Events

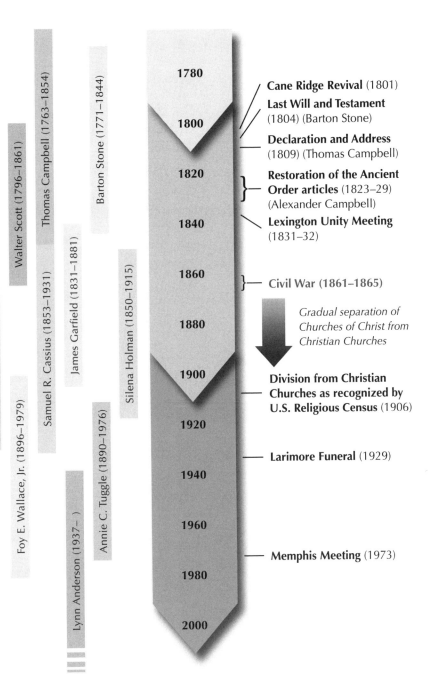

Alexander Campbell (1788–1866)

T. B. Larimore (1843–1929)

Walter Scott (1796–1861)

Foy E. Wallace, Jr. (1896–1979)

Thomas Campbell (1763–1854)

Samuel R. Cassius (1853–1931)

James Garfield (1831–1881)

Lynn Anderson (1937–)

Annie C. Tuggle (1890–1976)

Barton Stone (1771–1844)

Silena Holman (1850–1915)

1780

1800

1820

1840

1860

1880

1900

1920

1940

1960

1980

2000

Cane Ridge Revival (1801)

Last Will and Testament (1804) (Barton Stone)

Declaration and Address (1809) (Thomas Campbell)

Restoration of the Ancient Order articles (1823–29) (Alexander Campbell)

Lexington Unity Meeting (1831–32)

Civil War (1861–1865)

Gradual separation of Churches of Christ from Christian Churches

Division from Christian Churches as recognized by U.S. Religious Census (1906)

Larimore Funeral (1929)

Memphis Meeting (1973)

The Blue Hole

Just north of downtown San Antonio, about a twenty-minute drive from my home, under a thick canopy of vines and trees, lies a spring of cold, clear water, framed by a circular wall of stones in what looks almost like a wishing well plucked from a storybook.

The rock walls surrounding the spring form a structure about the size and shape of a backyard hot tub. A small stream flows out one side, spilling through a chute beneath the stone wall.

Joined by the waters from nearby Olmos Creek and other springs in the area, the little brook quickly grows in width and volume, wending its way beneath a charming wood-and-steel footbridge, past the old Pearl Brewery where restaurants and stores now flourish, past archways and artwork, museums, concert halls, amphitheaters, and gardens, gliding quietly among five old Spanish missions— including Misión San Antonio de Valero, which for more than three hundred years has been referred to as the Alamo, the Spanish word for the cottonwood trees that used to grow nearby.

As it passes downtown, the river threads through city parks and neighborhoods and into the South Texas countryside, ambling for 240 miles before merging with the Guadalupe River and emptying into the Gulf of Mexico.

Locally, the spring is known as the Blue Hole. It is the soul of the city, the beginning of the river, the reason the Spanish priests three centuries ago chose to build a mission and a settlement downstream, out of which the city would arise.

In truth, the Blue Hole had brought life to the area long before the Europeans arrived. The Payaya people had lived near the spring for generations. The Payaya were a small Coahuiltecan tribe consisting of no more than sixty families by the time the Spanish settlers arrived. Their staple foods were pecans, which they gathered in abundance from the native trees growing near the river, and prickly pear, which sustained them during the hot, dry summers.

At the center of Payaya life and culture was the Blue Hole, which in their day was a gushing artesian fountain. They called it *Yanaguana*—the Spirit Waters. From this spring flow the headwaters of the San Antonio River, on which the missions and the city were built.

But the Blue Hole is not itself the source of the river. The origins are elsewhere, remote, hidden. They lie almost 700 feet beneath the Blue Hole, in the expansive underground lake called the Edwards Aquifer. This massive body of water is 160 miles long and 80 miles across. Its waters are used every day in homes, restaurants, irrigation systems, swimming pools, golf courses, military bases, hospitals, and industries, providing life for millions of people.

And it is virtually invisible. A person could drive for miles, eat, work, sleep, and play without any awareness of the immense lake just beneath them.

Unless the water ran out.

If the water level of the great underground reservoir drops below 672 feet, the spring water at the Blue Hole ceases to flow. At 660 feet, drought restrictions kick in throughout the city. If the water level runs too low, lives and livelihoods are disrupted. Plants and animals die. But unlike an above-ground lake or reservoir, you can't tell what's happening. You can't see what's going on beneath you.

When the city declares drought restrictions, you are allowed to water your grass only once a week, so you grumble—my yard will yellow, my beautiful garden will wither.

But it's easy to complain when you are above ground and the lake is far below. You can't see how close to disaster you are.

In truth, life's most precious resources are often hidden. The river's origin is unseen. It lies beneath us. We drink from it. We irrigate the fields and power the mills by it. We run boats and barges, carrying freight and people up and down the river. The population grows. Neighborhoods are carved out of the nearby hills and woods. Freeways are built. Industry thrives. And over time, we forget the source of it all. We don't think about it until we need it or until it's too late. Until the river runs dry. Until the resources play out.

A person with exceptional drive and energy could go a long time sustained simply by her hard work and cleverness. A business could bask in its success for years, propelled by its innovative strategies and programs. A church could flourish as membership grows, as new folks move to the area, as the economy booms, during years when conflicts are small and failures are rare. As if each entity were completely responsible for its own good fortune. As if their successes were due solely to their brilliance. As if their futures were up to them.

But the difficult days will come. They always do. Drought sets in. The spring stops flowing. Water wells stop producing. Lakes shrivel. Lawns die. Businesses suffer. The groundwater stagnates. The earth cracks. The river runs dry.

But, we say to ourselves, how could this have happened? We have taken care of the Blue Hole. We have tended the stones. We have repaired the chute. We have trimmed the vines and trees. We have painted the footbridge and promoted the businesses. We have walked the archways and supported the arts and funded the museums and cultivated the gardens. We have venerated the old missions. We have built the city. We have honored the Spirit Waters. We have loved the river.

But the source of our bounty is not in the stones. It is not in our handiwork, not in our missions or our gardens or our innovations or our accomplishments or our organization or our programs or our size or our competence or our dreams. The source lies elsewhere, underground, remote, hidden, deep beneath the Blue Hole.

Peace, Death, Storm, and Fire: Churches of Christ on the Edge

History is not a random sequence of unrelated events. Everything affects and is affected by everything else. This is never clear in the present. Only time can sort out events. It is then, in perspective, that patterns emerge.

—William Manchester

Fieldnotes from the Blue Hole

We will begin our story in Lexington, Kentucky, with a handshake and a song, at an old cotton mill newly consecrated as a church house, on a cold New Year's Eve.

We could have begun elsewhere, at other times or places, because any event has a prior story, or many stories, that led to that moment. These stories are like a great underground lake made up of pools and streams that fill the crevices of the earth, receding and rising until, in a place and a way not entirely predictable, the water pours from the earth as a great spring, the headwaters of the river.

The place was Lexington in 1831, at the church house on New Year's Eve, when a handshake cracked open the earth.

Here is the "Blue Hole." Here is where Churches of Christ began. At least Churches of Christ as we know them today, by that particular name and history and disposition.

It might be difficult for a people who have often been told that history is irrelevant to acknowledge an origin story more recent than the Pentecost of Acts 2. But claimed or unclaimed, the events of Lexington, the story of these people, still shapes them, directly and profoundly.

What happened at the old cotton mill is part of the identity of these churches. Or should be, because if they don't know where their source spring is, it will be hard to understand where they came from, how the currents flow, how they might navigate the whitewater ahead, or where the river might lead. Because the currents are tricky. The rapids are treacherous. And the future is not guaranteed.

Said plainly, churches are in trouble. All churches are, but certainly Churches of Christ, for reasons we will soon see. Whether or not they recognize the threats they are facing is a different matter. The future is fraught with dangers. Many won't make it.

Our task is to find the resources that can help us along the way. Turns out, most of what we require is already in our possession. We just need a clear sense of what they are and why they are so important. That will be our quest.

These fieldnotes that introduce each chapter are designed to provide perspective and direction for our journey. I will point out key landmarks along the way. We will notice where the river zags, how the land slopes, the ways the cliffs alter the course of the riverbed. We will need to consult our compass from time to time to remind ourselves which way is north.

Our journey will take us through a landscape that is large and varied. The river's course is marked by stories both inspiring and troubling. We will see churches who believed peace and peacemaking was their most important virtue. There will be stories about death—funerals of beloved preachers and dirges for failed churches—and more than a few storms, where bitter disputes and shattering disappointments both scarred and empowered a people. And before all is said and done, there will be a story about fire, which may be our least-sought but greatest hope.

Our stories will converge around themes rather than chronologies. There will be some reflection pieces scattered among the stories, designed to cause us to stop and consider where we've been and where we might need to go. We will have some hills to walk around, streams to cross, a few wild beasts to avoid, and some interesting excursions to take. We will not be going in a straight line but, story by story, we will find our destination.

So, here are some of the directions we will be taking in chapter 1, the narrative paths that will shape the larger story that follows.

First, we will begin telling the story of the meetings at the Lexington church house. But I should prepare you. This story will take some time to tell. The story is too important to tell quickly. It will need to ripen, bit by bit, in its own time and way. Then we can come to see how that story has—or perhaps could—shape us in our time.

There will be a story about some farmers from Middle Tennessee who began to settle in western Arkansas just a few years after the Lexington meeting. They were looking for land and opportunity. But the first thing they did was start a church. This is my family's story. My story. We will not dwell on it long. I share it because I am serving as the narrator of our tale, and my story is like many of yours. I am not a disinterested observer. I have skin in the game. I care about how it all turns out.

We will also need to consider what condition Churches of Christ are in today. They have been in sharp decline for more than thirty years. The forecast for the next thirty is ominous. It will be hard to face these facts, but we must. This is not a time for myths and fantasies. There is too much at stake.

For that reason, we will need to stop and observe a funeral. What kind and for whom is not yet clear. But words of remembrance, the heartrending sounds of an elegy for the dead, still linger in the air. Are they words of praise? Grief? Comfort? Is there much weeping? Did the death come unexpectedly? What will it mean? What will it matter?

Finally, we will spend some time under a streetlight. Or, better said, we will try to move away from the streetlight so that we might, ironically, actually see what we are looking for. Churches are broken. Churches have problems. Some of them are relatively easy to fix. Some are so complicated, so stubborn, there seems to be no way out. The answers are hidden—by their nature and by God's design. Which is not to say they can't be found. But we will need to know where to look.

Those are the matters we will consider in chapter 1.

I am asked every now and then—more lately than in the past—if I think Churches of Christ are going to die. I will tell you my answer up front. I don't know. I really don't. It's possible. Some things are not looking good.

I don't mean that the eternal body of Christ for whom Christ is head might die. God has made promises about that. I mean, rather, the Churches of Christ that can trace their origins, decade by decade, congregation by congregation, to the American frontier in the early nineteenth century. Those churches, like a lot of other groups, seem to be in trouble, though they may not know it.

And nothing can be done to help them until they do. But there is hope. God's Spirit still dwells among them, even when they don't claim it. God is still gracious. Christ is still Lord. There are resources at the Blue Hole that could open up for them a new and vibrant future. If they knew it. If they listened. If they want it.

A Handshake and Tears

I finally arrived in Lexington late in the afternoon. My day had begun in the Northern Panhandle of West Virginia, in Bethany, at a cemetery, where I had lingered longer than I had planned. But there were still a few hours of daylight.

I cut off I-75 to Newtown Pike, slogging my way through thick downtown traffic, shouting at my phone as the exasperatingly pleasant voice of my map app kept urging me to turn into oncoming traffic. I maneuvered up North Mill Street, past Goodfellas Pizzeria and the Buddha Lounge, to the crest of a little hill. I turned right at the light and slid into an empty parking space next to the curb.

For several minutes I sat quietly—thinking, listening, trying to get a feel for the place, trying to grasp the significance of what had happened here. For bustling Lexington at rush hour this was just a normal day. But for me it was like finding myself at a thin place in the spiritual universe, as if a presence or a people were nearby, perceptible but just beyond my grasp.

It's not like I had never been to Lexington. I had come several times before. But those trips were different. I had been a visitor attending a conference or a guest speaking at a church. This time, I chose to come on my own. It was a personal quest, growing out of the longing of my heart.

I was looking for where my people came from, my spiritual family. More urgently, my soul was dry. I felt disconnected. Distant. Broken. I needed to be centered again. I needed to hope again. I needed fresh water. I was looking for my wellspring. Perhaps it was here, in Lexington of all places, a thousand miles away from my home, a couple of blocks south of Goodfellas Pizzeria, just off North Mill Street, at the crest of the little hill. I opened the car door and stepped into the sticky heat.

A few feet from where I stood, two churches had come together on a cold Kentucky night almost two centuries ago. Something astounding had taken place here, something that changed my life, indirectly but distinctly, miles away and decades later. They had met here, directly in front of me, at what had been, until a few months before their meeting, a cotton mill.

They had met at the newly consecrated Hill Street Church. They had come to sing and to pray. And to imagine a future.

It was New Year's Eve 1831. The people gathered not just as two congregations. They came from two distinct streams of Christians, with different histories, different temperaments, different beliefs and values.

Each group faced a crossroads. They had decisions to make, questions to answer. Could they talk to one another peaceably? Could they find common ground? Could they disagree and still work together? Could each group distinguish what they wanted from what was best? Could they worship together, pray together, share the Lord's table together? Could they, somehow, in the name of Jesus, become one?

For at least a year, some of them had begun to imagine the possibility of a union between the two groups. Several weeks before the meetings in Lexington, four men had met quietly in Georgetown, a small community just north of Lexington, to discuss what might be possible.

Two of the men belonged to the Georgetown congregation that Barton Stone had planted and where he still preached. The other two—one a leader of a congregation in west Georgetown, the other a popular Kentucky evangelist—were associated with Alexander Campbell from Virginia (now West Virginia).

All four men were named John. All four believed, in spite of the differences, that their churches had too much in common to remain separate. Whether the churches agreed with them was still an open question.

John Allen Gano was the grandson of George Washington's chaplain and the son of a general who fought in the War of 1812. As a young man, Gano had been baptized in a Barton Stone revival. By 1831, just twenty-six years old, John Allen Gano was already a powerful presence in the community, working to persuade folks who disagreed on many matters to at least come together to talk.

John Rogers, like Gano, was a member of Stone's Georgetown church. He had been an eighteen-year-old cabinetmaker's apprentice when he first heard Stone preach. A few years later, Rogers was one of the first members of Stone's churches to read articles written by Campbell. He became convinced that Campbell and Stone, in spite of significant differences in both doctrine and disposition, had more in common than what divided them.

John T. Johnson by 1831 had become a prominent figure in the state. He had served as an aide to General William Henry Harrison. He had been elected to the

Kentucky state legislature and to two terms in the US Congress. After leaving politics, Johnson had become captivated by the writings of Campbell, whose rational explanation of the gospel especially appealed to him. He soon rose to leadership in one of Campbell's churches on the west side of Georgetown.

John Smith, the only one of the four men who did not live in Georgetown, had been asked by Campbell to represent him in these conversations. Smith said he never liked the nickname by which he was known. According to legend, he acquired it while giving a sermon at Crab Orchard, Kentucky, telling the audience that he had grown up among the raccoons in Cumberland. It is often difficult to sort fact from fiction in the life of Raccoon John Smith. We do know, however, that he was an eloquent and persuasive preacher. We also know that perhaps no other sermon in Smith's life was as important as the one he gave to a crowd of Christians in a church house in Lexington on New Year's Eve 1831.

For weeks these men talked. And they prayed—for peace between their churches, peace among Christians. Their conversations and prayers began to bear fruit on Christmas weekend when the two Georgetown congregations—Gano's and Rogers's church where Stone preached and Johnson's church, which was part of the Campbell movement—convened for the first time to see if it made sense for them to unite.

These four days of conversation in Georgetown were promising, so they decided to have a second set of meetings to begin the following Friday, December 30. Because they anticipated a larger gathering than either Georgetown church building could hold, they set the meeting at the Hill Street Church in Lexington, ten miles south.

Things went well on the opening day of the Lexington meetings. On the next day, New Year's Eve, they agreed that two people, one from each group, would offer a speech stating what they believed was the basis for union. Raccoon John was chosen to speak for the Campbell churches. Barton Stone himself would speak on behalf of the congregation where he preached and the movement he had launched years before.

What Smith and Stone said at the meeting and what the two communities of faith chose to do are largely unknown by their spiritual heirs today. The story is rarely told. The astonishing climax of the gathering remains buried in obscurity, deemed to be trivial or irrelevant because of the distance of time and place.

But it should never have been forgotten. Not the words of the two humble men who sparked the moment. Not their trembling handshake nor their embrace.

Not the sound of newfound brothers and sisters, standing arm in arm, full-voiced, singing. Not their prayers, nor their tears.

That this story and other defining stories have largely been forgotten by their descendants is tragic, like the early onset of a communal dementia where the long-term memory of an entire people has withered and died. In this case, however, the malady seems to have been self-inflicted, the stories having been lost to them either through willfulness or neglect. If the story were known, if the impulse that brought the two movements together was recovered and embraced, a lot of churches today might have a different future.

The spiritual heirs of those who gathered that weekend in Lexington number today in the millions—by some estimates as much as ten million worldwide, at least three million in the United States. Most still wear at least one of the names by which these churches were originally known—Christian Churches, Disciples of Christ, and Churches of Christ—names that for the first decades of the united movement were largely interchangeable. Over time, however, each of these designations came to signify a particular group, which, in turn, often splintered into others.

Of the spiritual descendants of the Lexington meetings, Churches of Christ are the least likely to know what happened there. Most everything that had occurred in their history prior to the turn of the twentieth century has been stripped from their memory. But even if these churches have largely forgotten it, the main plotline of the story remains clear. In the years after the American Civil War, these people began a long and painful separation from the others. By the early twentieth century, the division was complete.

In the process, these churches began to use just one of the names by which they had originally been known—"Churches of Christ," or as some insist, "churches of Christ." Over time, some distinguished themselves from the others through parenthetical markers that identified particular doctrinal concerns, like Churches of Christ (non-institutional) or Churches of Christ (non–Bible Class), or through other self-designations such as International Churches of Christ. Each group remains to this day largely isolated from the others.

In recent years, some congregations have dropped the name Church of Christ altogether. Others have kept the name but downgraded it to a subtitle, like the Such and Such Church (a church of Christ). And more than a few individuals who grew up in a Church of Christ have become part of other faith traditions, seeding the other groups with pieces of their own story, like modern-day Johnny Appleseeds planting Church of Christ values and instincts wherever they go.

But whatever name appears on their church marquee, whether or not they claim it, all of them are part of a larger diaspora, a worldwide scattering of churches and people whose spiritual roots go back to the early American frontier. They can hardly avoid carrying within them at least some of the characteristics of that ancestry. The traits are part of them, part of their essence, like a religious genetic code. What they inherited from Churches of Christ may be intermixed with characteristics from other Christian gene pools, but their past has still nurtured within them certain perspectives, a way of seeing God and Scripture and one another and the world, a shared story that has largely made them who they are.

A Trail Where They Cried

My own spiritual journey, as far back as I know it, began in the early nineteenth century, in Middle Tennessee, in a little town called Flat Creek. The story eventually traveled to West Texas where it lingered for a few generations before scattering to the winds. But in between, my family's story was shaped and nurtured in a place called Corinth.

Not long ago, on an overcast summer afternoon, I drove the back roads of western Arkansas to the Old Corinth Cemetery near the town where my ancestors had settled. Until around 1840, that land had belonged mostly to Choctaw, Quapaw, and Creek as well as some Cherokee, Shawnee, and Delaware, before they were all forced out by the American government, resettling, at least for a time, in Indian Territory, now Oklahoma.

The first recorded White settlers in the area were my family, Jordan Reese and Davie D. Jones. They and their families benefited immensely from the involuntary removal of over 60,000 Native Americans and an unknown number of African slaves who were pushed out of Arkansas beginning in 1830. The Cherokees called this forced march *nunahi-duna-dlo-hilu-i*: "the trail where they cried."

The thousands of people who were deported from western Arkansas traveled with their horses and meager possessions, often walking barefoot through some of the coldest winters and driest summers in Arkansas history. Many died from cholera, dysentery, and smallpox.

Jordan and Davie were surely aware of the Trail of Tears. They entered the land in 1845 shortly after the last of the indigenous Americans had been forced out. What they thought of this tragedy, whether they grieved or were even concerned about what happened, history does not tell us. But they found the land rich and their own futures promising, so they wrote to their families and friends back in Flat Creek and urged them to come to Arkansas.

About forty families arrived in 1847, including Jordan's brother Sloman and his wife Eliza, who was Davie's sister. Sloman and Eliza are my grandfather's grandparents.

I walked among the gravestones in the old cemetery until I found a variegated gray obelisk about four feet high. Sloman's name was on one side: "Born Sept. 24, 1823. Died Dec. 6, 1917." Eliza's was on the opposite: "Born Apr. 1, 1827. Died Aug. 5, 1907." On one of the sides of the stone was the inscription, "Charter Members of the Church at Corinth when Organized 1850."

I knelt and wept. The emotional tie was deeper than I had prepared myself for. It wasn't just that they were family, distant ancestors, carriers of the family traits and name. They were spiritual forebears, the direct tie to my Christian roots, and largely the reason I grew up in Churches of Christ.

Sloman's parents, Billie and Catherine Reese, had, in their words, "joined the Campbell reformation" sometime before 1847, less than fifteen years after the Stone and Campbell groups had come together at the old Hill Street Church in Lexington.

Beginning in 1847, my family plowed, traded, bought, and sold. And they established and grew a thriving church, calling it the Corinth Church of Christ. The town, which was established many years later, was named after the church. By the end of the century, a Christian college was begun there, because that's what these people did, because they believed learning and reason mattered.

I am a child of this heritage unto the sixth generation. Within it, I was baptized. Through it, I felt God's urging to preach. Because of it, I learned to love Scripture, to pray, to teach, to serve. And to sing. In fact, I was encouraged not just to sing but to sing in harmony. Which is not the same as being harmonious. I grew to understand that much later.

My personal sensibilities about Churches of Christ come from deep inside the story, which likely means that both my love for these churches and my aggravations are magnified. Whatever the case, I consciously bring my experiences and values to this narrative.

My perspective here is that of an ethnographer, one who tries to understand the culture of a people from the inside out, through their own stories and experiences. My task is to look for the instincts and passions that have largely made them who they are, to try to figure out what is important to them and what is not. My desire is to serve as a bridge—between past and present, between scholarship and the daily life of the church, between those who have remained in Churches of Christ and those who have not, between Churches of Christ and other communities of faith.

My purpose is not merely to tell some stories from the past but to examine these churches' beliefs and practices, their patterns and meanings. I want to find the springs that fed them, their Blue Hole, in order to suggest a healthy way forward. It will not be easy. As we will soon see, the times call for tenacity, discernment, and courage.

To be honest, Churches of Christ are not an easy group to write about. We are diverse, complicated, and messy. In fact, we have exhibited far more variety over the years than the story we tell about ourselves usually admits. That variety is almost always interesting but not always pretty. Less like an English garden than, say, a Star Trek convention. We may share an overarching theme and a common set of values, but our actions and attributes often seem, well, peculiar to others.

My wife and I recently moved to a new neighborhood, the kind of place where friendly neighbors inquire about where you go to church, in part, we assume, because they care for our eternal salvation but mostly because they're curious. Our reply—we go to the such-and-such Church of Christ—is generally met with a marked silence after which they typically respond in one of two ways. Some of them say, "You don't seem Church of Christ," which we assume is intended as a compliment, though it's an awkward one at best. Or they say something like, "Oh, those are the churches that don't believe in music."

This last remark is usually the one that gets under my skin, though the neighbors never mean it unkindly. My mind sorts through an inventory of possible responses. Sure, our churches historically have been a cappella, but singing is actually music, you see. Church of Christ kids tend to fill their school choirs, bands, and orchestras because they learn to read music in church. (Or at least they used to. That argument is losing force each passing year.) Hey, you think we don't do music? Why, the Christian music industry in Nashville was started in large part by Church of Christ musicians.

But what good would those sorts of arguments do? We usually just smile and thank them for their interest in us. We understand what they are saying. They're not trying to be unkind. They're just being neighborly.

In his podcast series *Revisionist History*, Malcolm Gladwell, the author of *Tipping Point* and *Blink*, twice has made reference to Churches of Christ. I flinched both times I heard it. In the episode "King of Tears," Gladwell interviewed the country music songwriter Bobby Braddock who, Gladwell said, grew up "Church of Christ, just about the most fundamentalist of fundamentalist Christians." Ouch. In a later episode, "Analysis, Parapraxis, Elvis," Gladwell interviews Braddock again along with singer songwriter Kaci Bolls. He talks about "how they both grew up in the Church of Christ, the most strict of Southern fundamentalist denominations."

My reaction each time was, that's not the Church of Christ I know. I grew up in a loving, generous church, in a Church of Christ family that taught grace. I went to a Church of Christ university that prized critical thinking and that turned out nationally recognized medical doctors, research scientists, business leaders, educators, and public servants. In my field, a disproportionately large number of Church of Christ scholars have taught biblical studies, church history, or theology at some of the most prestigious universities and seminaries in the world. Fundamentalist we are not.

But when I am finally able to set my defensiveness aside and think about it for a moment, Gladwell is also right. The churches he refers to do exist. I know these churches. Their numbers, in fact, are legion. These are kind folks, conscientious believers who take the Bible seriously. They aren't trying to be mean or judgmental. They just want to be right with God. While they are not the whole story of who Churches of Christ are today, they reflect a significant strain of these churches that might be called exclusivist. In other words, they do not recognize other Christian groups as authentically Christian.

And when I say they are a strain of Churches of Christ, I fudge a little. For much of the twentieth century, most congregations in this group could be characterized this way. They lived in relative isolation, separated by choice and identity from other Christian groups. In other words, Gladwell's account, painful as it is to hear, has a measure of truth in it. Maybe more than a measure. Before churches in this movement can move forward constructively, they will have to come to grips with the stories told about them by the outsiders they rub shoulders with. Those stories, it turns out, reflect a certain reality.

But within the long and complex history of Churches of Christ, other impulses have also been at play besides the isolation by which we are often known. We have not always been what we appear to be today. There are other stories, other values, other commitments.

For example, Christians within this movement once encouraged one another to live as a separated people but not over-and-against other Christian groups. In fact, in the decades after the union in Lexington, most congregations that wore the name Church of Christ sought to unite with Christians everywhere, no matter what name they went by. The separation they sought, rather, was against the values and behaviors of the secular world around them. It was a separation marked by holiness, not exclusion. But this is a stream we hardly recognize today. We have little memory of it.

Churches of Christ, in other words, possess hidden, forgotten, and often rich resources that could serve us well—if we knew about them, if we knew something of our own story. Like a great underground reservoir, our story could bring us wisdom and life. But as long as it stays below the surface unsought and untapped, its most valuable energy will remain largely inaccessible and, therefore, useless to us.

At the Edge

What happened on the last day of the year 1831 and the following day—the first day of the new year, the first day of the week, gathered at table—is part of our living stream. Here the source waters once gushed from the earth like an artesian well, forming a great river. If we drank from this stream, if we knew our story, if we witnessed in our Christian ancestors a hint of Christ's heart, if we came to recognize among these people some of our own doubts and desires, or discerned in the stories a cautionary tale or two, then perhaps we might find for our own time wisdom and courage for a new day.

That's what we are seeking here. We are not collecting a photo album of dusty stories from the past so that we might look at it from time to time, remembering old vacations, reflecting on how young we once looked, or laughing at our quaint bell bottoms and poofy hair. Rather, we are seeking living resources for the future because we want to be healthy. We want to be alive, formed into the image of Jesus. It would be good news if we found those resources. But we better hurry.

Churches of Christ are teetering at the edge.

Certainly in America they are. Like other Christian fellowships, Churches of Christ are growing in some non-American contexts, particularly in Africa and South America. But in the United States, Churches of Christ are in serious numerical decline.

The total membership of these congregations in America today is a little over a million. Churches of Christ are the thirteenth largest Christian fellowship in the country. But they are in decline and have been, at least externally, for thirty years—since 1990 if not earlier.[1]

While Churches of Christ exist in every state and in more than three-fourths of US counties, they are concentrated in the states of the former Confederacy. In fact, five states contain more than half of the members of American Churches of Christ—Texas, Tennessee, Alabama, Arkansas, and Oklahoma.

Most of the congregations in the United States are small and getting smaller. Ninety-two percent of them have less than two hundred members. The average Sunday attendance nationwide is ninety-four. More than half of the congregations in the country average only thirty-four members.

You might need to let those numbers simmer for a minute before moving on. They are sobering. And revealing.

Churches in this movement have historically been rural, but like the rest of the country they have been moving to the city in overwhelming numbers. More than three-quarters of Churches of Christ are now in urban centers. In general, these churches have not adapted well to life in the city. They often seem out of place, disconnected from urban life.

The average age of members across the nation is growing older. Young people are not coming or are not staying. Around sixty congregations a year in the US are shutting their doors for good. That's more than one church closure a week.

And if the present looks bad, the future looks especially troubling. No one knows, of course, what the coming decades will look like. But according to the compelling research of Stanley Granberg and Tim Woodroof,[2] by 2050 Churches of Christ in the US will have declined to less than half of what they are today. That's the best-case scenario. When you take into consideration the exceedingly high number of older members in these churches and the comparatively small number of new members being added, church membership is expected to decline from 1.1 million to barely 250,000 in the next three decades, less than a fourth of what they are today. In thirty years.

Smaller congregations will be impacted the quickest—their average membership tends to be older and their critical mass more fragile—but almost every congregation will be impacted. Moreover, the research indicates that the number of Church of Christ congregations in the United States is likely to drop from 12,237 in 2016 to only about 2800 in 2050, an 80 percent decline.

And that's just the externals. It's not always easy to gauge the spiritual life and maturity of a congregation simply by counting heads. Bigger is not always better.

But if you think there is no correlation between the dramatic numerical decline of a movement and its future, I have some tickets to the Horse and Buggy Museum of America I would like to give you.

Churches have been given a wakeup call. It may already be too late.

But this is no time to throw up our hands in despair or, worse yet, try to construct an elaborate plan to turn things around. Truth be told, the numerical decline of Churches of Christ in America may be the best thing that could happen. As the dire state of these churches begins to sink in, it will become increasingly apparent that we can't fix ourselves. But here is the good news: God can. How and toward what end is what we will pursue in the coming chapters.

To be clear, no matter what Churches of Christ do, they will not likely recover their former stature or prestige. Nor should doing so be their goal. They will never become again what they once were. Even if rebuilding some version of a once-glorious past were possible, doing so would be both counterproductive and tragic. And attempting it would miss the point. But, congregation by congregation, Christian by Christian, they can become something different, something new, something healthier, something more humble, more Christlike, more faithful.

The rapid numerical decline of Churches of Christ in America is not unique, of course. Church attendance in virtually every Christian group is plummeting. These are the times in which we live. The larger culture is changing massively and quickly. Congregations everywhere are having a difficult time adjusting.

Churches of Christ, however, are facing some particular obstacles. Our longtime isolation from others and the growing polarization within the movement itself have made matters worse. We have historically cut ourselves off from other groups, so we missed what we might have learned in such a dialogue. More than that, we have cut ourselves off from our own story. We are thirsty and don't know why, and we can't seem to figure out who to blame for the drought.

But see, here is water. Plenty of it. If we looked up. If we were alert to it. We stand at the edge of a great stream, fed by Spirit Waters gushing from the earth, nourished from beneath by vast caverns of unseen resources. People and principles and values from our past, from our own story, could replenish us if we were open to receive them. If we sought them. If we remembered. At the Blue Hole we can find clues about our nature. And our future. God gave us unique gifts there. We may have squandered some of them, but we still have time to reclaim them. If we hurry.

But there is another gift at the Blue Hole, one less obvious, less direct, less intuitive. This gift will not be easy to find. It is hidden. It's not that God does not want us to have this gift. It's already ours, in fact. If we claimed it, it would change everything. But in order to receive it, we will have to die. Frankly, death will happen one way or another.

No one said the way would be easy.

Today, in Lexington, on what is now called High Street, at the place where the old church once stood, cars wait in line for the drive-through tellers at a local bank. Doing my best to ignore the withering heat and humidity, I stepped up on the curb and began to walk down the sidewalk, calculating where the old pulpit might have stood, the spot where Barton Stone and Raccoon John Smith shook hands.

I tried to picture among the waiting cars an old building filled with worshipers, arm in arm—two communities of faith choosing to become one, seeking together in full-throated song the harmony they had just pledged to one another. But I could hear no singing this day. Just the rumble of car engines idling on the hot concrete.

It is not that there are no sacred places in the area. Less than a block away stands Rupp Arena, where worshipers of a different sort often gather at one of America's iconic sports facilities, mostly to praise, though occasionally to lament. The arena is the home court of the University of Kentucky, whose institutional roots run deep into the soil of Stone-Campbell churches, though most of its students and faculty are little aware. History has a way of slipping from consciousness when you're focused on the thrill of yesterday's victory or the agony of today's defeat.

You won't find much that indicates anything of importance ever happened down the street from the arena, over at the bank where the drive-through tellers serve their customers. There are no remnants of the old Hill Street Church that could be memorialized. No historical marker tells the story. Then again, the movement never cared much about places or plaques.

But it is worthy of note that almost two centuries ago in what is now downtown Lexington, emerging from two distinct groups, a gathering of Christians, our spiritual ancestors, chose peace over conflict, unity over division. There, assembled in what had been an old cotton mill, this new movement of independent churches, including Churches of Christ, found its heart and its voice. Their union was sealed with a handshake, baptized in tears, animated in embrace, confirmed in song, and sanctified at table.

Does this story still have life? Can the song still be sung? Do these churches have a future? Perhaps. But time is running out. Our future may depend on whether, in our search for answers, we are able to detect the unsettling aroma of death.

A Casket and a Funeral

The two older children clung to their mother's hands. The two younger ones straddled their father's hips, snug in his arms, their small fingers clenching the lapels of his jacket. Their faces were attentive, trusting, eager, apprehensive as they made their way down the aisle through the crowd of chattering grownups to the figure lying lifeless in the coffin.

There is no right or wrong time for a child to view a body in a casket, no agreed-upon age of innocence to safeguard or societal norms to provide guidance. Some parents wait until their children are older. Some parents don't. But at some point, our children—all of us—have to come face to face with death.

Even then, understanding the whole mortality thing doesn't happen all at once. These smart, curious children viewing the body of their great-great-uncle at a family funeral visitation can only grasp so much. But over time, their understanding will deepen. Death happens to us all. Death is part of life.

Not that we don't try to conceal this truth. Modern societies largely sterilize death, keep it clean and distant, its reality obscured by euphemism—he is no longer with us, he has crossed over to the other side, gone to a better place, he checked out, met his maker, took the last train to glory. She passed away, you see. As if somehow, inexplicably, our friend slowly disappeared into the mist.

Our thoughts become more focused, however, when it's our own mortality we are facing. Family members of a terminally ill patient often don't know what to say about death. But the patient herself usually wants to talk about it, wants to process the imminent end of her life. There's something about facing one's own death that concentrates the mind.

Our churches are dying. This is a hard truth, difficult to grasp, difficult to say out loud. That our particular church is dying may not play well in the "News and Notes" section of this week's church bulletin, but it is true, nonetheless. And it would be to our advantage to come to terms with it, to talk about it, to figure out what's happening and why.

Knowing we were dying would focus us. We could set petty things aside. We could concentrate on important matters. But if we miss it, if we are blind to its reality or choose not to speak of it, there is a price to be paid. And too many churches are paying it.

If we don't know our church is dying we won't look for courage because we won't know we need it. We won't find faith, not grasping that our crisis, still hidden, requires it. We will waste time on piddling matters, like a dying man haggling over the price of a new suit, and miss the chance to do the things that might actually matter. We will obscure the truth about our predicament and ourselves. We will keep our imminent death distant, concealed by denial or doubt. Most importantly, we will stand in the way of the resurrection that only God can render, the new life our churches are counting on and desperately need.

The death of our churches will happen in different ways, of course. There will be a few congregations whose death will happen in plain sight. They will shut their doors and sell their property, their old members melding into new communities of faith, or, in a few cases, just disappearing from the kingdom altogether. You know, passing away.

But most churches will continue on, animated by their activities, business as usual. They will maintain their name, location, and legal status, operating week by week, year by year. They will worship and pray. They will hire and fire ministers, support missionaries, find teachers and supplies for their Sunday school classes, fill and dispense communion cups, fix the heating and air conditioning system, and change out the carpet in the back classroom. They will organize youth trips and Vacation Bible Schools, host meals for visitors, and provide social gatherings for singles looking for spouses and widows remembering theirs.

These churches are going to be around for a while, at least by appearance. Their death may not be visible or notable, even to themselves. The day-to-day business of church may very well continue uninterrupted. Not that they aren't seeing evidence of diminishment. They are. They're just not sure what to do about it. Or whose fault it is.

For many churches, Sunday attendance is dropping as the average age increases. There are fewer children, fewer families with teenagers, fewer Bible class teachers, fewer volunteers, fewer outreach efforts, fewer dollars in the church coffer, and, overall, less involvement by church members. In moments of self-awareness, these churches are able to catch a whiff of the fragrance of death. The odor can be unnerving.

More worrisome, perhaps, are the churches that cannot picture their own death, whose attendance is booming, whose resources are growing, whose programs are thriving, whose youth vans are full, whose futures are bright, whose reputations are made. These churches appear to be flourishing, but they may, in fact, be more vulnerable to their own demise because their busyness, their size, and their apparent successes mask their mortality.

But all of them, all churches, are facing death, and denying it will make matters worse. Our church, my church, church as we remember it, church as we like it, church as we want it to be is dying.

Churches that are propped up by our surrounding culture, where everyone we know basically believes alike and thinks alike, churches that keep strangers at arm's distance unless they are like us or want to be, churches that advantage us socially, that isolate us from pain or discomfort, churches that insulate us from hard people and hard truths are dying or already dead. Churches with brilliant marketing strategies. Churches with social media savvy. Casual churches. Cool churches. Contemporary churches. Megachurches. Back-to-the-Bible churches. Old churches and new churches. Liberal churches and conservative churches, big churches and little churches, city churches and country churches, all of them are facing death.

And this is just the regular and ordinary sort of encounter with death. The once-in-a-century pandemic that began in late 2019 put a whole lot of congregations on life support. Many will never recover. In the wake of a raging viral outbreak, old answers to church problems just don't work very well. Bring-a-neighbor Sundays and gregarious greeters wearing matching blazers somehow don't have that old sizzle. Weekly attendance for most congregations will never return to pre-pandemic numbers. Congregational stress is worsening. The risk level is stuck on critical. When churches don't attend to God's Spirit for decades, there are simply no ventilators adequate to treat the resulting shortness of breath. No wonder the death rate for at-risk congregations continues to soar. No church has been left unscathed.

To be clear, it's not that there are good churches and bad churches, some that are mortal and some that are not. Nor is it the case that if we could just figure out the cure, we could ward off the disease. In fact, that's the problem. We can't cure ourselves. We can't fix ourselves. Churches are filled with humans, and humans miss things. Humans mess things up. Humans misread and misunderstand. We are too willful, too shortsighted, too stubborn to fix ourselves.

It's that whole cycle-of-sin-and-death thing. I have no doubt that the gates of hell will not prevail against Christ's church, but that's no guarantee that any particular congregation is protected from the hell of its own making.

If we are not ready to deal with this reality, we will not be in a position to help our church. We will continue to believe that our futures can be planned, our successes can be secured, our conflicts can be managed, and that if we just figured out what the problem is and made good decisions, things would be better. As if church were about us, or up to us. Such a church is always on the edge of death.

But living in that sort of mess does not mean we are left hopeless. In fact, precisely because things are difficult, our hope should thrive. Our church is dying, hallelujah! We have hope because God is at work. Resurrection lies ahead if we have eyes to see. Our churches can be better. We can, in fact, become the kind of churches God desires, the kind of churches God promised.

"When the church faces the prospect of its own demise," Michael Jinkins has said, "it faces a critical moment . . . when its vocation is called into question, when it has the unparalleled opportunity to comprehend and to render its life. When the church faces death, in point of fact, it encounters a critical moment when it may know the power of resurrection."[3]

It is resurrection that our churches are hoping for. It is resurrection that we need. We may think to ourselves, if only we could get past what's holding us back, whatever our crisis du jour may be, then things would be better, then we could become the church we want to be. But here's the honest truth: if our churches keep doing what most of them are now doing, they are going to die. And for some of them, that death will be slow and painful. And some of them will never recover.

But here's the rest of it. If we don't die, there will be no resurrection. Make no mistake, there's going to be a death either way.

For some, death will come out of our own willfulness, our need to be in control. It will come out of a desire to preserve at all costs church as we want it, out of our understandable but tragic craving for familiarity and self-protection, like a man surrounded by a raging wildfire who shuts himself in his house, making a tall glass of tea with a slice of lime and two packets of Sweet 'N Low, calmly sitting on the old couch, reaching for the television remote, blind to the looming conflagration. It doesn't have to end this way, but when the drapes burst into flames it's likely too late to do anything about it.

Death comes when our church goes on about its business, head down, church as usual, picking songs and printing bulletins the way it always has, living out of its memory of what church is supposed to look like or how things used to be, propping up the beautiful façade by which it has always been known, oblivious to the encircling inferno. The smell of death is in the air, but the church ignores it like it's just meat cooking in preparation for the Fourth of July barbecue.

Death comes when we think we can keep from dying merely through good organization or good doctrine, when we think we can shape our own future, when we assume we can fix ourselves or keep things the way they are or the way we wish them to be, when we do everything we can to keep from dying or convince ourselves that we are not dying. This is death by avoidance, death by arrogance, death by stubbornness, death by self-infliction, death on our own terms.

But there's another kind of death, a death on God's terms. This sort of death grows out of what seems like God's weakness—part of the surprising, hidden, upside-down, the-first-shall-be-last, the-humble-shall-be-exalted nature of God. Death occurs when a church relinquishes control rather than seizing it, as an act of congregational discipleship, the whole church choosing to take up a cross rather than seeking its own way.

This death comes when our eyes are wide open, when we acknowledge the flames and grasp our circumstances, when, in an act of will and purpose, we give up our claim to do church the way we want it and find our place in the kingdom not as the ones who get things right but as those who are privileged to share in the suffering of Christ, proclaiming Christ's death until he comes—an elegy of gratitude and grace.

You have a decision to make. One way or another, you will have to choose. Not whether your church dies, but how. And why. Upon that decision rests your church's health and future.

The Streetlight Effect

You have likely heard this story before. A police officer sees a man looking for something under a streetlight. The officer asks him, "What are you doing?"

"I've lost my keys," the man says.

Wanting to help, the officer joins him in his search. After a few minutes with no success, the officer asks the man, "Are you sure this is where you lost your keys?"

"No, I lost them over in the park."

"In the park? Then why are you looking for your keys here?"

The man replies, "Because there's more light here."

This joke has been around, in one form or another, for over eight hundred years. The phenomenon it describes is so common that social scientists have given it a name: the "streetlight effect," a tendency among humans to search for something, not where it may be found, but where it is easiest to look.

David Freedman in his book *Wrong: Why Experts Keep Failing Us and How to Know When Not to Trust Them* describes this effect, pointing to influential scientific reports, economic forecasts, and medical research in which experts looked for answers where the light was good rather than where truth might be found.[4]

I know a little about this phenomenon. I've seen it at work in my own life, searching for answers where it was easiest rather than where the truth was hidden. I am not alone. It shows up in lots of places—in congregations large and small, Black and White, American and non-American, urban, suburban, and rural, among church leaders who have looked for answers under familiar lampposts where the search was most convenient rather than where they might find the truth.

It's a common malady, highly contagious and sometimes fatal.

That churches have problems shouldn't surprise anyone. Churches are made up of humans after all, and humans are fraught with problems. All our human-filled, people-led churches struggle with something. Every church faces problems. The question is why so many of them experience the same problems year after year with no apparent resolution. And often no idea where to look.

When they do, they tend to look in all the bright places: the latest book, the greatest expert, the splashiest conference, the hottest podcast, the compelling new blog. They imitate programs that seem to work for the big church across town. They write a new mission statement or create a strategic plan. They build a new building. Or they fire the preacher and get a new one—an up-and-comer maybe, someone who's in demand, on the circuit, someone who can pull in the crowds—only to discover after all the changes are made that the problems persist. While that streetlight was certainly bright, the keys to the church remain lost over in the park.

There's nothing wrong with a new mission statement or strategic plan or even, at the right time, hiring a minister or constructing a new building. But the truth is rarely found there. Rather, it is in the hard places, away from the streetlight. And few churches are willing to look for it.

That's not to say, however, that they don't know something is missing.

Marinated in Fear

I had never met the woman before, but she greeted me cheerfully. I was grateful. Serving as an outside consultant to a congregation has its upside. People are often more likely to speak with candor to a friendly stranger than to someone they go to church with every week. But that would be true only if they trusted me. This woman seemed to, or at least she was hiding her anxiety well.

"I'm really glad you're doing this," she said eagerly. "I'm glad the elders brought you in."

"Oh?," I asked. "Why?"

"Because the elders are afraid to make hard decisions. They're afraid to change anything. They're afraid that if they do, some members will leave—you know, some of their friends, some of the big givers. But if we don't do something, we're gonna lose a bunch of folks."

I tried to drill deeper. "What are your greatest fears about this church?" In other words, if you think the elders are afraid, then tell me what *you're* afraid of.

She didn't hesitate. "I'm afraid we will never change. We've got to change if we're going to stay alive. A lot of things stay the same around here because of tradition. But we have to change things as new generations come along. For my kids and my grandkids. I don't mean change the gospel but change how we do things. What we're doing now has become old and stale. People are leaving. I'm afraid if we don't change, we're going to die."

A few minutes later, after she had gone, I stepped into the reception area and looked for my last interview of the evening. An amiable, well-dressed man stood and greeted me with a firm handshake. He introduced me to his wife, now rising next to him. "I wanted her to join the interview," he said. He wasn't asking my permission. I invited them in.

Before we had even sat down, the man took hold of my arm and said to me, "Hey, I'm really glad you're doing this. I was thrilled when the elders said they were bringing in a consultant. They need help."

"Oh?"

"The elders are good people. I like them. But they don't seem to stand for anything. They're constantly changing things. They seem to just want to please some folks, mostly our new members, people who don't know our church very well. But the new folks don't have our history. They weren't here during the hard years. The elders seem to be making sure all of them are happy—mostly the younger members—making sure they aren't upset, that they get to have church the way they like it, no matter what it means for the rest of us. But we're losing touch with the truths of the Bible. We're afraid to say what the Bible says. And now a lot of the folks who care about the Bible are starting to leave."

"So," I asked, "what are your greatest fears about this church?"

His wife leaned forward. "I'm afraid that if we keep changing, I won't be able to recognize my own church anymore."

That such conflicting positions could be expressed by folks in the same congregation about the same leaders and the same issues shouldn't be surprising to anyone who has been paying attention. These sorts of tensions have been around for a while. All the way back to the beginning.

In first-century Corinth, the "I am of Paul" group thought the "I am of Apollos" and "I am of Cephas" groups were way off base. Totally wrongheaded. While the "I am of Christ" group, clearly superior to the others, looked down their noses at all of them. In the name of Jesus, of course. That's not accounting for the rich Christians who didn't want to share bread and wine with the poor Christians. Or the prophets and tongue-speakers who were yelling at each other after the closing prayer out in the back foyer. What a mess.

But there was conflict in all the earliest churches, even the healthier ones. The extraordinarily generous church in Philippi was slowly being torn apart because two strong and influential women were having a knock-down-drag-out. The house churches in Rome, reflecting their mixed membership of Jews and Gentiles, couldn't seem to resolve their differences over the eating of certain foods or whether it was mandatory to celebrate certain holy days. These were highly charged matters in which agreement seemed impossible.

Every church in every age has struggled to find agreement. But Christian unity is especially difficult today. The polarization among churches seems to have become more acute. In some places, a kind of paralysis has set in: if we don't change, we will die; if we do change, we will die. A classic no-win double-bind.

In the midst of the conflict, a lot of church leaders are wringing their hands, or at least scratching their heads. How do you get past the differences? Someone will be upset no matter what decisions are made. How can we move forward without offending one group or another, without half the church walking out?

A congregation went through a major change several years ago. Its members were polarized concerning a pressing issue of doctrine and practice. They couldn't avoid a decision. Some said if the church didn't make the change, they would have to leave as a matter of conscience. Others objected fiercely, also as a matter of conscience. So, when the change was eventually made, a bunch of folks left. The same thing would have happened if a different decision had been made, just with different members.

The loss hurt. Many who left were long-time members, the beating heart of the church. Good friends were separated. Families were divided. There was a lot of grief. Attendance and giving never fully recovered, which would have happened either way. Deep scars remain. The church is still having a hard time moving forward. It's more timid now, more cautious, more afraid. There are churches like it all over the country.

When I talk to church members, especially church leaders, in congregations large and small, fear is often the most tangible emotion on display. They are afraid to upset anyone, afraid of pushing outsiders away, afraid to make a decision, afraid to not make a decision, afraid they will change, afraid they won't change. And if fear is not the presenting issue it is often close by, unspoken, skulking just beneath a tranquil façade, preventing a church from addressing its problems or facing its demons.

That churches are often hamstrung by fear should not be unexpected. Fear seems to be the prevailing instinct of our culture. It has become the new Great American Pastime, the proverbial air we breathe. Spreading fear is how many politicians rise to prominence and cling to power. It's how a lot of news media expand audience size and advertising dollars. It's the common currency of political talk, the most effective strategy for policy change, the essential catalyst for Facebook gossip.

For years, Americans have been programmed to be afraid—afraid of the government, afraid of science, afraid of religion, afraid of the poor, afraid of the powerful, afraid of the other party, afraid of other races, afraid of strangers, afraid of immigrants, afraid of people with too much education, afraid of people with too little education, afraid of people from the wrong side of the tracks, afraid of people who don't see the world the way we do, afraid of confrontation, afraid of the unknown.

Our regular diet of public discourse is marinated in fear, breaded in worry, deep fried in hot dread, generously salted with fresh-ground suspicion, dipped in alarm, served on a heart-stopping plate of high-cholesterol anxiety, and capped by a seductive dessert of sweet anger.

No wonder so many churches feel paralyzed. No wonder the smell of death is in the air.

Four-Alarm Problems

To be clear, not every problem is grave. Not every issue is a crisis. Many of the problems we face in church can be fixed without provoking a congregational meltdown. Ronald Heifetz, the director of the Center for Public Leadership at Harvard, calls these sorts of problems *technical challenges.*[5] We can figure out what's wrong, and we have a pretty good idea what to do to fix it using the skills at hand.

A professor encountering a roomful of bored students can adjust her teaching strategy. A boss with an incompetent employee can provide remedial training or issue a pink slip. A church with an overcrowded parking lot can raise funds to expand it. Or hire shuttle vans to bring late-arriving members to the church from the bank parking lot down the street.

Adaptive challenges are different. They are highly complex problems that have no obvious answers, no easy solutions. Adaptive challenges may cause an acute, all-hands-on-deck, four-alarm pants-on-fire crisis. Or they may simmer for years because of inaction or indecision until the pot melts into a hot heap all over the stovetop because all the substance has finally cooked out.

In the midst of such a crisis, it is often hard to figure out what is actually wrong. And fixing one problem may make the others worse.

A new business venture rockets to the top because of the vision and charisma of the founder, but his public foibles are damaging to the company, but if he's fired the value of the company will likely plummet, but if he remains the company will likely fail.

A group of church members press to make changes in worship, causing another group to express alarm since this is not the way we have done things, causing the first group to threaten to leave, causing the second group to say that they were just following the Bible, causing the first group to say wait a minute we were just following the Bible too, causing the elders to try to appease both groups, causing some members from both sides to leave, causing the elders to panic and reverse their decision, causing the remaining members to hold on to their frustrations until a more opportune moment.

Dealing with these sorts of challenges is like playing a game of ecclesial Whac-A-Mole: you take care of one thing and then something else pops up, on and on, forever and ever, world without end, amen.

The problem is that most people, most systems—in this case, most churches—

look for technical fixes to their adaptive challenges. That is, they try to solve complicated problems by looking for easy answers.

Church leaders confronted by a deeply contentious and paralyzing set of intermeshed problems with a complex history fraught with overwhelming personal stress or grief, often find themselves on their hands and knees looking for the keys to the church under the streetlight. But the keys are not there. Adaptive challenges can't be fixed that way. They are too hard, too entangled, too sticky, too impenetrable. They may require years to fix. Or generations.

When we face problems this complex, we have choices to make. We can avert our eyes and hope the issues go away. Or we can resort to the usual solutions: convene some meetings, do a study, hire an expert, write a strategic plan. None of these responses are wrong in and of themselves. One or more of them may, in fact, be necessary before all is said and done. But they are rarely sufficient to actually fix things.

But for those who are confronting change or crisis, for churches facing an impasse or a significant conflict—in other words, for all churches—there are two places outside the ring of convenient light where they should begin their search. Both are hidden. One is hidden because we buried it. One is hidden because it is God's nature.

Losing Our Minds

I have a friend who is suffering from chronic traumatic encephalopathy (CTE). He is a delightful man. Full of life. Charming. Fun and funny. But he can't remember anything that happened more than a minute or so ago. He introduces himself again and again to long-time friends as if they're total strangers. He tells a story, then immediately repeats it, then tells it again with no awareness of what he just said. It's hard. It's tragic.

But he didn't choose it. That would be unimaginable, right?

Why would anyone choose to have no memory? Why would a church? Why would we choose to cut ourselves off from our past? Why would we set ourselves up to relive the same stories or repeat the same problems over and over again as if they were perpetually new?

Those who come from Churches of Christ, whatever name is on the church sign, have largely forgotten their own story. As a matter of choice, they have lost their memory, which is pretty close to saying they have lost their minds. The result is almost always tragic.

Some time ago, I sat at the back of a room while a working group discussed a document that contained a lot of organizational history. One person, exasperated by all the focus on history and anxious for the group to make a decision, finally raised a hand and said, "Can we just get on with it? Whoever wrote this doesn't live in the real world." In other words, all that history, all those stories about what happened a long time ago, why does it matter? Why would anyone care? What difference does it make? It's not the real world.

I get it. Looking at our past often doesn't come across as very practical, not when decisions are needed and action is urgent. But understood rightly, looking at our past may be the most practical thing a person can do. Or a church.

I am trying to imagine a stockbroker who thinks that what the stock market has done in the past has no bearing on today's decisions. While I am no expert on Wall Street, it's hard to think that what happened back in 1929, or in 2008, or last month, might not be of some use to a person whose livelihood depends on the rise and fall of the market.

Similarly, a farmer would surely find it useful to know what the yield has been when certain crops were planted in certain soils or would benefit from knowing when the first frost has historically occurred.

When a physician asks for a patient's medical history, she is not asking idle questions. Her decisions about appropriate care and treatment are affected by whether her patient has a history of, say, cancer or heart disease.

In virtually every part of life—from teaching to management, truck driving to space engineering—where things came from, how susceptible they are to change, and how corrosive or productive they have tended to be in the past are profoundly relevant. They are immediate and practical.

Knowing one's own story, then, is not about bringing to mind interesting morsels of information, fascinating incidents from the past that have little purpose other than to entertain or bore our friends. Rather, we engage our past because pieces of our story have nurtured within us certain instincts and inhibited others. The more we reflect on it, the more useful that knowledge can be.

Our past has shaped us, oriented us, liberated us, stifled us, empowered us, wounded us, enlightened us, and changed us. Our present realities are the offspring of our past experiences. Certain characteristics are passed down from generation to generation, whether in families or churches. Such as stubbornness. Or insecurity. Or arrogance, combativeness, hatred, and racism. Or integrity, tenacity, and courage.

But to affirm that we are shaped by our past does not mean that our history controls us, that there's nothing we can do. Past may be prologue, but it does not have to be destiny. History is not determinative. We can take a different road. We can choose a different way of being.

The son of an alcoholic or the daughter of a child abuser may very well have been impacted by their parents' behaviors, but each one still has choices to make—whether the harmful behavior is stoked or stymied, whether the family dysfunction is perpetuated or reversed.

What is true for families is also true for churches who have their own problems and pathologies. Churches have choices to make. Things don't have to remain as they are. Preserving the status quo is not their only strategy. Some things can be different, but a new future has to be chosen.

To choose it, we will have to move away from the streetlight, away from the easy solutions, over to where our keys were lost. It will be hard work. In the process, however, we may discover some things about Jesus and about ourselves we did not know. We may come to see some things differently.

We may have to live with some things we don't like. We may have to change. We certainly will have to figure out how to give up control. But when a crisis erupts or an opportunity emerges, we may also find fresh water from our own stream. We may discover the very qualities we need—the courage to make difficult choices, the vision to imagine what is not yet but can be, and the strength in the midst of it to live as cross-shaped people.

Glory and Cross

When we are pretty sure we know the answers, it's natural to feel confident. Knowing the answers can be a heady thing.

You understand what that feels like. You're a student, say, studying for the big test. You have the material down cold. There is no question you are not prepared for. The teacher puts the test on your desk. You look it over and smile. When you finish it and turn it in, all is well in the universe. You nailed it. You knew the answers. It's a great feeling.

If only faith were like that. Being smart. Knowing the answers to all the questions. Maintaining the GPA. But it isn't like that. It isn't at all.

One of Martin Luther's complaints about the church of his day was that it believed it had the answers. It lived, in Luther's words, by a *theology of glory*. His reference is to Moses's encounter with God at Mt. Horeb. Moses said to God, I want to see your *kabod*—your face, your glory.

God said to Moses, I will cause my goodness to pass in front of you. I will show mercy. I will show compassion. But you cannot see my face. No one may see my face. No one may see my glory and live.

Luther was reflecting on a church that believed it had seen God's glory. Everyone knew what God was like, what the church was for, what to believe, what to do. They thought they had the answers.

It's like they had constructed a tall tower, built on the certainty of their knowledge of God's ways, God's word, God's nature, God's laws, until they reached the heavens where God dwelt and peeled open the sky so they could see God face to face. They believed they had done so. They believed they had seen God's glory. They believed they had studied hard for the test and had aced it.

But that's not the world God has made. That's not God's nature or the nature of God's church. Scripture reveals a certain hiddenness about God. God has created a universe in which God's very presence cannot be irrefutably known, in which disagreements about God's ways are not just possible but inevitable. Tall towers into the heavens have never worked out very well. God isn't known in that way. God reveals himself in surprising ways, hidden ways. Luther refers to this God of hiddenness as a *theology of the cross*.

The message of the cross seems like foolishness, Paul told the Corinthians.[6] But God's foolishness is wiser than human wisdom. God's weakness is stronger than human strength.

Be careful when you think you know God. Believing in God requires a measure of humility because hiddenness is in God's nature. The immortal God entered the world not in grandeur but in poverty. God's power was at its greatest when the divine child was lying as a baby in an animal trough. God's hands were most able to save when they were nailed to a tree. It is in God's hiddenness, in God's upside-down wisdom, that God's heart and power are most visible.

In a time of spiritual drought, when a church is facing conflict or failure, we can be renewed. We can find fresh water at the fountainhead. We can find answers there, beneath the spring where hidden resources lie. But that's not to say that everything will be clear. It won't. Within the waters of the Blue Hole the wisdom of God flows. But God's wisdom can be murky, sometimes bitter, always costly.

And at the heart of God's wisdom is a death. The answers we seek will require a cross, both Christ's and our own. There's no other way.

The empty tomb is a central image in the New Testament story. But it means nothing if it is detached from wounds and thorns. Christ's victory makes sense only in the face of his humiliating condemnation and public execution.

Christ was disgraced before he was glorified. He was broken before he was raised. At the cross, in the ultimate display of Christ's humanness, we discover the crucial connection between his shame and ours, the merciful link that unleashes his divine power—not just in general but for each of us and in a way that addresses our particular brokenness and shame.

All of which means that before we can engage in resurrection living we better come to grips with our weaknesses—both our church's and our own. And it means that we find contentment not by having conquered our weaknesses but right smack in the middle of them.

But there is a measure of good news in this because, Paul asserts, when we are weak then we are strong.

We've all heard this truth, of course. I've preached it a hundred times. But preaching the whole self-emptying thing is not the same as living it. That's a lot tougher. This gift is not found under the nearby lamppost where the light is good. Self-emptying is a cross-shaped move, so it's difficult. And painful. And never fully realized in this life. But I'm learning to say with Paul that God's grace is good enough, because I'm not. I surely can't do it.

Nor can the church. Christians simply are not good enough. They are not right enough, strong enough, visionary enough, faithful enough, or obedient enough. None of us.

And no church, even one in the Restoration Movement, is restored enough.

Most of us are willing to admit that Christians are weak and sinful, that we are all in some way inadequate, shortsighted, imperfect, and, at least every now and then, mistaken. But somehow some of us have arrived at the conclusion, or we simply inherited the notion passed down from the generations before us, that God's vision of church has been faithfully and fully restored in our own time, in our own understanding of church. We have come to believe that our particular churches have deduced accurately and completely God's template for what a church should look like, now and forevermore.

Here is the adaptive challenge that churches must confront head-on before anything else can matter. If you think you can fix your church, it will never be fixed. If you think God will judge your church by whether you measure up to standards you arrived at, your church will never measure up. If being a Christian means getting it right, you will never be right. You can't.

Whoever you are, whatever the history of your congregation, whoever your preacher is, however great your worship is, however confident you may be of your conclusions, your church has not gotten all of it right. To believe you have is to undermine the gospel itself because salvation depends on God, not our ability to get everything right.

My grace is enough for you, God said, because power is made perfect in weakness. Therefore, when I am weak, then I am strong. Only then.

If a church is ever going to be strong enough to withstand the challenges it is facing—from rapid cultural shifts, the rise of uncivil speech and behavior, and the radical polarization in the nation and world, to declining congregational membership, generational conflicts, and our growing diversity—if a congregation will ever be spiritually healthy, it will have to begin by confessing it is weak, by admitting up front that it might be wrong. It will have to admit that it is broken, inadequate, incomplete.

Before an alcoholic can be healed, he has to admit he's an alcoholic. Before a church can be whole, its people will have to admit that they have not gotten everything right. They will need to take up a cross, together.

We will have to admit we may be wrong. We have been hurtful. We misunderstood. We looked to our own interests before someone else's. We have gone in wrong directions. We haven't lived rightly. And we can't. We are sinners. We are human. We are weak. We are broken. Our churches are broken—our people, our heritage, our past, our future. That's what the cross reveals. That's why we need Jesus. That's why we need the resurrection. That's why we need the Holy Spirit. That's why we need each other.

Churches are broken. That should go without saying, though church leaders seem to constantly be surprised by it. Churches are broken. Having said that, I feel no urge to pass judgment on them. Frankly, I have always belonged to such churches, which is to say troubled churches, difficult churches. Yet, in spite of their weaknesses, I have also been transformed by them. Through them, even amidst their brokenness, and certainly my own, I have found new insights and new courage.

The challenge is to look for a healthy way forward, to find the key to our best future. But to be clear, it is not under the streetlight, where it is safe, where the light is good, where we are comfortable. We will have to look in places we have not gone before, in hidden places, unfamiliar places. We will have to tell the truth about ourselves. We will have to look at our past for clues about how we got here. And before all is said and done, we will have to face death—our Savior's, our church's, and our own.

Perhaps that's the best place to begin. Not at the death of our own church—though we will surely have to come to grips with that prospect soon—but at a funeral nonetheless, in another time, another place, on a windy spring afternoon, near the ocean and the orange groves, on a day of remembrance, in a season of hope.

The Peacemaker and the Pallbearer: Choices and Consequences

Santa Ana, 1929

> If [people] have at last become incapable of seeing what they once saw, it is because they have gone for so long a time not looking at it.
>
> —Owen Barfield

Fieldnotes from the Blue Hole

Churches are broken. Churches are dying. There are no easy answers.

That's what we have tried to say to this point. Perhaps that's not the most cheerful way to begin a book about hope, but it is necessary. And true. If churches are going to get well, they will first have to acknowledge they are broken. Admitting we are weak, it turns out, is a prerequisite to being strong.

So, now we're going to wade into the river. We will need to look at where Churches of Christ came from. We will be searching for resources that might provide perspective and imagination for the coming days. But we're not going to step into the stream right at the Blue Hole. Not yet. We will explore those waters in the next section.

We will begin, rather, by putting our feet in the water further downstream. We will need to see what became of the river long after it first poured from the earth. We will look at how the terrain has affected the river's course. In other words, we need to see how the world around us has influenced our thinking, the kind of choices we make, how we view our past, how we see the present. We are products of our times and our location. All of us. Inevitably.

The problem is, we can't always see what our culture and context are doing to us. The world is complicated. We are blind to many of the pressures that shape us. But we can still make sense of some things. We can learn to see the bigger picture. We can aspire to act with wisdom.

But no matter what, we have choices to make, and choices have consequences.

Our framing story for chapter 2 is an ordinary event, at least on the surface. The story takes place in 1929, about halfway between the unity meeting in Lexington and today, at the midpoint of the river. We will join some Christians on their way to a funeral. It's not a tragic occasion. There were tears, of course. The one who had died was loved. But he was well into his eighth decade. His death was not unexpected.

The funeral, however, marked a turning point in Churches of Christ, though no one could have known it at the time. A mantle of leadership was symbolically passed that day from one preacher to another, from the peacemaker to the pallbearer.

The spirit of the peacemaker reflected the earliest impulses of the movement. The man whose memory was being honored had drunk deeply from the waters of the Blue Hole. But the young pallbearer had a different spirit. He would shape a different sort of church. In the years that followed, certain attitudes and values within Churches of Christ changed. Almost a century later, his influence still lingers.

Choices have consequences.

The Fragrance of Hope

The desert wind whipped over and down the Chino Hills, around the twin peaks of Saddleback Ridge, through the valleys and canyons, across the low plains that melt into the Pacific, carrying with it the scent of oranges.

The day was clear, the breeze warm and gusty. Women in proper hats and men in dark suits walked with purpose toward the wooden doors at the back of the church near downtown on Broadway Street. Most greeted the others, even their close friends, as Brother this or Sister that, titles that were both formal and intimate.

They came expectantly. They would always remember this day and the man they had come to honor. What they did not know, what they could not have known, was how much their lives—how much the world, in fact—would soon change. In truth, things were already different, though it would be years before anyone would know how much or why.

In Santa Ana, California, on the third Wednesday of March 1929, as worshipers made their way to the little church on Broadway and Walnut, life seemed good. Not necessarily easy, but good. These men and women were hopeful and optimistic. The world was moving forward. The country was vibrant. This city of almost 30,000 stood at the center of rapid growth and progress. And the future of their particular group of Christians seemed especially bright.

They had reason to hope.

In the decade since the end of the Great War, America had thrived, growing from a relatively isolated country of limited influence to a rising world power. Industry and wealth were soaring. Unemployment was down. The housing market was up.

For many Americans in the last year of the Roaring Twenties, everything seemed possible. Two years earlier, Charles Lindbergh had flown the *Spirit of St. Louis* from New York to Paris. A few months later, Babe Ruth batted his way into sports immortality by hitting his sixtieth home run in a single season.

In the spring of 1929, a decade after being granted the right to vote, American women were gaining a serious public voice, especially in education and health. And a new breed of women, reflecting—or perhaps fueling—the exuberance of the era, had become "flappers," discarding their corsets, shortening their hems, bobbing their hair, dancing to daring jazz music, and generally exuding a casualness and cool that many of their elders found scandalous.

The national optimism was stoked on March 15, less than two weeks after the inauguration of President Herbert Hoover and just five days before the Santa Ana funeral. Newspapers quoted Treasury Secretary Andrew Mellon saying that there were bargains to be found in the bond market. The nation went into a buying frenzy.

During his presidential campaign, Hoover had exclaimed, "We shall soon, with the help of God, be in sight of the day when poverty will be banished from this nation." Poverty in America totally eliminated. Progress, indeed. Now, with the stunning rise of the market, the president's words seemed to have the ring of prophecy.

Everything seemed to be getting better. The smell of progress was in the air. Even for the modest Christians in Santa Ana, there was a sense that, with opportunity and education—especially education—there was nothing they could not accomplish.

The American education system had become the envy of the world. Schools flourished. Learning was prized. For almost a century, colleges and universities had been established across the United States at an unprecedented pace. It was clear by the early years of the twentieth century that the future belonged to the industrious, the determined, and the informed.

The Christians in Santa Ana drank deeply of this spirit. Churches of Christ had founded almost 375 colleges, academies, institutes, and schools between 1813 and 1929.

One of the earliest of these colleges was established in the Western Reserve, the land along Lake Erie that had originally belonged to Connecticut. These three million acres of prime farmland became the northeastern part of Ohio and included the little towns of Akron, Youngstown, and Cleveland.

In 1851, a determined young man enrolled in the Western Reserve Eclectic Institute, which at the time was little more than a three-story redbrick building set in a cornfield just outside of Hiram. As a child of poverty, the young man had had few opportunities. Prior to beginning college, he had done hard and dangerous work just to bring food to the table.

In his first year of college, he had paid for the modest school tuition by sweeping floors and hauling wood. But he applied himself in his schoolwork so diligently that within a year, while continuing his own education, he was promoted from janitor to part-time professor, teaching mathematics, literature, Greek, and Latin in addition to the classes he was taking. He was so popular he was asked the next semester to add more classes to his load, including one devoted to the writings of the Roman poet Virgil. In 1857, at the age of twenty-five, he became the school's president.

Two years before enrolling in Old Eclectic, this resolute young man had been baptized on a cold March afternoon in the waters of Ohio's Chagrin River, about fifteen years after the unity meeting in Lexington.

His family was directly tied to what had happened at the old cotton mill. They were part of a group of Christians who took learning seriously. At the college, he not only became a popular professor and administrator, he was in demand across Ohio as a preacher. He was soon a leading figure among these churches.

Less than thirty years after entering the Western Reserve Eclectic Institute as a student-janitor, less than twenty-five years after being appointed the president of the school, this Christian leader would become president of a much larger entity. This time, however, he was chosen not by a handful of college trustees but by 4,446,158 voters across the country.

On March 4, 1881, James Garfield, a major figure in the early Stone-Campbell Movement and a tireless advocate of the merits of education and reason, of racial reconciliation and peacemaking, gave one of the most eloquent and prophetic inaugural addresses in American history, now mostly forgotten. Garfield denounced the widespread disenfranchisement of African American voters. He called for true equal citizenship of all the races and predicted with transparent joy that the descendants of American slaves would one day lead the nation. This is what an educated nation would do.

The Christians who gathered for a funeral in Santa Ana, California, less than fifty years after President Garfield's inaugural address also believed in the importance of education. Most of the children from the Santa Ana church, who came from the same Christian heritage as Garfield, were now regularly making their way back to Texas, Arkansas, and Tennessee where their families had largely come from, to receive their college degrees.

For these Christians, knowing was as important as doing. Like Garfield, they believed that calm and rational thinking was the hope not only for their future but also the nation's.

Throughout the country in those early months of 1929, hope prospered. It was a time of building and expansion, of problem-solving and achievement. Bell Labs created the first color television. Motorola began installing radios in cars. Upstate from Santa Ana, the San Mateo Bridge opened, linking San Francisco with the East Bay. It was the longest bridge in the world. In this momentous year, no dream seemed unfulfillable, no obstacle too great to overcome.

The citizens of Santa Ana embraced the spirit of the age. Business was good. In fact, it was very good. And the primary business was fruit. A hundred years earlier, the entrepreneur William Wolfskill moved to the area, establishing a large ranch on the land that eventually became Irvine and parts of Santa Ana. He began to grow grapes for winemaking. And oranges. Lots of oranges.

Wolfskill used his expertise in agronomy to produce a new orange hybrid, the Valencia orange, which was particularly good for making juice. By 1929, Orange County produced almost a fifth of the nation's oranges.

But fruit-growing was not the only concern of these residents. Throughout 1929, the citizens of Santa Ana had taken a keen interest in the filming of a new movie, one that would ultimately win an Oscar for Best Picture, a new award, just introduced to the nation and the world. And a few miles west, the last leg of the Pacific Coast Highway, running the length of California, was finished.

No one that spring, not even in this small Southern California town, could escape the sense of progress, the optimism and confidence that captured the nation. During the heady days of 1929, anything seemed possible, not just for the country, but also for those who had come to pray and remember at the Church of Christ on Broadway and Walnut in Santa Ana, not far from where the oranges grew.

Culture's Clothing

The funeral of a preacher, even a well-known preacher, may not seem to be a momentous event in the larger scheme of things. People live, people die. Besides, this story happened a long time ago. Almost a century ago. It's just history, after all. Why should we notice? Why should we care?

But don't rush past it. Don't look for conclusions too quickly. Linger awhile. Put yourself in their world. Slip into the back of the church house as the funeral begins. What do you notice? Who are these people? How did they understand church? Where did their views come from? What did they think was important and why? What were they passing down to their children and grandchildren?

Take a moment and look at what was happening in the world around them. What should they have seen? In what ways did their culture and language, their education and income, their race and belief system influence how they saw the world? And God? And each other?

In many ways, we can see the impact of their surrounding culture more easily from our modern perch than they could. We know that 1929 would end up being a momentous year. Within a few months of the funeral, the world would be shattered. A global economic depression would create havoc with their lives. In ten years, another global conflict would begin. A lot of the little boys at the church would become sailors and soldiers. Some would die.

From our vantage point, we can feel the future breathing down their necks. But how could they have known? They were living in the flow of their quiet world. Yet, they were being shaped by external pressures and world events, far more than they knew.

As are we. We also live in a time and a place that have shaped us. All of us have been influenced by having grown up where we did, speaking the language we do, reflecting the values of our times, our culture, our families, our church. We are not unusual.

Churches have always been influenced by their surrounding world. In the first century, Jewish Christians looked Jewish. Gentile Christians, well, not so much. That's why they had such a hard time getting along, especially when they worshiped in the same city, in the same house. The early Christians were deeply affected by how they were raised, how they spoke, how they saw the world. Their churches were profoundly impacted by it.

Greek-language churches were different than Latin-language or Syriac-language churches. The norms and customs of the host culture were reflected in the vocabulary and even sentence structure of each language. The languages themselves embodied different ways of thinking and acting.

That's as it should be. It's normal. It's inevitable. Churches in all places at all times, like the Son of God, are incarnational. God's church has human skin. The gospel message tows human baggage. God's transcendent power is poured into breakable jars.

So, it should not be surprising that Christians in our own time are affected by the world around us. We speak the same slang, we eat the same food, we wear the same clothes, we watch the same movies, we drive the same cars, we log on to the same websites, we download the same apps, we engage the same popular culture. In some ways, we will always look like the surrounding world. The question is not whether we will be influenced by it but whether we will be bound by it.

We will not know how to live across the grain of the prevailing culture, nor will we know how to choose the way of the cross in the face of culture's norms and pressures, until we come to grips with the fact that we cannot escape wearing culture's clothing. We are shaped by history and tied to our times, at the same time liberated from our history and our culture through the cross and resurrection.

The way forward, at the very least, will require us to fully grasp that our churches are not simply the result of being gospeled by Jesus Christ, though I have no doubt that the good news is central to our hearts. We are also shaped by how we live out there, what we watch and read, to whom we listen, what matters to us and our friends, and our primary cultural influencers.

All of that is difficult to see while we are in the midst of it. Some things only history's long lens will make clear, looking backward after we are dead and gone.

But that does not mean we must live today in total blindness, especially of the self-inflicted kind. If our vision of the world around us and of our future is blurred, it will do us no good to curse our eyes then poke them out with a stick.

There are some things we are still able to see if we stop long enough. If we listen first and talk later. If we discern our world with the clear-eyed rationality our people were once known for. If we pray with humility. If we seek peace with others.

Then, perhaps, we may be able to peer into the haze with purpose and grace. Maybe then we can claim the resources that could make us healthy again.

In the Santa Ana Winds

Not everyone saw 1929 as a year of opportunity. Michael was born two months before the funeral in Santa Ana. He was the second child of a Black family living in relative poverty in the heart of the Deep South. In 1929, the confidence of the nation had not seeped into all the neighborhoods of American cities.

And while the influence of women throughout the country was growing, those opportunities did not extend to Black women. During World War I, women had begun to work in offices and manufacturing plants, engaging in work once deemed inappropriate for them. Black women, who had historically been shut out of factory jobs, became part of the workforce during the war. Even then, most of them had to accept lower wages, longer hours, and heavier work.

After the war, most of these women were pushed out of their jobs. By 1920, more than 75 percent of Black women in the labor force worked as farm laborers, laundry workers, and domestic servants. They were not able to embrace the hope that seemed to be blossoming among the White families all around them.

And they were not alone. Prejudice against immigrants and Catholics increased, making life doubly hard for those of Irish, Polish, and Mexican descent. Verbal attacks on Asian Americans erupted into race riots in Watsonville, California. Native Americans were rarely thought of at all.

And so, in the midst of all the progress and optimism of that 1929 spring, a dank countercurrent sliced through the air. You could smell it in the wind, souring the fragrance of the oranges.

As the White worshipers assembled at their church in Santa Ana, others were preparing to gather for their weekly prayer meeting that Wednesday evening, just thirty miles northwest. Their church was at the corner of Compton and 95th in the Watts area of South Los Angeles, a few blocks away from where a college would later be built by the founder of Western Auto, George Pepperdine.

These Christians in Watts were led by A. L. Cassius. Cassius's father, Samuel Robert Cassius, had been born in 1852 on a Virginia plantation, the son of a house slave named Jane. In contrast to the myths about slavery that were created by turn-of-the-twentieth-century White supremacists, Jane was not happy or contented in her enslavement. Nor was any other slave. Jane was not free. She was forced to work, not for herself or her family but for her master. She had been ruthlessly raped by her White master. She carried the scars of her brutal life all the way to her death. In 1863, shortly after President Lincoln signed the Emancipation Proclamation, Jane and her young son Samuel escaped from their cruel master and walked across the Potomac River bridge to the city of Washington where, a few months later, eleven-year-old Samuel shook hands with President Lincoln himself.

As an adult, Samuel Cassius preached a message whose roots ran through the 1831 Lexington meetings. This powerful preacher, like James Garfield, was also fed by the springs of the Blue Hole.

At the age of seventy-two, after decades of preaching and writing, after having finally walked away from the White churches that had marginalized and humiliated him, Samuel joined his son, Amos Lincoln (A. L.) Cassius, at the new Church of Christ in South Los Angeles. By the time A. L. retired from his ministry in 1956, he had also seen his own share of marginalization and oppression, often at the hands of fellow Christians—less physical, perhaps, but hardly less impactful than what his grandmother Jane had known.

In 1963, seven years after his retirement and almost exactly a century after his father had shaken hands with President Lincoln, A. L. Cassius, like most Black Americans, had not fully experienced the breathtaking possibilities proclaimed so eloquently in the historic speech delivered on the steps of the Lincoln Memorial by the iconic Civil Rights leader who had been born Michael King Jr., just two months before the funeral in Santa Ana. Those words evoked a powerful longing for a day when he and his people would be free at last, free at last.

Clearly, the promise of this century had not been realized by everyone. Even in the optimistic glow of 1929, a shadow loomed, slowly obscuring the brightness of the future.

The exciting new movie people were talking about, the one being filmed near Santa Ana, was based on the bestselling German novel by Erich Maria Remarque, a German veteran of the Great War. His book was entitled *Im Westen nichts Neues*—in English, *All Quiet on the Western Front*. It was a realistic, horrific, sobering account of what war was like in the trenches of northern France.

Twenty-four-year-old Dietrich Bonhoeffer, who was doing postdoctoral work at Union Theological Seminary in New York at the time, saw the movie at a local theatre and was shattered by it. The movie deeply affected much of what he did and wrote over the next, and last, fourteen years of his life. It precipitated his opposition to an increasingly warlike Nazi government and pushed him to think more seriously about the kind of costly discipleship demanded by the Sermon on the Mount.

Across the Atlantic, Europeans, whose lives had been far more deeply affected by the war, had not enjoyed the same recovery, had not experienced the same measure of hope as their counterparts in the United States. The fetid odor of uncertainty and fear was more evident there.

In Germany, after foreign financiers withdrew their investments, the economy crumbled. Unemployment reached three million by the end of 1929. Taking advantage of the crisis, an Austrian-born firebrand soon began a rise to power. In Russia, Joseph Stalin consolidated power by exiling his chief rival, Leon Trotsky. In Korea, a student protest movement erupted against the occupying Japanese, leading to a violent crackdown of the Korean people.

And, of course, in America the calendar pages turned inexorably toward October 29, Black Tuesday, the day that marked the beginning of the devastating collapse of the global economy.

But these ominous signs were not so visible that spring. The citizens of Santa Ana were aware of world events, of course, but the history we know still lay in the future for them.

History in retrospect seems inevitable. We can hardly imagine that things could have turned out differently. But what happened—in the nation and among these Christians—was not inevitable. Different choices could have been made. And different choices lead to different futures, then and now.

March 20, 1929, was a critical moment within the Christian heritage of the Santa Ana worshipers who gathered that afternoon, though no one present could possibly have grasped its full meaning. In the coming days, new leaders would emerge for these churches, and the shape of their movement would change. The actions a few people took, or didn't take, barely ninety years ago continue to reverberate among their spiritual descendants. What they said then, and perhaps more importantly, how they said it, mattered. And it matters still.

I suspect that those who waited so reverently in the church house that warm Wednesday afternoon thought not at all about the stock market or a bridge in San Francisco or even the oranges that grew in the shadow of Santiago Peak a few miles to the east. They knew nothing of a boy named Michael, born that January to devoted parents in Atlanta, who, under a more familiar name, one day would dream great dreams.

I doubt they even thought much about the Santa Ana winds that blew so persistently that day. They had other things on their minds. They had come to a funeral to honor the greatest preacher they had known.

A Loose Confederation of Churches Acting in Freedom

The Church of Christ that met on the corner of Broadway and Walnut in Santa Ana, California, was not unusual. It was not particularly well known or large. It was pretty much like other churches of its sort. People there were born, baptized, and buried, just like at any other church.

What makes this church an interesting starting place for our story, in part, is because it is not unusual. It was just a normal church. Which is not to say it was unimportant. This church, in fact, is a significant link in a chain of thousands of congregations, past and present.

It is important because it is part of a larger narrative, a multilayered and some-times gripping story of accomplishments and failures, of growth, division, crisis, zealotry, apathy, triumph, and challenge. It is a story of ordinary people who, in the name of God, did remarkable things and of extraordinary people—often the same folks—who divided the church and wounded other Christians, also in the name of God.

That these people were both gifted and flawed should not be surprising. It is part of being human. But folks from this heritage have had a stronger-than-usual belief in the human ability to get things right. That impulse has often led to disappointment when they ended up disagreeing with one another or when someone acted, well, human. But clearly, both human failings and Christian graces were abundantly present from the earliest days.

Churches of Christ in 1929 were an optimistic group. The future seemed bright. They were optimistic about their churches, about the nation, and about the working of God in the world. They were especially optimistic about human ability, certainly their own ability, to get things right, to both understand rightly and live rightly.

They were children of their world. They were products of their times. Their worldview reflected what was going on around them, the sense of growth, progress, and accomplishment. They could not possibly have anticipated the events that would shatter the world in coming days—the collapse of the global market, worldwide political unrest, the Great Depression, and a second world war. But they knew who they were and what they believed.

In 1929 the conscious identity of the churches in this movement was not quite a hundred years old. In the early nineteenth century these churches had come together almost helter-skelter. There was no founding vision, no grand design, no denominational organization or plan. Even though it is commonly referred to today as the Restoration Movement or, more recently, the Stone-Campbell Movement, it was not even a single group. It was certainly not one founded by two men named Stone and Campbell. Rather, they were a collection of mostly independent congregations emerging from several diverse groups and movements.

Over the first few decades of the 1800s, these independent movements began to converge into two groups—some linked to Barton Stone and others to Alexander Campbell. By the beginning of 1832, these two movements had come together into one, though their union was shaky at best.

To be clear, their intention was not to become a new denomination. They desired to remain a loose confederation of churches acting in freedom. But they did come together and used a variety of names to describe themselves.

The churches in Stone's orbit generally referred to their congregations as Churches of Christ and their church members simply as Christians. Those who were connected to Alexander Campbell referred to themselves simply as Disciples of Christ. As they came together, they did not solidify around any one of these designations and used all three names interchangeably.

But while the Stone and Campbell movements had much in common, the differences between them were substantial. How, with all their differences, these groups united and how decades later, with all their common beliefs, they divided is central to our story.

It is difficult to look at what happened among these churches a hundred years ago apart from what these churches look like today. Three distinct fellowships or denominations, with various offshoots and subsets, have existed for so long it is hard not to read these distinctions back to an earlier era. But throughout most of the nineteenth century, the names Disciples of Christ, Christian Churches, and Churches of Christ were essentially interchangeable.

By 1929, however, those origins had mostly been forgotten. By then, some had already come to believe they had no meaningful history, no roots at all other than the Bible.

For this and many other reasons, few of those who gathered at the church that March afternoon in 1929 could have imagined how significantly this funeral drew from their own history, how it tied together many of the main storylines of their past. Nor could they possibly have anticipated what would unfold among Churches of Christ in the decades that followed.

While the funeral marked a significant turning point in these churches, there have been many turning points. At each crucial moment, like any traveler approaching a crossroads, they had to make a choice.

Could the early restorationists, for example, unite believers around common commitments while remaining, say, Presbyterians or Baptists, or would they have to leave those denominations—ironically for the sake of Christian unity? Could the friends and followers of the earliest leaders overcome their differences and unite their causes?

Perhaps most important, could they keep together the two fundamental impulses of the movement—the drive to unite believers and the drive to restore the ancient order—when those two passions clashed?

Every few years, it seemed, these Christians faced critical choices about what they thought most important. The traits that came to characterize the movement were not predetermined. They were chosen, and they had to be chosen again in each generation.

Choices were made about the purpose and meaning of Scripture, the significance of unity, the impulse for restoration, the place of baptism and table, the importance of congregational participation, the ability of each individual to understand and act, and the crucial place of reason and education, all of which reflected their views about humans and free will. In those early decades, they chose the people they would associate with or distance themselves from. And they chose what kind of churches they would be.

Similarly, in the years after the funeral in Santa Ana—in cities and small towns, in the United States and abroad, through sermons and editorials, and through lessons passed on to the next generations—churches continued to make choices. Some parts of the story that had shaped the movement were celebrated by these churches. Other parts were suppressed or forgotten. Some fires from their past were stoked. Some were doused.

But two things are clear. What happened was not inevitable. And our own future has not been set.

Ruin and Religion

The story of the Santa Ana funeral began a long way from the orange groves of Southern California. In fact, California played a relatively small role in the almost eighty-six-year tale. By the end, as the mourners gathered at the Fairhaven Cemetery singing "In the Sweet By and By," tens of thousands of lives across North America had been touched by the man they had come to honor.

But the earliest days had not appeared quite so bright. The great man's story began not with warm breezes and the scent of oranges but in wet, wilting heat and the pungent odor of sweat and cheap liquor, drenched in poverty, in a hovel in East Tennessee.

Nancy Larimore was a woman like a lot of others in the area. She worked hard. She was loyal to her friends and cared about her family. She left a significant imprint on her children and the generations of her family yet to come. Three relatives on the Brown side of her family were governors of Tennessee. At one time, she had been a woman of some means.

But in 1843, when she was thirty and living on a farm not far from Knoxville, her world collapsed. Her husband was with her, if he was in fact her husband—it's hard to tell from the records, and he didn't stay long. Some security debts had come due. They paid them off in full, owing nothing, but then again that's all they were left with. Nothing.

At the very depth of their devastation, on July 10, their son was born. Nancy named him Theophilus Brown Larimore.

The contrast between the world of T. B. Larimore's birth and that of his death is stark. The chronological distance between 1843 and 1929 is about the same as 1929 is from today, but the cultural distance is exponentially greater. In significant ways, what life was like when Larimore was growing up—how people traveled, how fields were plowed, wars fought, and news conveyed—was much closer to what it had been like nine hundred years before than it was ninety years later.

At the time of Larimore's birth, traces of the modern world were only beginning to be visible. In 1843 the first wagon train crossed the Rockies, marking the opening of the Oregon Trail. In March of that year, the United States Congress appropriated $30,000 to "test the practicality of establishing a system of electromagnetic telegraphs," though the telegraph was still several years away from common use. In December, in Erie, Pennsylvania, the United States launched its first iron-hulled warship.

The world of 1929, with its motion pictures and car radios, was inconceivable in the year Larimore was born. In fact, few people in 1843 could have conceived of still photographs much less movies or automobiles, certainly not ones with radios.

A little more than ten years before Larimore was born, up north in Hiram, Ohio, where the Western Reserve Eclectic Institute would later be established, an angry mob of Christians gathered at their church building. It was a congregation that some of James Garfield's family belonged to, as well as members of the Booth clan, the family of Lucretia, who in 1881 would serve for a tragically short time as the nation's First Lady. Before the evening was over, these Christians had tarred and feathered Joseph Smith, after which he decided to find a more welcoming place for his band of Latter-day Saints out West. A number of Alexander Campbell's friends and associates went with him, infusing more than a few of Campbell's ideas into the doctrines of the Mormon Church.

Just a year after Larimore's birth, many within the Stone-Campbell Movement finally distanced themselves from the self-proclaimed prophet William Miller when his predictions that the world would end did not come to pass.

In the Larimore household, however, no one had likely heard of Stone or Campbell, much less Mormons or Millerites. Their concerns were more immediate and even desperate. Young Larimore would grow up with the demands and constraints of his family's crisis, which would shape his life profoundly.

The family's financial ruin was not borne well by the young son's father. Many of Larimore's earliest memories were about his father stumbling home. "I can well remember when the yell of the drunken one coming home in the otherwise still hours of night would start all of us from the hut to the woods. . . . [Then] we would slip, like little partridges after a scare, back to the gloomy nest."[1]

That he developed a lifelong aversion to debt and drunkenness is no surprise. But it was his intellectual curiosity that marked young Larimore as unusual. In a family that apparently did not go to church much, his soul was fed by reading books.

When he was sixteen, Larimore entered Mossey Creek Baptist College (now Carson-Newman College) in Jefferson City, just east of Knoxville. While there, surrounded by faculty and students of strong commitment, he became interested, for the first time, in religion.

But he did not become a Christian. Not then. The prevailing revivalism of the day persuaded him that he needed to wait for a religious experience, some sign of God's favor that would lead to his conversion and validate God's election of him as a Christian. None came. Years later, when he was baptized, it resulted not from an emotional experience, not some sense that he, rather than some others, had been chosen by God. Rather he made a decision, a commitment born of reason, reflecting the values of the Stone-Campbell churches whose teachings ultimately nurtured his faith.

Larimore's young life was hard, but the burdens of adulthood came down on him even harder. Three months before he turned eighteen, the Union garrison at Fort Sumter in Charleston Harbor was shelled by South Carolina artillery, and the world changed.

The Civil War and Churches of Christ

This is a good place to stop for a moment and think about the American Civil War. The further away we get from it, the clearer it becomes that the war was a pivotal event in American life and culture. Its effect on our lives and institutions remains deep, though mostly in unconscious ways.

But the war and its long, divisive aftermath probably had a greater impact on Churches of Christ than most are aware.

In those rare moments that the history of the movement is discussed by church members, a storyline persists that justifies the great division of this unity movement at the turn of the twentieth century. The Church of Christ side, the story goes, was committed to just being New Testament Christians. We just followed the Bible. The other side became liberal, what with their organs and missionary societies and all.

But those explanations—or self-justifications—came later. The story is much more complex. Perhaps the most immediate cause of the division in the Stone-Campbell churches is the same as what divided the rest of American society: the War Between the States.

We will see that story unfold in more depth in the coming pages. But here's a good beginning.

When the war began, James Garfield was an Ohio state senator, in addition to being the president of the Western Reserve Eclectic Institute. A month before the opening cannon shots at Fort Sumter, Garfield and other Ohio legislators had met with Abraham Lincoln as the President-elect made his way from Illinois to Washington for the inauguration. Later that summer, still several months away from his thirtieth birthday, Garfield received a commission as colonel of the 42nd Regiment of Ohio Volunteers.

Garfield recruited hundreds of students from the school he had long served to join his regiment. Almost all of them were Disciples of Christ (which is also to say, Christian Churches or Churches of Christ). This regiment, led by a Stone-Campbell Movement preacher and filled with Stone-Campbell Movement soldiers, played a significant role early in the war.

On January 10, 1862, Garfield led his outnumbered troops to victory in the Battle of Middle Creek, the decisive battle for Eastern Kentucky, helping keep the state in the Union. As one of the North's first war heroes, Garfield was soon promoted to brigadier general.

Richard Montgomery Gano was also a Civil War officer with strong ties to Stone-Campbell churches. His father, John Allen Gano, had helped convene the 1831 unity meeting between the two Georgetown, Kentucky, churches when Richard was just a toddler.

When the war broke out, the thirty-year-old Richard was a member of the Texas State Legislature. He lived in Grape Vine Springs, near Ft. Worth. In 1862, as a captain in the Confederate Army, he recruited almost two hundred men for his regiment, virtually all of whom were from Churches of Christ, which is to say Christian Churches or Disciples of Christ.

In September 1863, Colonel Gano led Confederate troops at the Battle of Chickamauga in southeastern Tennessee, the bloodiest two days of the war. Gano's fellow Christian Church preacher James Garfield and a number of Christians from Old Eclectic were serving on the Union side of the line, just a few miles away.

Since both Gano and Garfield were relatively high-ranking officers, and since each of them had become a prominent preacher among their churches, it's almost inconceivable that they would not have known each other. At the same time, it's a little hard to fathom that soldiers from this Christian unity movement might have been shooting at one another from opposite sides of the battlefield.

General Garfield's heroism at Chickamauga further fueled his popularity in the North, contributing to his eventual election as President seventeen years later. After the war, General Gano returned to Texas to preach, establishing the first church in Dallas, downtown, on the corner of Pearl and Bryan, and baptizing over seven thousand before his death in 1913.

Chickamauga, as far as we know, was the only Civil War battleground where so many Stone-Campbell Movement soldiers faced one another across battle lines, but it was not the last time that figures from the movement would encounter one another as combatants. Except later, the lines drawn were theological in nature. And personal. And they were conflicts of their own making.

Still a teenager when the war began, T. B. Larimore enlisted in the 35th Tennessee Infantry. In April 1862, his scouting report for General Albert S. Johnston provided important information about Union gunboats on the Tennessee River. Soon afterward, the Confederates under Johnston's command attacked General Grant's forces near Shiloh, where James Garfield also commanded Union troops. How close Larimore came to Garfield, we don't know.

A year later, while stationed at Chattanooga, a few dozen miles from Richard Gano's brigade, Larimore was sent on a scouting expedition where he was captured by Union soldiers. Given the choice of going to prison or taking an oath to be a noncombatant, Larimore chose the latter and returned home.

These incidents are more than just interesting tidbits from a long-ago war. They are pieces of a larger story, the significance of which can hardly be overestimated. The Civil War, with its long prelude and even longer aftermath, was a defining event, perhaps *the* defining event, for the nation and for virtually every Christian group in the country.

Within the American story, the war was the culmination and consequence of the divisions that had marked the nation from its beginning. The most profound division had been codified in the US Constitution.

In this founding document, as the result of the bargain between slave states and free states, slaves were calculated as three-fifths of a person. By that formula, the slave states could include sixty percent of the slaves in their population count. In this way, the slave states increased their electoral power. At the same time, they denied their slaves the right to vote. Or the right to be free.

Slaves could be bought, sold, beaten, and bred. Husbands, wives, and children could be separated. Masters could rape their slaves without legal consequence. Though the Thirteenth Amendment, which was passed and ratified at the end of the war, abolished slavery, the societal and personal costs of slavery continue to this day for both nation and church.

Among the Stone-Campbell churches, preachers and editors from both North and South boasted that their churches had not divided as other Christian groups had. Before the war, and for many of the same causes as the war, Baptists divided into Northern and Southern Baptists. Methodists did the same. Every denomination had its story of conflict and division. But the Stone-Campbell churches did not divide.

Or so they believed. But underneath the surface, the war played a crucial role in defining the issues they faced. The roots of almost all their disputes over the last decades of the nineteenth century, the disputes that ultimately divided these churches, began before the war in the clash between the impulse toward unity and the impulse toward restoration. But the war and its bitter aftermath became the wedge that split the movement wide open. And to be clear, the division was not only doctrinal and cultural, it was also racial.

When the long spiral of disagreement finally erupted in division by the turn of the twentieth century, most Churches of Christ, which were concentrated in the former Confederate States, rejected the other names by which they had once been known—Disciples of Christ and Christian Churches—just as they had rejected the groups those names now represented.

And tragically, most White Churches of Christ rejected Blacks. Since the Civil War, African Americans among these mostly Southern churches were forced to worship separately from Whites. A distinct, predominantly Black fellowship of churches was created, perpetually disadvantaged by culture, income, and opportunity.

Even today, the cultural differences that exist between Black and White Churches of Christ are so significant that worshiping separately has become the norm. And while more than a few predominately White congregations include people of color, little if anything is done to honor African American culture, worship style, history, values, communication, or relationships. Whites remain the dominant culture.

Without realizing it, for the most part, White members expect everyone else to assimilate and conform to their culture and style. And they wonder why ethnic minorities often feel uncomfortable in their churches. These are among the many consequences of American slavery.

While much has changed since 1865, the identifying characteristics of Churches of Christ—doctrinal, cultural, and racial—can hardly be understood apart from the causes and consequences of the Civil War.

The Peacemaker

T. B. Larimore's long and effective ministry took place in the wake of the war. Less than a year after his capture by Union troops, Larimore was baptized. A year after the war ended, he preached his first sermon. His hard work, intellect, and eloquence eventually thrust him to national prominence among the Stone-Campbell churches. Throughout his decades of preaching, as the divisions among these churches became more visible, so did his influence. And his heart for peace.

Unlike most of the frontier revivalists of his day, Larimore was not a highly emotional preacher, though his sermons were powerful and often moved listeners to tears. He never used notes and rarely gestured. He spoke simply and rationally but with great verbal artistry. Words mattered, and few preachers of his generation were better at words than he. But spirit and tone mattered as well.

Larimore's sermons, as his life, were marked by humility. He was humble before God—one contemporary called him "the most self-forgetful preacher"[2] he ever knew—and was unpretentious with people.

He believed his primary task as a preacher was to get out of the way so that God's Word could do its work. He respected people's intelligence and their innate human worth. Preaching, he believed, was about educating people, not manipulating them. Not surprisingly, then, one of his earliest endeavors was to build a school.

When the war was over, Larimore had enrolled at Franklin College in Nashville, studying under Tolbert Fanning, one of the most influential leaders of the day among Christian Churches, especially in the South. After he graduated, Larimore taught school and preached in Tennessee and Alabama. In January 1871, seven years after his baptism, five years after preaching his first sermon, he established Mars Hill Academy in Florence, Alabama. He was twenty-seven.

For sixteen years he led the school, taught classes, preached several times a week, and often spent weeks away from the school in evangelistic work. A significant number of his students became preachers. To be one of "Larimore's boys" was a badge of honor. He reluctantly allowed the school to close in 1887 so that he could devote full time to evangelistic preaching.

For the remainder of his life, Larimore's ministry focused primarily on preaching at gospel meetings. His practice was to continue a meeting as long as he and the host church thought the preaching was still effective. During these events, he preached twice every day and three times on Sunday.

One such meeting in Los Angeles began early in January and lasted until the middle of April. His longest evangelistic meeting was in Sherman, Texas, in 1894. It began on January 4 and continued for five months, during which he preached more than 325 sermons. He held his last evangelistic meeting at the Sichel Church of Christ in Los Angeles in November 1928, preaching his final sermon on December 2, a little more than three months before his death.

Between the end of the Civil War and the beginning of the Great Depression, roughly the years T. B. Larimore preached, churches in the Stone-Campbell tradition grew substantially. Churches flourished in every region of the country and increasingly abroad. But there were also disputes and ultimately division.

In the decades following the Civil War, the various disagreements began to solidify around three questions: Does the Bible authorize mission societies, musical instruments in worship, or paid local preachers?

But the cultural divisions played at least as substantial a role in the growing separation: North versus South, urban versus rural, rich versus poor. Over the remaining years of the nineteenth century, the rhetoric around these matters became increasingly heated, and preachers across the country were pushed to take a stand.

Larimore refused.

In the last quarter of the nineteenth century, a growing voice of women began to be heard throughout the nation, challenging the prevailing views about women. They believed women had intelligence equal to men and advocated, among other things, for the right to vote.

Silena Moore Holman was a leading voice in this regard among Churches of Christ, and she was a major figure in the Woman's Christian Temperance Union. For twenty-five years, she wrote numerous articles in the *Gospel Advocate*, challenging traditional interpretations of the Bible that women could never teach men.

When Holman died in 1915 in her hometown of Fayetteville, Tennessee, over a thousand people attended her funeral. She had requested that Larimore preach her funeral, saying, "I want no man to apologize for my work, and I know he will never do that."[3]

Though Larimore had opinions about the issues of his day—whether missionary societies, instrumental music, or women in leadership—he did not believe they were gospel concerns. He refused to divide the church over them or condemn others with whom he disagreed.

His gentleness and humility, which had marked his entire ministry, appeared to some detractors to be signs of cowardice, or what they considered worse, liberalism. For others, Larimore was a deeply entrenched conservative, stifling growth and subduing the voices of Christian liberty. But in the face of growing public pressure, he would not give in to either side.

In July 1897, at a crucial moment in the growing rupture of the Stone-Campbell churches, an open letter from one of Larimore's former students was published in the *Christian Standard*. The letter was written by Oscar Spiegel, who issued Larimore a public challenge.

It is not best to be silent when we see our fellow men, and especially our own family, drifting apart. Thousands of your friends believe you owe it to yourself, your family, your friends, your Saviour and your God to speak out on some matters now retarding the progress of the cause of Christ.[4]

To be clear, Spiegel's views on the issues of the day were not the same as Larimore's. Spiegel was a young, progressive preacher. He led the state missionary society in Alabama and pushed openly for the use of organs in churches. His frustration with Larimore was not that he was too open-minded but that he was too narrow, too timid. Spiegel's letter seemed designed to call Larimore out, to force him to take a stand, either to push him over the divide to the progressive side or undercut his influence.

His questions to Larimore can be boiled down to the three we have already encountered. Is instrumental music in worship permissible? Can churches work with one another to create societies or coordinate mission efforts? Is it in harmony with Scripture for congregations to contract with ministers and pay them to serve as their regular preachers? There is little doubt what Spiegel's position was on these issues. He wanted Larimore to come clean about his own. Spiegel concluded with a final challenge.

I assure you that nothing but the purest and best of motives have prompted me, in good faith, to ask these questions. Rather, a confiding brotherhood has asked them through me; for thousands of your brothers and sisters believe it is your duty to speak out on these questions, and strive to unite, if possible, the people of God. And surely when duty calls you will respond.

Larimore would not be pushed. He refused to take sides. He offered a public reply to Spiegel.[5] His words reflected not only Larimore's tender heart, but they emerged directly from the fountainhead of the movement, from the Blue Hole itself.

My dear brother, if you deem it possible . . . for a man to be in no sense a partisan, but just simply and solely a Christian, in this intensely partisan age, please try to believe that I am not a partisan. . . .

It cannot follow from the fact that I have never "spoken out" on these or similar matters, or taken part in a bitter controversy over them . . . that I am or am not either for or against them. . . I have, always, everywhere and under all circumstances, JUST SIMPLY LEFT THEM ALONE: and can, therefore, never be justly or truthfully counted, in any sense, in that fight. I have always been busy, however—busy "about my Father's business."

. . . When Brother [B. S.] Campbell took my confession, on my twenty-first birthday, he questioned me relative to none of these "matters now retarding the progress of the cause of Christ." While thousands have stood before me, hand in mine, and made "the good confession," I have never questioned one of them about these "matters." Shall I now renounce and disfellowship all of these who do not understand these things exactly as I understand them? They may refuse to recognize or fellowship with ME; but I will NEVER refuse to recognize or fellowship or affiliate with them—NEVER.

. . . Some good brethren may deem it their duty to denounce, renounce, criticise [sic], censure, condemn, boycott and abuse me, and refuse to recognize, fellowship or affiliate with me, because I am as I am or do as I do, and especially because I have written what I have written in answer to your "open letter," since, unfortunately, such spirit seems to be a popular and prevalent substitute for the spirit of Christianity, in these degenerate days of discord, division and strife among the people of God. If so, may the Lord abundantly bless, sanctify and save them. I shall certainly never retaliate. I shall simply do as I have always done: "love the brethren"; be true to my convictions, endure as patiently as possible whatsoever may come upon me; go when and where I am wanted and called, if I can; carefully avoid all questions that "do gender strifes" among God's people; PREACH THE WORD; try to do my whole DUTY, and GLADLY leave ALL results with HIM from whom all blessings flow.

Neither side was happy with Larimore's position. Conservatives criticized him for not taking a stand. Progressive preachers, like Spiegel, were exasperated. But Larimore would not budge. He had stated his position years earlier: "Criticise freely, brethren, if you wish; but do not hope to provoke unpleasant controversy with me. This you cannot do."[6]

At the turn of the twentieth century, as controversy raged among the churches of this unity movement, as conflict decayed into division, T. B. Larimore refused to engage in it. Larimore was accused by both sides of caving in to the other, of avoiding conflict, of taking the easy way. But his heart for peacemaking was, in fact, the difficult road. He took it not as an act of compromise but of conviction. He saw it not as the cowardly way but the Jesus way.

Larimore would be remembered for his strong convictions spoken not merely with eloquence but with grace. "When my final farewell to the world I have said," he went on to write, "no one shall truthfully say, 'by his death I have lost an enemy;' but be it carefully cut, in characters of truth, by request of those who love me, on the cold white stone that may cast its shadow on my lonely, gloomy grave, 'The World Has Lost A Friend.'"[7]

These were the emotions and the memories of the worshipers who gathered at the church on Broadway and Walnut in Santa Ana that windy March afternoon in 1929. Letters and remembrances poured in from all over the world.

The most prominent paper of the a cappella Churches of Christ in that day, the *Gospel Advocate*, devoted three full issues to tributes and reminiscences of T. B. Larimore. Perhaps more significantly, the two national papers representing the Christian Churches also carried tributes to Larimore.

The *Christian-Evangelist* ran a long obituary, estimating that Larimore may have baptized more than 10,000 people in his lifetime. The article also noted that the self-effacing Larimore did not keep a record of such things.

The *Christian Standard*, which had been established after the Civil War in part because of Garfield's strong influence, was the most prominent paper of Christian Churches and Disciples of Christ at the time. That a stirring obituary came from the *Standard*, then, was especially meaningful. Referring to Larimore and his former student E. A. Elam, who had died a few days earlier, the editor of the *Standard* wrote,

It is exceedingly unfortunate that more of our readers will not at once feel the shock that comes to so many with the information that these two Christian leaders have been called from the scenes of their earthly labors. This is due to the fact that a group to whom these brethren ministered faithfully and a group composed of the rest of us have drifted apart in recent years as we should not have done.[8]

Larimore had contributed many articles to the *Christian Standard* over the years and had loved the churches from that part of the movement. When he first started preaching in 1866, of course, there had been no division. He had not wanted to drift apart. He had refused to play any part in the "unpleasant controversies." But by the time of his death, the groups were hopelessly divided.

Most of the *Standard's* readers in 1929 had never heard of T. B. Larimore. Today, few in Churches of Christ know his name. Yet he played a substantial role in the history of these churches, serving as evangelist and teacher, bridge-builder, and peacemaker.

His funeral marked a significant transition in the movement, an unintentional passing of a torch to another leader, one with a different temperament, who chose a different road and a different future.

Timshel

I was somewhere east of Eden.

It is hard for visitors to the small West Texas town not to smile at the town's ironic name. The citizens of Eden are kind and welcoming, to be sure, but the stark, arid landscape of the area is scarcely gardenlike. My bemusement that day, however, had a different cause.

I wasn't aware that I was even on the road to Eden. I was coming from San Antonio, driving through Brady on the way to Abilene, a route I had taken many times before. But the route does not pass through Eden. I was distracted, listening to an audiobook. The thought that the scenery was not familiar hung for several minutes just outside my consciousness until I saw the cut-off to Melvin. I'm sure the 179 souls who live in Melvin are delightful. But I had never heard of their town. I was clearly on the wrong road.

I opened my map app to figure out where I was. Turns out, I had missed the right turn just outside of Brady. I was not on the road to Abilene as I had intended. I missed the cut-off. I found myself a few miles east of Eden. I smiled.

East of Eden. I knew that title. The great John Steinbeck novel derives its name from a line in the Cain and Abel story: "Then Cain went away from the presence of the Lord and settled in the land of Nod, east of Eden." God's interaction with Cain provides the framework for Steinbeck's classic tale.

In a crucial scene in the book, Lee tells his neighbor Samuel what has made the story of Cain and Abel so hard for him to understand over the years. In the King James version of Genesis 4, God tells Cain, "If thou doest well, shalt thou not be accepted? And if thou doest not well, sin lieth at the door. And unto thee shall be his [that is, sin's] desire, and thou shalt rule over him."

Lee explains to Samuel, "It was the 'thou shalt' that struck me, because it was a promise that Cain would conquer sin." But in the American Standard version, Lee noted, God's word to Cain is not a promise but an order: "Do thou rule over him."

The difference is neither small nor irrelevant. Did God make a promise—sin will be overcome? Or did God issue a command—you must overcome sin? Lee had spent years trying to solve the dilemma. It finally came down to one word, a word upon which everything in the novel rests. Steinbeck writes:

Lee's hand shook as he filled the delicate cups. He drank his down in one gulp. "Don't you see?" he cried. "The American Standard translation orders men to triumph over sin. . . . The King James translation makes a promise in 'Thou shalt,' meaning that men will surely triumph over sin. But the Hebrew word, the word *timshel*—'Thou mayest'—gives a choice. It might be the most important word in the world. That says the way is open. That throws it right back on a man. For if 'Thou mayest'—it is also true that 'Thou mayest not.' Don't you see?"

The word is *timshel*, Lee said. You may. But it is possible that you may not. It is neither a promise nor a command. The way is open. You have a choice.

As inconsequential as my missed turn was, I had made a choice. In my mind, distracted by other things, I was just going straight ahead to Abilene. But straight ahead did not lead to Abilene. And so, I found myself east of Eden.

In the years following T. B. Larimore's funeral, most Church of Christ folks did not know they had come to a junction. They were not aware that they were taking a different road. It felt like they were just going straight ahead. But they had changed course. They had made a choice. It would be a while before some would look around and notice the terrain was different.

Timshel.

The Pallbearer

It was the middle of March, 1929. Hope was stirring in the Santa Ana winds. The economy was booming. Incomes were up. National confidence had reached new heights. But the worshipers did not seem to notice or care. And in the long run, none of it mattered. They spoke this day of less transitory things, of the working of God and the gift they had received from having known the godly servant whom they remembered with joy.

The service was short, as Larimore had wanted. Brother James H. Sewell, whose relationship with Larimore had been long and sweet, preached the funeral sermon. Everyone said his words were beautifully spoken. Brother S. E. Witty read a few verses from Hebrews 11. Brother E. C. Fuqua led the closing prayer. As the worshipers departed the building and headed to the cemetery, the sun shone bright in the afternoon sky.

In the wake of Larimore's death, a new era would unfold. The courageous champion of peace was dead. What kind of people would they now be? Though they did not fully grasp it, they had come to a critical juncture. Two roads diverged just ahead. Which one would they take? Their future was not yet written. They still had choices to make.

Would it matter that their lives had been touched by this man? Would these people, in Santa Ana and throughout this fellowship of churches, catch the spirit of kindness and peace so vividly lived in their midst? Would they choose not to engage in unpleasant controversies? Would they be able to discern the echoes of their past, already grown faint? Would they recall the memories of a time when the unity of all Christians was the primary concern of this people? Would they remember to be gentle? Would they remember to listen?

At the cemetery, eight pallbearers carried the casket from the hearse to the gravesite. One was Larimore's grandson, another his son-in-law. Several were friends or fellow ministers.

One of the pallbearers was the new preacher over at the Central Church of Christ in Los Angeles. Larimore had not known him well, having met him for the first time just six months earlier. He was thirty-two years old but had started preaching when he was fifteen. Some still referred to him as "the boy preacher." He would soon be the most powerful editor and preacher in Churches of Christ, whose often-harsh spirit stood in stark contrast to Larimore's marked gentleness, a polarizing figure who was both revered and reviled by those who knew him, whose judgments dominated these churches, directly or indirectly, for the rest of the century.

But on this day, this man had been asked to play a small role at the funeral of the most gentle-spirited, peace-minded preacher of the era. The pallbearer's name was Foy E. Wallace Jr.

Ninety years ago, Valencia orange trees, growing under the hot sun in orderly rows, painted the mountain slopes and coastal plains of Southern California a rich green and gold. But things soon changed. Growers began to sell their land to developers who had other priorities. Soon the soil was no longer cultivated for fruit. By the end of the century, almost all the oranges were gone.

Takeaways from Chapter 2: Patterns and Meaning

In his book *How We Believe*, Michael Shermer argues that humans are "pattern-seeking story-telling animals . . . quite adept at telling stories about patterns, whether they exist or not."[9] Cognitive scientists have been making this point for years. Patterning and meaning go together.

"People make sense of experience by their mind's drive to find and create patterns and relationships," Shermer says. We see dots on a page, or we discern two or three data points in our life experiences, and then our minds form connections, which may or may not actually exist. From the pattern we have perceived we ascribe meaning and thus make sense out of the world.

We are sometimes right. Sometimes we are tragically wrong.

I have seen this phenomenon firsthand. Someone says something. Soon after, another person, a friend of the first, does something. I assume that one action must have led to the other or that both individuals are working together to undercut my purposes. Then I construct a story in my mind about what the truth is. In retrospect, "truths" such as these are rarely true. But they seem true to us and so we cling to them, confident of our grasp of the truth.

A church member hears that some change is being made in a plan or program, something new or different for this congregation. Motives are ascribed. Patterns emerge—folks just want to do what they like or copy what other churches do rather than following the Bible; this is not what Churches of Christ do, this is not who we are.

A church member hears that there is opposition to some new plan or program in this congregation. Motives are ascribed. Patterns emerge—some folks are always against anything new or different, they just want to do what they like, they care more about preserving a tradition than they do about following the Bible; this is not what Churches of Christ do, this is not who we are.

In part, the patterns we perceive in the world reflect a sort of template in our brain about what is normal or right, about the way things have always been or about the ideal shape or practice of the church. But our brains have a way of seeing something as present when it is not, or seeing something as constant when it is, in fact, in the midst of dynamic change.

It's like we take a picture in our heads about a particular moment in time, one that was for whatever reason meaningful, then extrapolate that moment to the way things have always been. On that basis, many consequential church decisions are made. But as with ancient Heraclitus, no man (or woman, for that matter) steps into the same river twice, for it is not the same river and he is not the same man.

The church as we have always known it does not actually exist. It never did. The church we once experienced was only a piece of the whole, never all of it. That church was always changing, never standing still. Just as we were changing. Others who were part of the same church experienced a different church than we did, and they were changing as well.

The meanings we construct from the patterns we see are only partial and are notoriously unreliable. That's why humility is so critical. That is why we need other perspectives, more input, different voices to help us see more clearly.

Until now, we have focused on choices and consequences, context and culture. Perhaps this is a good time to admit to ourselves that each of us has a particular angle of vision on such matters, only a piece of the truth. If we insist on our particular view of things, if we believe in our hearts that we are right and others are wrong, then congregations will remain stuck, dysfunctional, unhealthy, even if it turns out we are right on the issue itself. A key part of healthy church leadership is admitting—and believing—that our perspective on almost any issue is partial and may be wrong.

So, I have a perspective on what happened to Churches of Christ, how we got to where we are today, a perspective that stems from my own experiences and my fallible research. I might be wrong. But here is what I see.

In the years after the Civil War, what came to be called exclusively Churches of Christ, mostly in the South, began to fragment from the churches, mostly in the North, who retained the other two names of the movement, Disciples of Christ and Christian Churches. The decades leading up to the turn of the twentieth century revealed increasingly divergent streams until everyone had to recognize, by around the turn of the century, that the movement had split in two.

As the subcultures of the movement drifted apart, fueled by the bitter aftermath of the Civil War, some leaders felt a need to clarify what made their own stream distinct. Others refused to embrace the growing division. While Larimore's was not the only voice of his era promoting unity, and certainly not the loudest, his character was unassailable and his influence strong. As long as he lived, his heart for peace lived. His tender spirit would subdue the more strident voices that were stirring up these churches.

What made Larimore's gentle voice so powerful was not that he reflected a moderate position. He wasn't trying to be middle of the road. He was making a cross-driven decision. He was trying to live like Jesus.

When Paul told the Philippians to let their gentleness be known to everyone, he wasn't making a moderating move but a radical one, stemming directly from the self-emptying nature of Christ, who took the form of a slave, who humbled himself and became obedient to death on a cross—the ultimate witness of someone looking not to their own interests but to the interests of others. Larimore's spirit of peacemaking stemmed not primarily from his temperament but his discipleship.

When Larimore died, choices had to be made about the identity and character of Churches of Christ. Would anyone pick up his mantle? Would these people choose the path of gentleness, the road of discipleship? While other voices were growing louder, would a peaceable spirit be allowed to lead or at least remain in the conversation?

By the early 1930s, as the influence of Foy Wallace increased within the movement, Larimore's spirit waned. The identity of Churches of Christ as articulated by Wallace and others like him began to be seen as the norm, the way things had always been.

It was not.

Voices like Larimore's, however, while often muffled, were never completely silenced. For churches today that are dealing with their own particular challenges, Larimore's spirit may serve as a particularly valuable resource.

Some readers, no doubt, have never heard the name Foy E. Wallace Jr., and may wonder what the big deal is. Did one man really make that much difference in a worldwide fellowship that numbers into the millions? Is it fair to put what happened to Churches of Christ in the twentieth century on one man's shoulders?

Other readers will have memories of Wallace. Some of these individuals will come quickly to his defense—Wallace was a brilliant preacher, an uncompromising defender of the faith. Others will remember him as one of the most divisive individuals they ever knew. Decades after his death in 1979, Wallace is still a polarizing figure.

By the time I knew who he was, he had become almost a caricature of himself, a larger-than-life figure who could still draw crowds but seemed a throwback to another era. My most vivid memory may be his long mane of silver hair, an attribute that, on more than one occasion, was used by some male college students in Church of Christ colleges to defend their right to have long hair. If

Foy Wallace could wear his hair down over his collar then, surely, we should be able to. It's possible I made just such an argument. I don't recall it making any difference. With age, I grew to understand Wallace's more substantial impact on these churches.

But the larger issue remains. Was one man responsible for what happened to Churches of Christ in the twentieth century? We will have an opportunity to assess that question more thoroughly, but the answer for now is yes. And no.

Wallace was a singular figure. There were other preachers with influence. There were other editors with power. But Wallace was both editor and preacher, and his impact was unusually broad. As front-page writer or editor of several influential journals, including the *Bible Banner* and the *Gospel Advocate*, Wallace shaped many of the issues of the day. What raged on the pages of these journals also raged in the churches influenced by them. And he had an opinion on most issues.

But Wallace did not just argue the issues, he often publicly shamed those with whom he disagreed. More than a few preachers in his day, as well as some college presidents and faculty members, had their reputations destroyed by a stab of Wallace's pen. More than a few lost their jobs. And what he said in writing, he amplified with devastating impact from pulpits across the nation.

Throughout much of the twentieth century, churches east of the Mississippi and those west of the Mississippi largely lived in different worlds. Powerful Tennessee preachers typically had little sway in Texas, and big Texas preachers had little influence in Tennessee. But Wallace's stride left deep footprints on both sides of the river, not merely on the issues of the day—pacifism, premillennialism, church cooperation, among others—but more insidiously on deep cultural issues such as race.

Though Wallace wielded considerable influence, especially in the middle third of the twentieth century, he was not alone. He might be a symbol of what happened, but he is not responsible for all of it. Which raises the larger questions of choice and consequence.

Wallace displayed a different spirit than Larimore and, by so doing, was instrumental in creating a new pattern for those who came after—a new meaning, a new identity. Said more bluntly, Wallace did not merely exhibit less peaceable behavior than Larimore, he consciously and utterly rejected Larimore's reconciling spirit and worked all his life to undo Larimore's more openhearted vision of the church.

A century later, we are still attempting to make meaning of what happened. We have to, because that's what humans do. But if our view of what has been handed to us from the past is faulty or is mostly created in our own imaginations, we end up clinging to a narrow or even false notion of our own identity. If so, the scaffolding beneath us cannot hold.

A century ago, in a time of massive transition both in culture and church, Wallace and other church leaders made decisions about how they would behave and what was important. The direction they chose created a new reality for the churches they influenced.

In the century prior to Wallace, two primary impulses defined the movement—a desire for Christian unity and a drive to restore the church of the New Testament. These two impulses lived side by side, often in tension. Folks like Larimore worked to preserve both. Folks like Wallace worked to destroy the unity part in order to promote the restoration part, or at least their particular vision of it. Wallace prevailed, or at least seemed to. As a result, these churches became, and still remain, something they had not previously been, a restoration movement, not a unity movement.

Churches of Christ in the early twentieth century were on a long journey. To stay on the road, to reach their destination, they would have to make a turn. If they drove what seemed to be straight ahead, they would go off course. Here was a decisive moment. They had to choose.

You may, Lee said to Samuel, but it is possible you may not. The way is open. You have a choice.

At the critical junction, these churches chose to go straight. It seemed at the time that they had stayed on the same road, but they hadn't. They were now east of Eden. The new road would take them to a very different destination.

Timshel.

In our time, we do not know what the future may look like. We are on our own journey. We have been on the road a good long while. The way ahead is unfamiliar. We need to have our eyes open. There are choices to make—about whether to turn or when, about where our destination lies.

We can still decide what is important and what is not. We can decide how to speak to one another, what we should value, what we should relinquish, where we should go. Our future is not inevitable. The journey ahead is not set. We have choices to make.

And choices always have consequences.

A Timeline of the Movement

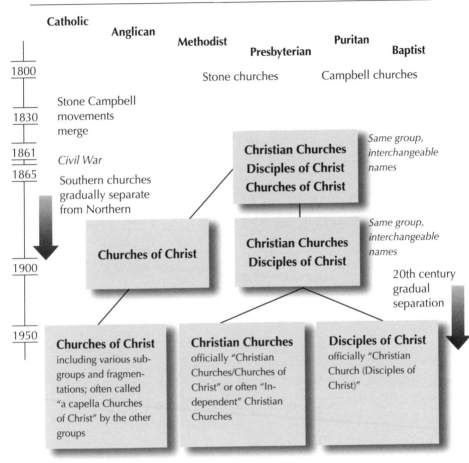

Any visual representation of the history of this or any movement is overly simplistic and therefore flawed, but it may be helpful to see the broad historical sweep. After the joining of the Stone and Campbell groups in the 1830s, this unity movement used three names interchangeably. After the Civil War, Southern churches, mostly choosing the name Churches of Christ, gradually separated from the other, mostly Northern, churches. A gradual separation of Independent Christian Churches (known organizationally as Christian Churches and Churches of Christ) and the Christian Church (Disciples of Christ) took place from the early to mid-twentieth century.

There are substantial differences among the groups, to be sure, but also significant similarities. In many cases, the lines between the groups are blurred or overlap. There are also a significant number of fragmentations within what began as a unity movement. Among Churches of Christ these include International Churches of Christ, noncooperation, and non-Bible class Churches of Christ, among others. Many Northern churches kept the name Churches of Christ but were not affiliated with the Southern churches of that name. They remain part of the group known as Christian Churches and Churches of Christ.

CHAPTER 3

Pray More, Dispute Less:
The Road to Christian Unity

Lexington, 1831

> When the mariner has been tossed for many days in thick weather, and on an unknown sea, he naturally avails himself of the first pause in the storm, the earliest glance of the sun, to take his latitude, and ascertain how far the elements have driven him from his true course. Let us imitate this prudence, and before we float farther on the waves of this debate, refer to the point from which we departed, that we may at least be able to conjecture where we now are.

> —Daniel Webster

Fieldnotes from the Blue Hole: Part Three

The shape and direction of the river is starting to come clear. We can now see that the river diverges downstream from the Blue Hole. Less than a century after the Lexington meetings, the unity movement split in two.

T. B. Larimore lived almost three decades beyond the division, well into the years when Churches of Christ had forged an identity separate from the others. But even after the split, Larimore stayed in relationship with those who ended up on the other side. As long as Larimore and people like him were alive, the spirit of peace and the heart of peacemaking remained.

But when Larimore was gone, most Churches of Christ chose a different way.

Churches of Christ are still making choices. Each church—in its own way, within its own context—has things to decide. We are not just figuring out what to do about our many technical challenges, like whether we expand the auditorium or change the worship hour. Those are not always easy choices, but they are mostly manageable. It's the adaptive challenges that can tear us apart.

What do we do when we disagree on big issues? Can we talk about disputable matters? If we can't agree, does one group or another have to leave? Can matters decided long ago by our spiritual ancestors be reasonably reconsidered in our own day? Can we do church in such a way that all generations of Christians can work and worship together? What will be the consequences of the choices we make?

Those are questions not just about our future but about our identity. Who are we, really? What's important to us? What do we value?

And so, we are thrust back to the beginning. Now we need to wade into the stream at the Blue Hole, to the story of the unity meetings where the disagreements among Christians were far more profound than what most of our churches experience today.

But we will also need to explore what happened before, in the waters that nourished the river from below. What led to the unity meetings? What made these people a peacemaking community? What difference might those stories make for our own churches?

There are many tales to tell here. The framing story in this section will be the meetings at Georgetown and Lexington. That story is dramatic. It might even evoke a tear or two. But we will also discover a shipwreck and a near drowning—two different stories, mind you, but ones that might serve as an apt metaphor for our own churches. We will encounter some Old Light Seceders, whose Old World disputes slopped over into the New, perhaps creating a pattern for how we deal today with some of our own divisive matters.

We will meet old Thomas Campbell, carrying with him the divisions of his former homeland, who set them aside to embrace the heart of unity two decades before Lexington. We will meet Thomas's son, a young Alexander, who will have a more pronounced presence in chapter 4.

Finally, we will walk alongside Barton Stone, who sparked a national spiritual awakening at his church at Cane Ridge, Kentucky. Three decades after this massive revival, Stone became the beating heart of the union sealed in Lexington, where the Spirit Waters spilled from the earth at the Blue Hole.

In the years after the meeting, even though Stone's temperament and teachings seemed to be overwhelmed by the younger, more aggressive Campbell, Stone's spirit of peace continued to live, long after his death. It showed up in sometimes unexpected ways, quietly but persistently, generation by generation, in men and women of peace.

Like the old preacher buried in Fairhaven Cemetery, in Santa Ana, near the ocean and the orange groves.

Like anyone in your church?

The Road through Georgetown

The early story of the Stone-Campbell Movement in its various streams and tributaries, in all its influences and instincts, traveled from continental Europe to Scotland and Ireland for a season, then crossed the Atlantic into New England, Virginia, and North Carolina, and on to the upper reaches of the Ohio River, making its way town by town and sermon by sermon into the bluegrass country of central Kentucky. There, on Christmas and New Year's weekends in 1831–32, two groups of Christians came together to see if they could make their way together as one people.

The choice they had to make was not easy, though they could scarcely have been aware of all that was at stake. What these churches did in two weekend meetings still echoes, however faintly, among their spiritual descendants two centuries later.

T. B. Larimore had begun to preach within living memory of the Georgetown and Lexington meetings. During his long ministry, unity with other believers was still a vital part of the movement's identity, even in the difficult years after the Civil War. And so, unity was important to Larimore.

The way he thought and acted reflected not only his discipleship and his temperament but also the times in which he lived. His people, his community of Christians, valued harmony among believers. From Larimore's earliest days, his family and his life situation had helped him distinguish what was important from what was opinion. His instincts were to look for common ground whenever possible and not to argue over what he considered personal judgment rather than pure gospel.

Foy Wallace, on the other hand, was born in the late nineteenth century, at the critical moment of division between the mostly Southern Churches of Christ and the rest of the Stone-Campbell Movement. He had not known a unified movement and had no personal memory of the unity meetings in Georgetown and Lexington nor anyone who was there.

In other words, Wallace—like Larimore, like all of us—was shaped by the times in which he lived.

One of the crucial concerns for Churches of Christ at the turn of the twentieth century, as they worked to find their footing in the wake of the division, was how they were or should be distinctive. In other words, what set them apart from the other side of the movement. The drive to be distinctive from everyone else remains in the gene pool of the movement to this day. I still hear it from time to time. If we make this decision or adopt that practice, how will we be distinctive from all the other churches?

But the language of distinctiveness was not present at the beginning. It was added later, sometime after these churches missed their turn.

For Wallace, being distinctive meant choosing what was right, which meant everything else was wrong. Seeking unity, on the other hand, was to Wallace an expression of compromise. It revealed weakness, even cowardice.

Wallace began to emerge as an influential preacher shortly after the Larimore funeral, just as the nation fell into years of fear and uncertainty. The stock market collapse launched a worldwide economic depression. The world seemed to be hurtling again toward war. Churches of Christ were not immune to the anxieties of the day.

In such difficult times, people often look for commanding leaders, sometimes autocrats or even despots, who see the world in black and white. These sorts of leaders provide unambiguous answers in uncertain times. They soften people's fears by slaying the people's enemies, whether real or imagined.

And so, Wallace's talents and temperament were custom-made for his times. By 1950, barely twenty years after Larimore's death, the memory of a movement that had been established on the basis of unity among diverse peoples, one that cherished cohesion and harmony, had virtually disappeared. But these developments could not have been anticipated by the leaders of the Kentucky churches who started down the road toward unity less than a century before Larimore's death.

That road wound through Georgetown.

In the beginning, this small town in central Kentucky was barely more than a hamlet nestled on the seventy-five-mile-long North Elkhorn Creek in what had once been the hunting grounds of the Shawnees. The village seemed inconsequential on the surface. But over a twenty-year period, between 1819 and 1839, this sleepy little town came to play an unusually large role in shaping the future of the Stone-Campbell Movement.

When Elijah Craig established the town in 1784, he named it Lebanon, but changed the name to George Town six years later in honor of the nation's first president. Craig was a strong-willed, outspoken Baptist preacher from Virginia, whose stamp on the community was immense.

Among Craig's numerous initiatives were two that particularly marked the town: he produced the first bourbon in America, at least according to legend. (There is a bourbon today bearing his name, or so I'm told.) And he established the first classical school in the state of Kentucky, the Rittenhouse Academy.

Georgetown fell into decline after Craig's death in 1808. Its resurgence began, at least in part, when Barton Stone moved there a decade later to become the principal of the Rittenhouse Academy and to preach at a new church.

Stone, at first, was not thrilled with the little community. He found Georgetown "notorious for its wickedness and irreligion,"[1] and so he set his mind to change things. As principal of the school, he would be able to leave a deep imprint on the community. And so he did.

The Baptists in the area were not enthused. It's not that they embraced the "irreligion" of the local citizenry. They were just concerned about the growing influence of Stone and his fellow church members. And so, Baptist leaders founded Georgetown College in 1829 to educate Baptist clergy, solidify the Baptist presence, and resist the growing presence of Stone's Christians. Soon, Stone's group would found its own college, almost next door to the Baptist school. It was the first in a wave of new colleges established by the fledgling movement and would later spawn three significant schools in Lexington, a few miles to the south.

The identity of the Stone-Campbell churches, which first came together in Georgetown, can hardly be understood apart from their interaction with other Christian groups. Especially Baptists. Especially in Kentucky.

An Incubator of Revival

In the late eighteenth century, in the years after the Revolutionary War, Kentucky was ripe for an uprising. The question was what kind—the armed variety or something more spiritual in nature. It would take a few years for that to be sorted out.

Many of the first settlers to the new territory of Kentucky were old soldiers who had been promised land in return for having served in the Continental Army. At their arrival, a decade of disorder and lawlessness began.

But a new group of settlers soon started to move in, mostly families of Scotch-Irish ancestry from Virginia and North Carolina. These were quiet and religious folks, Presbyterians for the most part, who soon sought ministers for their new towns.

Among the preachers who accepted the call to preach to these new settlers were several who had been a part of Caldwell's Academy, a school licensed to educate Presbyterian ministers in Guilford, North Carolina. This school, as it turns out, was an incubator of religious revival.

David Caldwell, the school's founder, had been profoundly shaped by what we now call the First Great Awakening earlier in the century—think Jonathan Edwards and the New England Puritans. In turn, many of Caldwell's students would spark the next Great Awakening soon to burst upon the hollows and hills of Kentucky, preaching fiery sermons and exhorting the people with shouts and tears.

For the next few years, such revivals began to be held throughout central Kentucky, becoming larger and increasingly enthusiastic. The meetings were usually held outdoors because of the size of the crowds and were striking because of the physical signs of renewal, including shouting, laughing, and falling.

Though such demonstrative behavior would never characterize later Churches of Christ, the beginnings of these churches, nonetheless, run through the raucous, Spirit-drenched world of Kentucky revivals.

Barton Stone had been a student at Caldwell's Academy. He began preaching in 1796 in central Kentucky, in country churches a few miles east of Lexington. In June 1801, Stone hosted a revival in Concord in one of the churches where he preached. Around four thousand were present. They heard sermons by a number of ministers, mostly Presbyterian, Methodist, and Baptist. The revival centered on communion services, held in smaller groups on the church grounds. One hundred fifty folks were said to have "fallen" or in some other way physically manifested certain "exercises" of the Holy Spirit.

Later that summer, Stone hosted another revival, this time at his church at Cane Ridge. For almost a week, beginning on August 6, between ten thousand

and twenty thousand people—some witnesses said even more—gathered inside
the little church and all around the grounds, crowding together acre upon acre
across the rolling farmland, thickets, and meadows. They listened to sermons,
sometimes as many as seven preaching events at the same time, on tree stumps
and makeshift platforms across the grounds.

The preachers were mostly Presbyterian and Methodist. Perhaps as many
as 1100 slaves and freedmen were present. A Black pastor, probably a Baptist,
was among those who preached, as were a number of women. Several hundred
took communion in the log cabin church as well as in groups scattered across the
nearby fields. And again, there were many physical evidences of a great outpouring
of the Holy Spirit.

What was happening in Kentucky, the so-called Great Revival of the West,
lasted until 1805. But the revitalization of Christianity in America, what was
later referred to as the Second Great Awakening, continued for several decades
more. Many would mark its beginning at Cane Ridge and the preaching of Barton
Stone.

After the camp meeting revivals began to wane, the Awakening continued
to be fueled by the rapid growth of Methodism as well as by Baptists and other
independent movements. One of these independent movements was led by Stone
and emerged from his experience at Cane Ridge.

But Stone had come to have a conflicted relationship with the Presbyterian
Church. On one hand, here were his teachers, his friends, his family. The Presbyterians had formed him, and he was grateful. But he had begun to disagree with
some of their central doctrines. He had to make some decisions about what his
future would be with them.

These doctrines were carefully spelled out in the Westminster Confession
of Faith, to which Stone and all Presbyterian ministers were accountable. The
Confession had been approved by the British Parliament in 1646. This government action had taken place during the English Civil War, after Charles I, king of
England, had been deposed. Which is to say, he lost his head.

With the king now gone, various church officials and political leaders drafted
the Westminster Confession, whose purpose was to reform the Church of England. The Scottish Parliament adopted it the following year. When the British
monarchy was restored in 1660, the Westminster Confession was overturned in
England. But it continued to be accepted by the Church of Scotland and all of

its spiritual heirs, including American Presbyterians, as their rule of faith and order.

Stone's troubles with Presbyterian Church officials began shortly after the revival at Cane Ridge in the summer of 1801. By this point, he and several of his associates were no longer able to fully accept the Westminster Confession. As a result, they had to answer to their presbytery, the ruling body of elders in the region where they served.

Among Stone's concerns were the doctrines of election and reprobation. According to the Confession, God gives faith to the elect, that is, to those whom God had previously chosen to be saved, but God does not give faith to the reprobate, to those who are rebellious or morally unworthy. Stone struggled with how a God who loved sinners could choose to give faith to some sinners but not to others. He had come to believe that every individual had the power to have faith and that no previous work of the Holy Spirit was necessary to convict them of their sin.

God gives faith, Stone believed, not primarily through a prior mystical experience but through the gospel story itself. A person could choose to receive it or not. Therefore, those who ignored the message of the gospel and who rejected God's love were responsible for their own condemnation, which the sovereign God had promised and will accomplish.

But Stone had another concern, which added to the tension among the Presbyterian leaders at the time. He had inherited two slaves from his mother upon her death. He had decided to free them.

For some time, he had been making strong and public anti-slavery appeals, which had created more than a little discomfort in some of the churches. He said that slavery was "a moral evil, very heinous, and consequently sufficient to exclude such as will continue in the practice of it from the privileges of the church."[2]

In other words, he believed slave owners should not be allowed to take communion or have any sort of leadership in the church. Moreover, during the Kentucky revivals, a large number of slave emancipations had taken place, which Stone saw as evidence of the work of God. Many of the Presbyterian officials were not pleased.

Stone had to come to grips with his differences with the Presbyterians and his deep concerns with the institution of slavery. What he did next is not just an item of interest in the historical record. Stone's heart still beats, however weakly, within the churches that bear the stamp of his influence.

What Happened to the Holy Spirit?

It may seem strange to a reader steeped in present-day Churches of Christ, with their history of reason and intellectual sobriety, of decency and orderliness, to fully grasp that the roots of the movement ran so deep into the soil of exuberant frontier revival. In these early meetings there was a lot of shouting, laughing, and falling. All attributed to the work of the Holy Spirit.

Even some of the early restoration leaders struggled with the revivalistic spirit. These displays were not Alexander Campbell's thing, to be sure. Campbell's hyper-rationalism—as well as his later, less noble efforts to diminish the role of Barton Stone's group of Christians before they united with Campbell's Disciples—may have fueled the almost two centuries of neglect of the Holy Spirit among Churches of Christ.

Well into my adulthood, too much talk about the indwelling of the Holy Spirit was frowned upon. If it was too vocal, it often resulted in professional banishment. The majority opinion was the so-called "Word Only" view, essentially that the Holy Spirit wrote the Bible, then went away. As if the Spirit had finally found a nice retirement home in Palm Beach and mostly spent his time playing golf and remembering the good old days.

Some courageous preachers in the late 1960s, including a grace-talking young firebrand with a shock of blonde hair from the prairies of Canada, began talking about an indwelling Holy Spirit. And a new batch of New Testament scholars among Churches of Christ began to actually address the evidence from Scripture.

Today, the memory is dim of a time these churches ever denied the present work of the Holy Spirit. Still, it is hard for stories about the Spirit-filled Kentucky revivals at the turn of the nineteenth century not to make modern Churches of Christ squirm a little.

But something was going on. The Holy Spirit certainly seemed to be at work. But it wasn't only in the stories of revival. Somehow the Spirit of God was creating among people who strongly disagreed about many matters a heart for unity, a spirit of peace.

Pray More, Dispute Less

Stone's frustration with the Presbyterian Church came to a head in September 1803. He and five other pastors with similar objections to the Westminster Confession withdrew from the denomination before any disciplinary action could be taken against them.

They decided to form their own presbytery, naming it after a town in Ohio, where some of their past experiences had been especially positive. But the newly formed Springfield Presbytery did not last long. The ministers became concerned that all they had done was form a new sect, another division, while their desire had been for the unity of the whole church.

So, on June 28, 1804, they wrote and adopted a document of remarkable power and simplicity. It was a clear and sharp call for unity, a commitment to stop creating new sects and denominations. It is one of the most important religious documents ever drafted on American soil. Its message serves as a founding principle of Churches of Christ, the source water of these people.

The document is entitled *The Last Will and Testament of the Springfield Presbytery*. It lists twelve statements of concern or commitment, beginning with the item of primary importance:

> We will that this body die, be dissolved, and sink into union with the Body of Christ at large; for there is but one body, and one Spirit, even as we are called in one hope of our calling.

Let those words wash over you for a moment—let this body sink into union with the Body of Christ at large. What a difference it would make if our churches were committed to such a spirit. Among the remaining items are the following:

We will that our power of making laws for the government of the church, and executing them by delegated authority, forever cease; that the people may have free course to the Bible, and adopt the law of the Spirit of life in Christ Jesus.

We will, that the people henceforth take the Bible as the only sure guide to heaven. . . .

We will, that preachers and people cultivate a spirit of mutual forbearance; pray more and dispute less.

Now that's a prayer that should be uttered often in our assemblies, in our elders' meetings, Bible classes, and prayer groups.

In the concluding section, describing why they took this action, these pastors said,

With deep concern [we] viewed the divisions, and party spirit among professing Christians, principally owing to the adoption of human creeds and forms of government. While [we] were united under the name of a Presbytery, [we] endeavored to cultivate a spirit of love and unity with all Christians.

A deep concern about a party spirit among Christians. A spirit of love. Unity with all Christians.

The words of this remarkable document are deeply embedded in the soul of the churches that soon emerged—the church of James Garfield, the preacher, general, congressman, and president; the church of Samuel Robert Cassius, the former slave, who fought against massive prejudice in order to preach the gospel; the church of Richard Montgomery Gano, the Confederate general, physician, and church planter; the church of Silena Moore Holman, the writer and advocate, whose powerful words taught and transformed both men and women; the church of T. B. Larimore, the evangelist and peacemaker; and the church of countless women and men who have served the kingdom faithfully over the decades.

These words helped create the road upon which Churches of Christ have walked, even though most members today have never heard them.

Until his death forty years later, Stone led a growing group of Christians who believed they had a responsibility to study the Bible for themselves, to share the gospel with others, and to actively pursue Christian unity. They believed in the sovereignty of God who alone granted salvation. But they also believed humans had free will to make choices and that those choices had consequences. Like the Presbyterians from whom they had come, Stone and his fellow pastors argued for the independence of local congregations and believed congregations should ordain their own ministers and make decisions about their own futures. They scorned all denominational names, urging folks to simply call themselves Christians.

Over the years, Stone's opinions evolved on many issues—the atonement, the Trinity, and baptism, among others—but his primary focus did not change. Until his death in 1844, he would champion, with diligence, purpose, and considerable energy, the cause of unity.

But the way was not smooth. The conversations with other church leaders about God and doctrine were not always amicable. His interactions with the Presbyterians who did not join this new movement of Christians were sometimes difficult.

But it was with the Baptists that the tensions seemed to have been greatest. Many of those tensions were evident within the Baptist community itself, especially among those who thought of themselves as Regular Baptists in contrast to a new group of Reforming Baptists.

For Stone's Christians, the road to the unity meetings of late 1831 in Georgetown and Lexington led through the Reforming Baptists. The road to the Reforming Baptists began in Ireland, in County Armagh, in the villages of Ahorey and Rich-Hill, in the preaching of a son of the Campbell clan.

Jubilee

A number of years ago, several Churches of Christ in the Nashville area sponsored an event called Jubilee. A few thousand people came together each summer for worship, preaching, classes, and fellowship. I was able to be present two or three times and remember it with fondness. Like most who went, I knew it was controversial.

Some preachers in the area had branded Jubilee speakers as false teachers. Among other issues, these opponents were concerned that Jubilee organizers believed in the active presence of the Holy Spirit and seemed to accept folks from other Christian groups as full-fledged, authentic Christians. Some of the issues were personal and petty. Local Churches of Christ began to publicly take sides. The religion editor at the Nashville *Tennessean* ran a series of articles highlighting the squabble. Not understanding all the church issues in Middle Tennessee, I wasn't completely sure what all the fuss was about.

A few years later, one of my former students was on a mission survey trip to a city in Ukraine. He was part of a group thinking about planting a church in the area. These young Americans went to a worship service one night that was made up mostly of new Ukrainian Christians.

One of these new Christians, whose thick accent was barely understandable to a non-Ukrainian-speaking American, apparently felt a need to check these Americans out, to see if they would be a good fit with the Christians already there. He asked my student, "So, what is your opinion about Jubilee?"

I still shake my head when I think about it. How could an event in Nashville possibly be a test of fellowship for a group of Christians in Ukraine?

It happens all the time. A congregation of Christians somewhere makes a decision of expedience or forms a judgment about what is right or best for them at the time. This belief or practice is then passed down from generation to generation, from one congregation to another, becoming, over the years, a defining characteristic of the church. Long disconnected from the reasons it was first introduced, or totally removed from the local context in which it first arose, the belief or practice now approaches gospel from which it would be close to heresy to change. And no one can remember why. It's just the way things have always been.

It's the Pot Roast Principle at play.

You know the story. A young girl watches her mother prepare a Sunday roast dinner. Each Sunday, the mother cuts the ends off her pot roast before popping it into the oven.

"Why do you do that?" the daughter asks.

"Well, that's just how you make pot roast," her mother replies.

"But why?"

You know, you shouldn't have to stop to justify how to cook a pot roast. You're a good cook. You certainly know how to cook a pot roast. You've been doing it for years. It's how you've always done it. It's simply how it's done.

But the daughter is persistent. The mom finally provides the only answer she can come up with: because it's how my mother made it.

So the daughter calls her grandmother. "Grandma, when you cook pot roast, why do you cut the ends off? Does it make the meat more tender? Does it give you more room for the vegetables? Does it cook the roast more evenly?"

Her grandmother scratches her head. "When I first married your grandfather, we had a tiny oven. The pot roast didn't fit unless I cut the ends off."

Apparently, the new Christians in Ukraine didn't know about pot roasts.

No Uncharitable Divisions among Them

Thomas Campbell began preaching at the Presbyterian church in Ahorey, Ireland, in 1798, about the time the revival was breaking out across the Atlantic in Kentucky. Campbell's family was Scotch-Irish. That is, they had been part of a great migration of Scots to Ireland.

Campbell had been raised in the Church of England, but he found it cold and rigid. So, as a young man, he decided to become a Presbyterian. And then, against his father's wishes, he decided he would become a minister.

Campbell spent three years in Scotland, at the University of Glasgow. His studies included not only the traditional course in ministry preparation, including literature, theology, Greek, and Latin, but also medicine. Perhaps his most formative studies were in philosophy.

He was deeply influenced by the works of Thomas Reid, George Jardine, and Dugald Stewart, towering academic figures of the day, whose Scottish common sense philosophy would play a significant role in the churches Campbell later influenced in America and the colleges those churches would establish.

We need to stop for a moment to try to understand what was going on in Thomas Campbell's church. Perhaps if we understood the Scottish Presbyterians of his day, we might better understand why Churches of Christ are what they are today.

Campbell's church in Ahorey, Ireland, was part of a division of a division of a division. Scottish Presbyterian churches had fought for years over a number of issues, mostly having to do with their relationship with Scottish national and local governments.

Because of all the controversies, some congregations seceded from the main Presbyterian church. These were known as Seceder churches. Among other things, these Seceder churches appointed their own ministers while Anti-Seceder ministers were appointed by the Scottish Church.

Some of the Seceders supported church members becoming burgesses, that is, city officials. Some did not. These were called Anti-Burghers.

Of the Anti-Burghers, some followed new interpretations of the Westminster Confession. These were called New Lights. Old Lights did not.

Campbell's church in Ireland was of the Seceder, Anti-Burgher, Old Light Presbyterian variety. They didn't fellowship with Anti-Seceders, Burghers, or New Lights, you understand.

The ironic thing is, these issues had almost nothing to do with Ireland. They were relevant almost entirely to Scotland. I do not know what their position was on Jubilee.

Campbell's experience with the divisiveness of his church in Ireland set the stage for what would happen on American soil. Not only did he have to deal with the sometimes petty, often irrelevant, disputes among the Presbyterians, he also had to face the political turmoil in Ireland, which was roiling toward full-blown revolution. He chose to disengage from the politics.

While Thomas Campbell remained distant from political affairs, his instincts toward unity in the midst of a divided Christianity were stoked by his growing involvement with an independent congregation in nearby Rich-Hill, where he had established a small school. The church was part of a large and growing group of independent churches throughout England, Scotland, Ireland, and the New World.

Campbell was a much-loved preacher at the Ahorey Presbyterian Church. He was hospitable in his pastoral work and engaging in his sermons. But on many Sunday evenings he visited the church in Rich-Hill, taking advantage of the privilege of "occasional hearing," which the Presbyterians allowed if not encouraged.

Campbell visited the Rich-Hill church so often he was sometimes jokingly referred to as Nicodemus, "who came to Jesus by night." There he experienced a congregation with no denominational affiliation, serving only under its own authority.

The independent congregation at Rich-Hill observed the Lord's Supper weekly and was led by a group of elders. The church took up a collection each week for the poor and was known to be largely free of a dogmatic or controversial spirit.

The preaching that was common there was of the new style popularized by John Wesley and George Whitefield, the so-called "methodists." Campbell was clearly influenced by what he experienced at Rich-Hill. On his visits to the church in this village, he often brought his oldest son Alexander.

In 1807, Campbell's doctor urged him to get out of Ireland for health reasons. And so, he caught a ship to America, leaving Alexander, who was nineteen at the time, in charge of his affairs.

When Thomas arrived in Philadelphia, he discovered the old issues were still at play. He was soon commissioned by the Seceder Presbyterians to preach out on the western frontier of Pennsylvania where the divisions of the Scottish church were even less relevant than they had been in Ireland.

The church authorities made it clear that Campbell should not minister to, and especially should not serve the Lord's Supper to, anyone who was not a Seceder, Anti-Burgher, Old Light Presbyterian. But Campbell felt a need to serve all the people out on the frontier. Even those who were not his type of Presbyterian. Even those who were not Presbyterian at all.

It did not take long before some fellow preachers brought charges against him to the governing church authority in Philadelphia. They apparently did so not simply because of Campbell's church transgressions but likely because he had become so popular. In other words, he had become a threat to them.

After a long messy trial, the governing officials chose not to suspend Campbell. But they did censure him. It quickly became apparent that because of this public rebuke, no church within the synod would allow him to preach. And so, he formally withdrew.

But Campbell still had lots of preaching opportunities. He was too respected to lose his influence. Soon he was in conversation with several others about establishing an organization whose purpose was to encourage Christians to disconnect from their various creeds, seeking unity based on the Bible alone. On August 17, 1809, the Christian Association of Washington, Pennsylvania, was formed.

Over the next six weeks, Campbell wrote the introductory statement for the organization. It expressed his new understanding of the nature of the church, growing out of his education in Glasgow, his experiences in Rich-Hill in Ireland, and all that had happened to him since he had come to America.

The document was a fifty-six-page booklet, published in December 1809. It was entitled simply the *Declaration and Address*.

This profound statement of unity was Thomas Campbell's most important literary work. It stands, along with Stone's *Last Will and Testament of the Springfield Presbytery*, written five years earlier, as one of the most influential documents of American Christianity in the nineteenth century, part of the bountiful underground lake beneath the Blue Hole, the wellspring of the Stone-Campbell Restoration Movement.

Though most modern Churches of Christ know nothing about it, the *Declaration and Address* remains in the DNA of these people. If it were spoken of, if it were part of our story, it might make a difference in the kind of choices we make today.

Here are some excerpts:

Oh! that ministers and people would but consider, that there are no divisions in the grave; nor in that world which lies beyond it: there our divisions must come to an end!

What gratification, what utility, in the meantime, can our divisions afford either to ministers or people? Should they be perpetuated, 'till the day of judgment, would they convert one sinner from the error of his ways, or save a soul from death?

The document concludes with thirteen powerful propositions, which include the following:

1. That the Church of Christ upon earth is essentially, intentionally, and constitutionally one; consisting of all those in every place that profess their faith in Christ and obedience to him in all things according to the Scriptures, and that manifest the same by their tempers and conduct, and of none else; as none else can be truly and properly called Christians.

2. That although the Church of Christ upon earth must necessarily exist in particular and distinct societies, locally separate one from another, yet there ought to be no schisms, no uncharitable divisions among them. They ought to receive each other as Christ Jesus hath also received them, to the glory of

God. And for this purpose they ought all to walk by the same rule, to mind and speak the same thing; and to be perfectly joined together in the same mind, and in the same judgment.

9. That all that are enabled through grace to make such a profession [of their faith], and to manifest the reality of it in their tempers and conduct, should consider each other as the precious saints of God, should love each other as brethren, children of the same family and Father, temples of the same Spirit, members of the same body, subjects of the same grace, objects of the same Divine love, bought with the same price, and joint-heirs of the same inheritance. . . .

10. That division among the Christians is a horrid evil, fraught with many evils. It is antichristian, as it destroys the visible unity of the body of Christ; as if he were divided against himself, excluding and excommunicating a part of himself. It is antiscriptural, as being strictly prohibited by his sovereign authority; a direct violation of his express command. It is antinatural, as it excites Christians to condemn, to hate, and oppose one another, who are bound by the highest and most endearing obligations to love each other as brethren, even as Christ has loved them. In a word, it is productive of confusion and of every evil work.

Like Stone's *Last Will and Testament of the Springfield Presbytery*, Thomas Campbell's compelling language and unflinching commitment to unity fueled the movement that birthed modern Churches of Christ. The trajectory was set. Beginning in Pennsylvania and then western Virginia, another independent movement was launched whose purpose and identity were centered on Christian unity.

But its full impact would not become evident until Thomas's son joined him and began to assume leadership of the movement.

Seceder Churches Today

Reading the story of Thomas Campbell and the Seceder, Anti-Burgher, Old Light churches is painful. It's hard not to cringe a little that churches could divide over such issues.

But let's be fair. The issues seemed important at the time. People had to decide where they stood. Neutral positions were difficult, if not impossible. You agreed with the Westminster Confession or you did not. You supported Christians in civil leadership or not. You were part of either this church or that one.

When you are immersed in the issues, when they genuinely matter to you, and when they become personal, they begin to feel like gospel concerns.

A few years later, on American soil, some Christians in Union states urged support for the Union cause in national missionary society meetings. Christians in Confederate states found the national and church politics within the missionary societies intolerable. Over time, these Christians felt they could no longer work together. Southern churches, including some who earlier had participated in, led, or even founded missionary societies, now condemned them.

Many post-war churches in the industrial North, after the war had been won, had money to build big new buildings, with stained glass and pipe organs. Many post-war churches in the rural South, which had lost the War, were desperately poor and saw the seemingly gaudy expenditures of their Northern brethren as offensive and unbiblical. Organs and expensive buildings became a wedge issue. The rift between these churches grew.

In post–Civil War Stone-Campbell churches, the old Seceder, Anti-Burgher, Old Light causes were largely forgotten. The new hot concerns were about societies and organs.

During World War I, several Church of Christ members chose the way of pacifism. Pacifism had a long history within the movement, especially among those who were influenced by Barton Stone and David Lipscomb. But the treason laws of the era made such acts suspect if not illegal, and patriotism pushed some church leaders to ban members who chose to be conscientious objectors or who advocated Christian pacifism.

While many early nineteenth-century leaders believed in a literal thousand-year reign of Christ, early twentieth-century leaders who held premillennial views were viewed by many as heretics. Most of them were kicked out, or they finally left.

Those who believed the Bible did not authorize churches working together to support orphans' homes or other parachurch institutions left. Those who believed the Bible did not authorize divided, age-distinct Bible classes left. Those who believed the Bible did not authorize paid preachers left. Each of these groups forged their own network of churches.

Likewise, beginning as a small network of interconnected Churches of Christ near state university campuses, International Churches of Christ emerged as a separate worldwide fellowship, walking away from the so-called mainline Churches of Christ. It wasn't long before this group itself divided.

Generation after generation, decisions of conscience, often fueled by matters of context and culture, have propelled churches toward division, whether for eighteenth-century Seceder Presbyterians or modern Churches of Christ. The very existence of a worldwide fellowship known today as Churches of Christ, in all its various forms, can only be accounted for by the fact that people at one point in time chose to divide from their larger body for reasons they thought were important, for reasons at least some believed were gospel.

In each case, by the second generation the reasons for the division crystallized. Congregations aligned themselves with one side or another. Arguments were bolstered. Justifications were made. And over time, the churches that had left lost their memory of life before the division. The new configuration of churches became the norm, the way church, in their minds, had always been.

And the grandmother who cut the ends off the pot roast could no longer be asked why. She was dead and long gone.

After his censure at the hands of the Pennsylvanian Presbyterians, Thomas Campbell faced his own crossroads moment. He chose a different path. He believed unity itself was a vital Christian doctrine. There ought to be "no uncharitable divisions," he said. "They ought to receive each other as Christ Jesus hath also received them." Even when they disagreed.

"Although the Church of Christ upon earth must necessarily exist in particular and distinct societies, locally separate one from another, yet there ought to be no schisms, no uncharitable divisions among them," he said.

Throughout the history of the movement, two impulses existed side by side, always in tension—the impulse to remain united even among profound differences and the impulse to stand for truth even if it meant tearing churches apart.

These two competing impulses grew in visibility and intensity as Thomas passed the torch of leadership to his son Alexander.

But at the beginning, as Thomas Campbell walked away from the Seceder Presbyterian churches, as he joined likeminded Christians who no longer desired to be controlled by petty disputes, a movement of independent churches was launched, centered not on their differences but on what they share in common, on their unity in Jesus.

From the *Hibernia* to the Redstone Baptist Association

When you think you are about to die, your priorities become clear.

As a young man, Alexander Campbell had been very religious, but he wasn't sure he wanted to preach. His father had taught him Greek, Latin, French, and philosophy. Under his father's tutelage, he learned to love John Locke and John Milton. He had heard his father preach and had assisted him in his ministry.

At sixteen, Alexander had served as his father's assistant at the Rich-Hill school, where his excellence in teaching was largely responsible for the school's growth. And he had run the school when his father left for America. But however competent this now twenty-one-year-old was, Alexander's future and passions were still unclear.

As a young man, Alexander was "tall, athletic and well-proportioned," as his friend Robert Richardson later described him. "He had an air of frankness about him, blended with decision and self-reliance, which at once inspired respect; yet he was affable and fond of conversing with others and eliciting information."[3] With his father away, he became the head of the household and the headmaster of his father's school.

Thomas had been in America for several months. When his home and position in western Pennsylvania were sufficiently stable, he summoned his family to join him. And so, Alexander, along with his mother and siblings, departed Londonderry (now Northern Ireland) on October 1, 1808, bound for the New World.

The *Hibernia* was a small but solid ship whose crew was perhaps less competent and more inebriated than might have been best for an ocean crossing.

The ship was soon caught in a terrible storm, which pushed it off course, north and east toward the rocky Scottish coast. For days, the unsteady captain tried to maneuver the ship out of danger.

On October 7, at nightfall, Campbell had a premonition that something terrible was about to happen. He and the family secured their luggage, the most precious of which were his and his father's books. They retired for the night, but Campbell remained fully dressed.

During the night they heard the crash of timbers and the sound of rushing water accompanied by screams and terror. The winds had driven the ship onto sharp rocks, cracking open the hull. To try to keep the ship from capsizing, the crew and passengers worked with the only axe they could find, and along with a few broadswords they cut down the masts. Filling rapidly with water, the ship finally settled hard onto the rocks, listing badly.

All the passengers had to crowd onto the upper deck, exposed to the rain and wind. Large waves crushed against them, the ship increasingly vulnerable to total destruction. It would be hours before the dawn and any possibility of rescue.

In the darkness, Campbell, having gathered his family to a secure place on the deck, sat on the stump of the mast, faced the gale, and thought about how little of his life's ambitions mattered to him at this moment. He thought of his father, whose care of others and sense of divine calling seemed the noblest of all possible human engagements. In the face of death, his priorities became clear: if God granted him safety, he pledged to spend his life in the ministry of the gospel. From this commitment he never wavered.

The next morning, residents of the Isle of Islay, where the ship had grounded, helped bring the passengers ashore. Over the next several days Campbell worked to salvage as much of the family's luggage as possible, including most of his books. They stayed for a while on this island, a twenty-five by fifteen-mile strip of land among the Inner Hebrides Islands of Scotland.

They were welcomed into the home of a fellow Campbell clansman. Finally determining they could not embark for America anytime soon, they left the island, making their way to Glasgow, where Alexander's father had once lived and studied. It would be almost a year before they would attempt the crossing again.

In the three hundred days between voyages, Campbell's newly focused life grew in depth and scope. He began studies at the University of Glasgow, twenty-five years after his father had enrolled there. He worked under George Jardine, as his father had done, and became equally captivated by the Scottish philosophers.

He also studied French and English literature, logic, Greek, and Bacon and Locke. He wrote in his journal daily, mostly in Latin, and began to mature as a scholar and thinker.

But it was his exposure to several independent churches, like ones started by John Glas and Robert Sandeman in Scotland and England, that may have affected him the most. These churches had influenced the independent church in Rich-Hill, Ireland, where his father had often visited. Now the younger Campbell began to see what it was about the independents that had so captured his father's interest.

During the months Campbell was in Scotland, his interaction with the independent churches pushed him to grapple hard with such issues as the restoration of primitive Christianity, baptism of believers by immersion, weekly communion, and local congregational leadership by a plurality of elders. By the time he departed for America, he was no longer a Presbyterian.

In 1809, after a less than tranquil Atlantic crossing, Alexander, with the rest of his family, joined his father in America. It was just days before Thomas's *Declaration and Address* was to be published. The reunion of father and son was sweet, though both feared what the other would think about the significant changes each had made since they had last been together.

Their anxiety turned to surprise and joy when they discovered they had independently chosen to walk the same spiritual road. Alexander got to see the proof sheets of the *Declaration and Address* just before its release, giving it his enthusiastic support. In the days after its publication, Thomas began to increasingly play a supporting role to his brilliant son, working together to accomplish the goals they now both sought.

The plan was for the Christian Association, which Thomas had helped establish, to meet twice a year. Its purpose was not to become a new church but to work within the various denominations for reform. The ultimate objective was unity.

But the effect of their efforts was negligible. Few seemed interested in joining them. Certainly, their old Presbyterian associates were not. So, practical matters made it necessary to constitute the Christian Association as a church. Thomas was appointed elder. Alexander was licensed by the church to preach. Four deacons were named. In early summer 1811, they met in a half-completed church building in Brush Run, Pennsylvania.

But Alexander and the Brush Run Christians were not interested in functioning as an isolated congregation. They were focused on unity and worked zealously to bring together like-minded Christians.

When they began to adopt believer's baptism as the normal practice of the church, it made sense for them to seek to align with the Baptists, who not only practiced believer immersion but also, like they, placed the authority of the church within local congregations, not within a church hierarchy. So, young Campbell and the Brush Run Christians began a conversation with the churches of the nearby Redstone Baptist Association. Campbell's group wasn't looking to form a new denomination, nor, frankly, were they particularly desirous of becoming Baptists. But they did care about Christian unity.

In 1813, when the churches in the Redstone Baptist Association voted to affirm the application of these new, self-described "Reforming Baptists" for membership in the association, Campbell and his group were accepted. It would not be easy. A strong, vocal minority of the Baptists opposed them. The issues were not small. One of the most difficult of these issues was young Campbell himself.

The Edge of a Rope

When you think you are about to die, your priorities become clear.

Alexander Campbell was not the only one in the movement whose life was altered when he came face to face with death. Forty years after Campbell's escape from the shipwreck, James Garfield had his own encounter with mortality.

Even though his mother wanted more than anything else for him to go to college, the sixteen-year-old Garfield had other things in mind. His mother's expectations were not ill-founded. Though her current state of poverty may have made it difficult for her friends and neighbors to recognize it, Eliza Ballou Garfield's family was brimming with intellectuals, including a president of Tufts College and an editor of a Boston newspaper.

But young James had read a lot of books about the sea, and that's where he wanted to go. Ohio is a long way from the ocean and he was too poor to get there, so he went to the nearest body of water he could find. He decided to work on the Erie and Ohio Canal.

A strange choice, perhaps, since Garfield could not swim.

In the first few weeks, after having been promoted from mule driver to bowman, he had fallen into the canal at least a dozen times. But it had been daylight each time, and someone had always been there to pull him out.

But one night, as he was working on the bow of a barge trying to wrangle a coiled rope, he lost his balance and fell into the water. It was almost midnight, and everyone was asleep. He screamed for help, but no one could hear him.

He reached frantically for anything that he might hold onto, anything that might save him. His hand suddenly found the edge of a rope, the rope that had caused him to trip in the first place. He grabbed it and pulled himself back into the barge.

Cold and wet, Garfield noticed that the rope was not tied to anything. It should have fallen into the water with him. "Carefully examining it," he wrote later, "I found that just where it came over the edge of the boat it had drawn into a crack and there knotted itself." He felt God's hand in the episode and decided to do something more meaningful in his life than to serve as a bowman on the Erie Canal.

Garfield returned home and enrolled in Geauga Seminary, a secondary school nearby, where he decided he loved learning after all. It was there he met Lucretia "Crete" Rudolph, a devout member of a local Church of Christ who would later capture the hearts of the nation.

Garfield then went to Western Reserve Eclectic Institute (now Hiram College) and upon graduation enrolled in Williams College in Massachusetts, one of the most rigorous and prestigious schools in the country, where, late in the century one of his sons would serve as president.

After his decisive episode on the canal, Garfield had become unusually devoted to education. He learned multiple languages. He embraced science, even the new theories and discoveries, because there is nothing to be afraid of when people of good will are willing to reason together. Garfield's love of books and his commitment to learning prepared him to be, among other things, an effective preacher, a beloved college president, and ultimately the leader of the nation. A remarkable life for a barge hand on the Erie and Ohio Canal.

When you think you are about to die, your priorities become clear.

Church can go on as usual, year after year. People come and go. Preachers are hired and retired. But church life proceeds as normal. Just keep everything running smoothly. You don't need folks rocking the boat. Every now and then, of course, someone will complain about something, but it usually doesn't last long. People learn to adjust to the way church is. Or they move on. But church remains the same.

Unless it looks like the church is going to die. Then your priorities start to change. Then, floundering in the cold, dark water, you start looking for a rope.

Battling with Baptists

The Regular Baptist churches of the Redstone Baptist Association and the Reforming Baptist congregation at Brush Run, founded by the Campbells, came together reluctantly.

While the Campbells' view of baptism and congregational independence fit well with the Baptists, they intensely opposed any creed or confession of faith. The Redstone Baptists, on the other hand, were aligned with the Philadelphia Confession of Faith, which was not only a creed but one that included elements of Calvinism that the Campbells intensely opposed.

For his part, Alexander was not impressed by many of the Baptist pastors. He thought they were less concerned about what the Bible taught than their own church members were. Besides, Campbell believed, the pastors were less educated than he thought they should be, certainly less than he was. Humility was not Campbell's strong suit.

Campbell was not shy in expressing his concern about the pastors' doctrinal positions. At the same time, some of the Baptist pastors believed Campbell was teaching heresy. In 1816 they tried to exclude him from the annual meeting of the association. But when one of the speakers became ill, pressure from Campbell's supporters caused the organizers to invite him to speak.

His sermon on that occasion, his "Sermon on the Law," was a turning point in Campbell's life and the reformation he led. It was no subtle piece. It was not meant to appease. In it, Campbell directly called into question key doctrines of the Philadelphia Confession. His arguments were in direct opposition to what most Baptists believed. Leading Baptist pastors soon began working to kick Campbell and his churches out.

In 1823, when it appeared they might have enough votes to exclude him, Campbell preempted them by moving his membership to a nearby church that belonged to a different group, the Mahoning Baptist Association. By the end of the decade, when most of its churches in this new district had accepted Campbell's teaching, the Mahoning Baptist Association officially dissolved.

Throughout the 1820s, the tension between the Regular Baptists and Campbell's Reforming Baptists deepened. A couple of debates with Presbyterian ministers made Campbell's anti-Calvinist positions more widely known. His arguments against Presbyterian positions challenged certain Baptist positions as well, adding to the growing concern. At the same time, he began to publish a new journal, the *Christian Baptist*, in which his strongly worded attacks on Baptist doctrine sometimes became pointed and personal.

And so, as Campbell's influence spread westward, tensions among the Baptists increased. In 1825, a Baptist Church in Louisville renounced the authority of the Philadelphia Confession and claimed the Bible as their only guide, becoming the first church in Kentucky to identify with Campbell's movement. By the end of the 1820s, as many as a fourth of the Regular Baptists in Kentucky had joined the Reformers— perhaps as many as 10,000 people, including a number of entire congregations.

It is not surprising, then, that these Baptists became increasingly wary of Campbell's new independent movement. Baptist associations throughout the Ohio Valley kicked out many individuals and even entire congregations who advocated and practiced Campbell's reforms.

By 1830, after years of argument and counterargument, the break had occurred. The Reforming Baptists increasingly began to refer to themselves simply as Disciples of Christ. Though a drive toward unity was at the heart of Campbell's churches, finding common ground with the Baptists was becoming more and more difficult. Friction between the two groups, particularly in the South where the name Church of Christ was most common among Stone-Campbell churches, would continue well into the twentieth century. Among a few, the judgments and animosities between the two groups remain to this day.

Differences neither Small nor Insignificant

As Campbell's Disciples of Christ spread westward, they began to run into a number of Stone's churches, especially in Kentucky. Both groups saw things they shared in common. Both movements, for example, rejected the Baptists' Philadelphia Confession of Faith. Both groups battled with Baptists.

Perhaps the old proverb was at play—the enemy of my enemy is my friend. Whatever the case, there was soon talk about union between Campbell's Disciples and Stone's Christians.

Campbell, however, was not enthusiastic about a union with Stone.

During a trip to Kentucky in 1824, Campbell had met Stone for the first time. Face to face and in subsequent articles in their respective journals, they had spoken kind words about each other. But for several years, the back-and-forth between them in Stone's *Christian Messenger* and Campbell's *Christian Baptist* revealed substantial concerns.

It was one thing for them to be united, in the sense that they recognized the other as Christians and cooperated where they could. It was another to seek union, to converge the two movements into an organic whole.

The differences between the two groups were neither small nor insignificant.

- *What to call the churches.* Stone's churches had long used the name Christian Church and Church of Christ (though many Baptist churches also used the name Church of Christ). Campbell preferred Disciples of Christ. Stone thought Campbell was using Disciples of Christ in a sectarian or denominational way. Campbell thought the name Christian Church could be confusing, since every group referred to themselves as Christian. Moreover, some groups who used the name "Christian" did not believe in the Trinity, and Campbell was not interested in being associated with them. As much as anything, Campbell may have been concerned that no one think that the churches under his influence, shaped by his faith and intellect, had simply been absorbed into Stone's Christians. Ultimately, all three names were used, usually interchangeably, often confusingly.
- *The nature of the Trinity.* Campbell was concerned about Stone's beliefs about the Trinity. Stone rejected the classical language concerning Father, Son, and Holy Spirit, believing the notion of the Trinity was not found in Scripture. Campbell's views were more orthodox in this regard. They never came to agreement. It took many years before Campbell was convinced that Stone's views were not heretical.
- *Reason and emotion.* Stone's churches grew out of the religious revivals of the early nineteenth century. Their evangelism, rooted in the miraculous

work of the Holy Spirit, was generally more emotional and experiential than Campbell's churches, which focused on reasoned preaching and calm decision-making. Campbell was never comfortable with Stone's views on the Spirit nor the spiritual fervor that Stone's churches often displayed. Stone never insisted on it but never apologized for it either.

- *Ordination of clergy.* Both Stone's and Campbell's churches believed in the authority of local congregations, not any sort of denominational system. Stone, reflecting his Presbyterian roots, argued that a minister should be ordained through examination and calling by other ordained ministers but that only an individual congregation could call a person to serve as its minister. Campbell, on the other hand, argued that congregations should choose their ministers from among their own members and that only individual congregations could ordain them.

- *The non-immersed.* Both movements had come to believe in baptism by immersion. But Campbell's Disciples of Christ, at least early on, required everyone to be baptized. Without it, no one was allowed to be a member. Stone's Christian Churches and Churches of Christ, while teaching baptism by immersion, allowed non-immersed people to be members. Almost everyone in these churches had been immersed, they made clear, but they allowed freedom of opinion and believed that over time most of the un-immersed in the church would choose to be baptized.

- *Open communion and the role of clergy.* Stone's churches opened the Lord's Supper to all believers but allowed only ordained ministers to preside at the table. In contrast, Campbell's group barred all un-immersed believers from the table but allowed any (male) member of the congregation to preside.

The issues were even more complex than these, of course, and the differences between the two movements were substantial, far more than most churches today experience. For this reason, Campbell was not in a hurry. He wanted to move toward union cautiously, if at all. The urgency toward the union of the two movements came primarily from Stone.

By the end of 1831, the quiet conversations of John Allen Gano, John Rogers, John T. Johnson, and Raccoon John Smith bore fruit. A meeting was planned between two churches in Georgetown, one associated with Stone, the other associated with Campbell.

The meeting was to take place in Georgetown on Christmas weekend. After four productive days, they arranged a second meeting for the following weekend. It would begin December 30 in Lexington, ten miles away. A public announcement of this meeting was placed in a Lexington newspaper: "We are requested to state, that a four days' meeting will be held in the Christian Church on Hill Street, commencing Friday the 30th inst. Messrs. J. Smith, of Montgomery County, and J. T. Johnson are expected on the occasion."

This second weekend, then, would bring together not just members of the two local congregations but leaders from both groups throughout Kentucky. What happened that weekend would affect the churches of these two movements in ways they could never have imagined—then and now.

Stone's Voice

I think a lot about Stone, about his emotions as the Lexington meetings approached, about what he thought would happen. Of the two most prominent leaders of the movement, Campbell and Stone, Stone seemed to be in the least vulnerable position, at least on the surface. He was a generation older than Campbell, a more established and better-known preacher at the time. The churches associated with his movement had been around longer and were more widespread. And in Georgetown and Lexington, in the state of Kentucky, Stone had home field advantage.

But in many ways he also had more to lose. He had met Campbell before and had read what Campbell had written. Stone surely had a sense of Campbell's dominating personality and competitive spirit. Campbell controlled most every conversation and relationship he was in. It would not be difficult to imagine that Campbell would exert his considerable influence over Stone's churches, far more than the soft-spoken Stone would exert over Campbell's.

It would have been easier, surely, for Stone to have pulled back a little, not working particularly hard toward union, speaking graciously about Campbell's churches but from a distance. His reputation was made. No one would have condemned Stone for being cautious.

But Campbell was the cautious one as these meetings began to unfold.

Campbell seemed to want to know the answers first, before any union could take place. He wanted to minimize the risk. He wanted to make sure that what he had worked so hard at—the churches he had established, the doctrines he had worked to protect—would not be compromised in the unity talks.

The differences between the two groups seemed too great. Perhaps they should take their time. When the unity conversations moved forward without his express approval, Campbell was frustrated. There would be a day when Campbell would be the public champion of unity, but his voice was quiet during the unity talks of Georgetown and Lexington. Stone, on the other hand, was all in.

I don't know what wisdom looks like when people who have considerable differences seek unity. I suppose it depends on the people and what's at stake. I know that in our own times, especially in our fraught political climate, finding compromise in the midst of conflict is rarely prized or sought. National leaders are rewarded for hardening their positions, not in seeking harmony with the other side, not in compromise, not when they have to give up something in order gain something. It's a zero-sum game today, and only one side can win.

It doesn't have to be this way.

Several years ago, I sat down beside Stone's gravestone at Cane Ridge. I tried to hold back the tears. Stone had sacrificed much for the sake of unity. Campbell's dominating spirit was overwhelming at times. Stone didn't fight it. He wasn't in it for the glory. He didn't need to win. He clearly had strong convictions about important matters all the way till his death. He was not a doormat. He could hold his ground.

But there were a lot of things that didn't matter as much, not as much as Christian unity. People could simply disagree with one another on a lot of things without becoming enemies. Stone could love them anyway. They could remain in the same congregation. They could remain friends. Loving one another was more important than agreeing.

At a crucial moment, as two very different groups found a way to come together, Campbell's influence increased. And Stone's waned. Less than three years after the union of the two groups, Stone moved to Jacksonville, Illinois. Among other reasons, Stone wanted to free his slaves in a state where they could remain free. He wanted to push his revival west. And, frankly, there was just no need to stay around and compete with Campbell.

When Stone arrived in Jacksonville, he found two restoration churches already there—a Christian church that was a part of his movement and a Disciples church that was part of Campbell's. He refused to meet with either of them unless they joined together. When they did, he did.

His ministry continued another ten years until his death in 1844. The older he got, the more content Stone was to just to be a good minister to folks and a good evangelist for the kingdom. To the end, he chose unity over division, compassion over conflict.

I hope his voice is not lost.

A Great Stream Bursting from the Earth

The church building on Hill Street in Lexington where the unity meetings took place had, until recently, been a cotton factory. The Lexington Christians, when they acquired it, dedicated the building for the work of the kingdom. That dedication would bear fruit on this New Year's weekend.

On the first day of the Lexington gatherings, the building began to fill, and the meetings commenced. They knew each other now. They had worked through a number of issues the previous weekend. Trust between the groups began to grow.

On the second day, New Year's Eve, it was agreed that two people, one from each group, would offer a speech stating clearly what they believed was the basis for union. The Disciples chose Raccoon John Smith. The Christians selected Barton W. Stone.

The two men withdrew from the meeting for a while to plan their remarks. Before they reemerged, Stone asked Smith if he preferred to go first or last. Smith said he did not care either way. Stone said, if it was all right he would like to go last. Smith agreed, and the two men walked back into the crowded room.

Smith walked to the pulpit and looked over the crowd, sensing their tension and their hope. As he began to speak, Smith felt a great weight of responsibility on his shoulders. He wanted union. Raccoon John, far more than his friend Campbell, believed the two movements should unite. He also knew that the ties between the groups were fragile and that, with poorly chosen words, he could shatter the possibility of union.

He took his time. He talked about the long history of Christian speculation and dispute. He told them that he had long ago decided that he would try to speak about complex doctrinal subjects only with language from Scripture itself. The kind of unity God desired, he said, had to be "based on the Word of God, as the only rule of faith and practice." He continued,

> While there is but one faith, there may be ten thousand opinions; and hence, if Christians are ever to be one, they must be one in faith and not in opinion.... Let us then, my brethren, be no longer Campbellites or Stoneites, New Lights or Old Lights, or any other kind of lights, but let us all come to the Bible, and to the Bible alone, as the only book in the world that can give us all the Light we need.

One in faith, not in opinion. When people come together, their opinions will not likely align perfectly, but they can unite on the basis of the faith they share. The one faith.

Stone listened intently. Smith was not a stranger to him. Stone knew they could work together. But what kind of spirit would Smith bring to this occasion? Would he be hesitant? Would he express concern about their differences?

But in the words Smith spoke, Stone heard his own commitments, his own heart. He heard in Smith's words the grace of God and the blessing of the Holy Spirit. When Smith finished, Stone rose slowly from his seat, stepped to the pulpit, and faced the crowd.

It had been twenty-five years since he had helped dissolve the Springfield Presbytery in order that he and his churches could "sink into union with the Body of Christ at large." For decades, Stone had admonished folks to "pray more and dispute less." He had urged them to take seriously God's desire that Christians everywhere be united.

The time was now. Speaking simply and briefly, he seized the moment.

> The controversies of the Church sufficiently prove that Christians never can be one in their speculations ... which, while they interest the Christian philosopher, cannot edify the Church....
>
> ... I perfectly accord with Brother Smith that those speculations should never be taken into the pulpit; but that when compelled to speak of them at all, we should do so in the words of inspiration....

. . . I have not one objection to the ground laid down by him as the true scriptural basis of union among the people of God; and I am willing to give him, now and here, my hand.

Then, as the crowd of believers watched in silence, Stone turned and offered Smith his trembling hand. Smith grasped it. And through this sign of accord, they made to each other their pledge of unity.

They then turned to the crowd and invited them to offer one another signs of their willingness to work together in this union of churches. The gathered leaders—elders, preachers, and teachers, women and men—rushed to one another. They joined hands and embraced. A song rose spontaneously among them, attended by tears.

And the union was confirmed.

On this day—and the next day, the first day of the week, the first day of 1832, as they shared together the Lord's Supper—and at crucial junctures in the days ahead, these Christians made choices. Their choices had consequences.

That is not to say that these Christians did not believe that God was present in all that happened that weekend. They did. They trusted that God was at work—Stone and his associates, perhaps, a little more than Campbell and his. They believed salvation was a gift from God, as was this new union. But they also believed that God gave humans the gift of choice.

Some of the choices they made were about the nature of the unity they shared. While most of them recognized that their unity thrived among their differences, a few seeds were planted early on about a type of unity that could take place only if everyone agreed. In fact, some of those seeds had already begun to sprout even before this union of churches. Decades later, those seeds would grow and blossom, bearing bitter fruit.

But at their best, these men and women believed that Jesus called them to be one, as he and the Father are one. They believed that the unity of God's people was a cross-shaped, Spirit-filled doctrine, that it lived at the very core of the gospel. They believed that the nature of the Good News was people joining together despite their differences, that unity itself is God's desire and God's gift. And that Christ's disciples, knowing God's heart, would want it and choose to receive it, now and here.

For many years, in the wet caverns and crevices just beneath the surface of the earth, a great pressure had built, a drive to unite God's children. And now, for this people gathered in an old cotton mill, with a handshake and a song, through tears and at table, a great spring burst from the earth.

Takeaways from Chapter 3: Unity Matters

On the whiteboard, scribbled with an anemic dry-erase marker, was a single word: *unity*.

My wife and I had walked into the Sunday morning Bible class as visitors. It was a large class, attended mostly by older adults. The room was alive with friendly banter. Good-natured teasing was lobbed across the room and was often returned with a little extra topspin. These folks clearly enjoyed being with each other.

As class started, visitors were welcomed, and announcements were made. The designated doughnut-bringer was chosen for the following week, an important assignment, to be sure. Considerable time was spent in prayer.

Then the teacher, one of the elders of the church, found his place behind the podium and surveyed the room. He gestured toward the single word on the whiteboard.

"That was last week's lesson."

His slow drawl seemed to settle, little by little, into a barrel of thick molasses.

"I know we're the old folks' class," he drolled, "so we may not remember what we talked about a week ago."

Pause. A few chuckles flitted around the room.

"It was unity," he said, smiling. "So, let me remind you what we said. We have a lot of young folks at this church. Most of us aren't going to agree with them about everything. Shoot, we can't even agree with each other about everything. We're not going to like some things."

Pause. He leaned over the podium.

"And we may not like everything the elders decide to do."

Protracted pause.

"But the point is not that we like everything. The point is that we figure out how to stay together, how to love each other. That's a whole lot more important than whether we like it. This church has got to be united. Period."

And that was that.

It's no small thing for a leader among a church's older members to say church isn't about getting our way. Church isn't about our liking everything but about honoring and serving others, even when we disagree. Such a sentiment—from across the generations, from across ethnicities and genders and opinions on everything from carpet color to the nature of God—could make a difference in churches.

But only if Christian unity matters.

Unity, as we have seen, was at the heart of both the Stone and Campbell movements, the driving impulse behind the formation of Churches of Christ as we know them today. But for the past century and more, the call to Christian unity among these churches has weakened. Like arms or legs that have atrophied for lack of use over a lifetime, a desire for unity within this heritage has withered to the point of uselessness. Whether the patient is terminal is not yet clear.

The desire for unity that precipitated the union of Stone's and Campbell's churches beginning in 1832 was no small matter. Their differences of doctrine and practice were great. Yet they found a way to make it work.

Their union grew directly from the sentiment found in Thomas Campbell's declaration that Christians "should love each other as brethren, children of the same family and Father, temples of the same Spirit, members of the same body, subjects of the same grace, objects of the same Divine love, bought with the same price, and joint-heirs of the same inheritance."

The trajectory for this union began, in many ways, twenty-five years prior to the union, in Barton Stone's *Last Will and Testament of the Springfield Presbytery*: "We will that this body die, be dissolved, and sink into union with the Body of Christ at large; for there is but one body, and one Spirit, even as we are called in one hope of our calling."

This is the unity that these Christians sought. But we should be clear, the immediate goal of that union was limited. They welcomed others to join them, but they did not aggressively seek unity with everyone—not with the Presbyterians from whom most of them had come, and not with the Baptists with whom many of them had journeyed for a while.

Ideally, they thought Christians everywhere should unite, rejecting their creeds and confessions and following the Bible alone. Many of them believed that the miracle of such a union would help usher in what they believed was a literal thousand-year reign of the kingdom of God on earth.

But despite the union of the Campbell and Stone streams, the newly united movement did not sink into union with the Body of Christ at large. In fact, many of the leaders of the movement were not particularly known for their peaceable ways. While hundreds of churches from Stone's and Campbell's groups eventually came together, they did not ignite a global movement of churches joining together in Christian unity.

But what they did was nevertheless remarkable. Their successes at unity were certainly greater than what most of us have ever experienced. It's worth thinking about. How can churches today be better at this?

First, it has to matter. Seeking unity has to matter. For Churches of Christ, Christian unity has typically been pitted against the other dominant impulse of the movement: the restoration of the early church. The churches that became Churches of Christ by the twentieth century focused more on the latter than on the former, more on the truth of Christian doctrine, as they understood it, than on the impulse for Christian unity. As if by accomplishing one the other would be negated.

The main problem with this view is that Christian unity was itself a key doctrine of the early church. One would assume that a restoration-driven church would want to restore a doctrine so central to the gospel.

Of all that was on Jesus's mind in his last night with his disciples, in the hours before he was arrested, the day before he was crucified, the unity of his followers was chief among them:

> The glory that you have given me I have given them, so that they may be one, as we are one, I in them and you in me, that they may become completely one, so that the world may know that you have sent me and have loved them even as you have loved me. (John 17:22–23)

But Christ's compelling call for his followers to be united has largely been muffled among Churches of Christ over the years. Like a muted trumpet or a padded cymbal. Not silent, but diminished. Gagged. Tamed.

In early twentieth-century Churches of Christ, as the desire to restore the ancient order overtook the commitment to embrace Christian unity, unity was not completely jettisoned, but it was increasingly seen as Christians coming together in agreement. In other words, unity may be important, but we can be united only if we agree with one another.

An alternative sentiment was often expressed in the phrase, "unity in diversity." But to many church leaders such a slogan seemed to threaten the movement's very reason for existing. To be united even when you disagreed seemed self-contradictory to them. Surely, they believed, a sincere back-to-the-Bible people could agree on what was true. On all of it. Without disagreement.

But unity makes no sense if there is no diversity, no differences of opinion. To say we are united only when we agree undercuts the essential nature of Christ's plea for unity. It denies the power of the cross and the witness of his church. The world will know that the Father and Son are one because God's children, in spite of their profound differences, love each other no matter what. Because, in spite of everything, they are one.

Loving each other in the midst of differences cuts against the grain of the world because it stands in stark contrast with what the world considers normal. Anyone can be united with friends when they all agree. It takes a different kind of love to be united with people with whom we acutely disagree. But that's what unity is. And it is precisely what Jesus calls us to do.

Living in contrast to the prevailing cultural norm is, at least in part, what draws people to Christian community. "They will know you are Christians," Jesus told his disciples, "by your love."

At the heart of the biblical witness is the shocking truth that people with profound differences can be united in Christ. Rich and poor can love one another. And slave and free. Men and women. Jew, Gentile, Black, White, Asian, and Hispanic. Republican and Democrat. Americans and non-Americans. Pro-missionary society and anti-missionary society. Pro-instrumental music and anti-instrumental music. Pro-praise teams and anti-praise teams. Pro-women in church leadership and anti-women in church leadership. Those who eat meat offered to idols and those who believe it's a sin. Those who drink moderately and those who do not. Those who endorse displays of patriotism in church and those who cannot. Those who embrace other Christian groups and those who do not. Those who want to build a new education wing or fire the youth minister or start a daycare center or have two services or create small groups or support a new mission team or launch a ministry for refugees or sing more contemporary songs or fund a program for the homeless, and those who do not.

Working and worshiping alongside folks with whom we disagree can be awkward. And extremely hard. Harder than most of us can manage on our own. Because doing so would mean that everyone would not be able to get their way, that all of us would have to give up things we care about.

But what a witness! No wonder so many people in the first few centuries of the church wanted to be part of such a movement. And in unity's absence, no wonder so many churches today appear to be in decline.

Philip Hallie, in his extraordinary book *Lest Innocent Blood Be Shed*, tells the story of the little French village Le Chambon. During World War II, these villagers saved thousands of Jewish children and adults, smuggling them into Switzerland right under the noses of the Nazis. None of the other villages in France were risking their lives in this way. Only Le Chambon.

After the war, when these villagers were asked why they had done so, why their village was different, they all spoke about their church and their pastor André Trocmé. They talked about the sermons they had heard much of their lives, lessons that had called them to be compassionate, to help one another, even those who were not like them. Above the church door, chiseled in stone, were the words of John 13:34: "Aimez-vous les uns les autres." "Love one another."

That was their highest value. That's the message that had shaped their hearts. And when the time came to live it, they did.

To be clear, seeking Christian unity is not a church growth strategy. It is simply what the cross demands. Christians, by recognizing their own brokenness, reach out to other broken people to love them and serve them, because that's what Christ in his brokenness did for us. Love One Another. That's the cross way.

The way of the cross, mind you, is not a conflict-averse way. It is not a mealy-mouthed, tepid, weak-kneed, give-in-to-the-loudest-member response. Unity is not about denying or avoiding differences. It is about seeing those differences, even embracing the differences, then seeking for the other the highest good, even when it's painful, even when it's costly. This cross-shaped way of living grows directly out of what the ancient Hebrews called *shalom*.

Shalom is often translated into English as "peace." But it's not just any peace. *Shalom* is not about personal contentment. It is not some sort of easy, peaceful feeling. Rather, *shalom* is about restoring relationships, welcoming strangers, reconciling with our enemies, and being reconciled with God.

To seek *shalom* is to pursue wholeness—the wholeness of the Christian community, the wholeness of our enemies, the wholeness of those with whom we disagree. To seek *shalom* is to desire the healing of the broken body of Christ, to pursue divine healing for the wounded and bruised, the discouraged and afraid, the angry, hurting, abandoned, abused, doubting, greedy, arrogant, apathetic, incompetent, impatient, sick, and sinful. In other words, so that all of us may be healed.

For a church to engage in *shalom* means its members will need what Lewis Smedes called "the miracle of the magic eyes," seeing others not as ones who oppose us but as fellow sufferers, not as ones who hurt us but as ones who, like us, need to be made whole. We cannot acquire such eyes on our own. They have to be given to us. And we have to choose to receive them.

We used to see one another from a worldly point of view, Paul told the Corinthians. But we do so no longer. We have been given new eyes. As broken people, living in a broken world, serving in a broken church, redeemed by a broken Savior, we can choose a path of healing. And God grants us wholeness, resurrection, and life.

In a world marked by unspeakable polarization, of intolerance and incivility, hostility and hatred, communities of *shalom* will have an unusual place. We may be seen by the culture as out of step, odd, irrelevant. But by living as people of peace, a few, by God's grace, will see something unusual, unexpected, transforming.

They will see in us a glimpse of the inbreaking kingdom of God.

Come, My Christian Friends and Brethren
(hymn by Barton W. Stone, 1829)[4]

1. Come, my Christian friends and brethren bound for Canaan's happy land,
   Come, unite and walk together, Christ our leader gives command.
   Lay aside your party spirit; wound your Christian friends no more.
   All the name of Christ inherit, Zion's peace again restore.

2. We'll not bind our brother's conscience, this to God alone is free,
   Nor contend with one another, but in Christ united be:
   Here's the Word, the grand criterion; this shall all our doctrine prove.
   Christ the center of our union, and the bond is Christian love.

3. Here's my hand, my heart, my spirit, now in fellowship I give.
   Now we'll love and peace inherit, show the world how Christians live;
   We are one in Christ our Savior; here is neither bond nor free.
   Christ is all in all forever; in his name we all agree.

4. Now we'll preach and pray together, praise, give thanks, and shout and sing;
   Now we'll strengthen one another, and adore our heavenly King;
   Now we'll join in sweet communion round the table of our Lord;
   Lord, confirm our Christian union by thy Spirit and thy Word.

5. Now the world will be constrained to believe in Christ our King;
   Thousands, millions be converted, round the earth his praises ring;
   Blessed day! O joyful hour! Praise the Lord, his name we bless.
   Send thy kingdom, Lord, with power; fill the world with righteousness.

Freedom and Conformity:
The Quest to Restore the Golden Age

Memphis, 1973

> Lord, grant that I may always be right, for thou knowest I am
> hard to turn.
>
> —Traditional Scotch-Irish prayer

Fieldnotes from the Blue Hole

In chapter 3 we discovered a movement of churches formed in the crucible of union. It's important to get our minds around that. In the beginning, Churches of Christ were a unity movement. That was how they saw themselves. They were a people of peace.

In this section, we will have to come to grips with the other side of the story. Here we will find less peace and more storm. And certainly some death.

Our framing story here takes place in Memphis at a time of unrest, both in the nation and among Churches of Christ. This story, like the union of the Stone and Campbell churches in Lexington and T. B. Larimore's funeral in Santa Ana, will not be well known to most readers.

What happened in Memphis in 1973 serves as a symbol for what happened to Churches of Christ in the twentieth century when we lost our memory of the Blue Hole, when we lost our thirst for unity.

To understand what happened, we will need to spend more time with Alexander Campbell, a character more complex than what we have seen thus far. To the day he died, Campbell was devoted to Christian unity. He fought hard for it.

At the same time, Campbell introduced another instinct into the movement—the search for a golden age, the restoration of the ancient order—that was captured in a series of articles Campbell wrote as a young man just a few years before the Lexington meetings.

These two drives—both to unify and restore the church, both to pursue freedom and maintain conformity—were deeply embedded in the heart of the movement. These competing impulses became a kind of bipolar disorder among the churches. Ultimately, the fabric of unity split in two.

We will meet some other key characters here. We will be introduced to Walter Scott, Campbell's younger colleague, evangelist, and writer. Much to Scott's dismay, one of his most memorable accomplishments ended up playing a major role in crystallizing the restoration impulse and undercutting the cause of unity that he cared about so deeply.

We will meet David Lipscomb who, in the hard post–Civil War years, served as a bridge between Stone and Larimore, keeping the spirit of peace alive and promoting holiness as a counterbalance to the self-serving nature of the prevailing culture. And we will meet Lipscomb's nemesis, Austin McGary, a hard-talking, gun-toting Texan who had little patience for peacemaking and who paved the way for Foy Wallace and a type of restoration that neither Campbell nor Scott would have recognized.

All these forces came together at Memphis in 1973, forces that were darker than what any of those who were present that day surely intended. What was meant to occur was a conversation among church leaders. But before the day was over, it felt more like an inquisition.

Lynn Anderson, a young preacher only a few years removed from the prairies and ranchland of Saskatchewan, found himself in the heat of the cauldron. With his friend and former classmate Landon Saunders and two elder statesmen, Batsell Barrett Baxter and Harold Hazelip, Anderson worked to respond to the accusations against him. He tried to speak with grace, but he was told he needed to conform. No one went home satisfied.

But perhaps that hot day in Memphis marked a turning point, even if small, for at least some Churches of Christ who were trying to find their way back to the unity of the Spirit and the bond of peace evident at the Blue Hole.

Chapter 4 is a pivotal section. Without it, we will have a hard time understanding who Churches of Christ are today and how we came to be this way. The stories can be unsettling. But don't be discouraged. In the midst of the setbacks and frustrations, you may discover a ray of hope.

You will not find it, however, in the usual places. There will be no powerful sermon, no heart-wrenching story, no viral video involving puppies or babies. If you look closely, however, you may be able to spot the hope you need. Not in yourself. And not in your church. But where God put it in the first place. Smack dab in the middle of the fire.

The Memory of an Earlier Day

The meeting had begun earlier that morning but had moved to Robilio's Restaurant for lunch. By early afternoon, more than two hundred had shown up. They soon had to move to a nearby church building just to handle the crowd. More than a few who were present that day say they had never experienced anything like it, before or since.

It was Monday, September 10, 1973, and things in Memphis were not okay.

There were questions that needed to be answered and statements that needed to be explained. Four national church leaders faced the gathered group of ministers. Three of them represented a prominent parachurch organization. The fourth was the preacher of that organization's home church.

These four men had prepared statements laying out what they believed concerning several issues of the day. Troubling rumors had begun to circulate about their doctrinal positions. Then again, the days were ripe with troubling rumors.

At its narrowest focus, the subject for the meeting was the Holy Spirit. Does the Spirit work within the lives of Christians beyond the words of Scripture? And did these four national leaders believe miracles were possible today? To be clear, there was only one acceptable answer to this last question.

These were not new concerns for the movement. Disagreement about the nature and work of the Holy Spirit had taken place from the very beginning. Alexander Campbell and Barton Stone had expressed serious disagreements with each other about the Holy Spirit.

Campbell thought Stone was too open to the present and miraculous work of the Spirit. Among other things, Campbell was concerned about what had happened at the Cane Ridge revival earlier in the century, an event that Stone had never distanced himself from.

In contrast, Campbell himself was more inclined to see the Spirit's work primarily in the writing of the Bible, a position Stone could never agree with but one that was shared by most of the folks in the crowded room in Memphis.

Beyond the Holy Spirit, many of the gathered preachers were concerned about the nature of congregational cooperation, an issue with a long history among these churches. Congregations that coordinated their efforts to send and support missionaries—the nineteenth-century name for this sort of cooperation was missionary societies—soon became a wedge issue within the movement. By the mid-twentieth century, concerns about congregational independence and cooperation escalated among Churches of Christ, precipitating a division that remains to this day.

Most of the ministers in the room believed some degree of congregational cooperation was appropriate. But they were concerned about the level of control and especially the doctrinal positions of the home church, the primary supporting congregation, across the Mississippi, over in Texas, out in Abilene, at the Highland Church of Christ.

But other issues were also at play. Some of the questions that day were about the internal politics of the Highland Church. Some of the questions by the Memphis preachers were more doctrinal in nature, like whether the Church of Christ was one of many denominations—anathema to most of the preachers present—or was the one and only true church. And some of the accusations were personal. They felt harsh, demeaning, at times even hateful.

But the division in the room was as much about the times as the topics. It was about change and fear. It reflected the mistrust and anxiety that had become prevalent among Churches of Christ and within the larger culture.

And it evoked the memory of an earlier day when things seemed not so broken. In another, earlier, glorious golden age.

Not the Way It's Supposed to Be

Golden, that first age, which, though ignorant
of laws, yet of its own will, uncoerced,
fostered responsibility and virtue.

Ovid was Rome's favorite poet. The Roman people might have considered Virgil their greatest, but Ovid was their most loved. His epic poems were sensuous, witty, and vivid. He was a spectacular storyteller. Through Ovid, many of the great myths of Greece and Rome came alive in the imaginations of the people of his day and were passed down to the coming generations and to history.

The Romans of the day divided the history of the world into four ages, each one worse than the one that came before it. Ovid described these ages with characteristic eloquence. The present world, Ovid said, was the Iron Age, the worst of the ages, in which humans were greedy, immodest, disloyal, vicious, and shameful. Before Iron was the Bronze Age, when humans were violent, presumptuous, and haughty to the gods—in other words, brazen. Before Bronze was the Silver Age in which humans first rebelled against the gods.

But in the beginning was the Golden Age, when citizens chose things that were good and right, when responsibility and virtue were fostered, when the world was "golden honey dripped."[1]

The idea of a golden age has been part of the mental and emotional framework of Western civilization from the earliest days of our dim past, before literacy, before recorded history. And now, after age upon age, it is fashioned deep in our imaginations, this memory of a time greater than our own from which the world degraded into our own days of disorder and injustice.

Even at the most personal level, most of us remember earlier days when things seemed better, times we sometimes recall with painful longing. In a 1668 doctoral thesis, the medical student Johannes Hofer coined a term to describe the sense of severe, often debilitating homesickness that Swiss mercenary soldiers sometimes experienced. He mashed it together from the Greek words *nostos* (a return home) and *algos* (pain, grief, distress)—*nostalgia*.

For the next two hundred years, physicians commonly diagnosed their patients as having nostalgia, a label that covered numerous symptoms including chronic fatigue, severe weight loss, anxiety, and depression. By the early twentieth century, nostalgia had come to refer to no physical disease but to a type of homesickness for an earlier, happier day, a condition sometimes as agonizing as any illness.

For my parents and many in their generation, that time was the 1950s, the post–World War II period, when the world reflected a more innocent time, when life seemed less threatening, at least to people like them. The days of nostalgia for me were the 1960s. Most people, I suppose, recall the days of their youth somewhat wistfully. But as any Baby Boomer will tell you, the sixties was no ordinary decade.

In terms of its cultural impact, the decade of the sixties did not really begin until late 1963, with the March on Washington in August and the assassination of John Kennedy in November, and in early 1964 with the appearance of the Beatles on *The Ed Sullivan Show*. I was twelve, and thanks to the generosity and fairly good judgment of my parents, I was allowed to watch this latter event along with seventy-three million other viewers, thereby hastening my coming of age as well as my parents' general anxiety.

The decade of the sixties ended somewhere around 1974–75, with the resignation of Richard Nixon and the fall of Saigon. But the effects of those years linger still. It was a time of significant social change, marked by audacity and candor, idealism and rebellion, cynicism and hope.

On college campuses, in urban neighborhoods, and in centers of cultural power, long-held views were challenged and new ideas advanced. It was the dawning of the Age of Aquarius we were told, not having any idea what that meant, but at the time it seemed like a really great ride.

Not for everyone, of course. My parents and many in their generation found the times frightening, or at least confusing. The culture felt like it was coming apart. The Vietnam War seemed to be dividing the nation across generations, geographic regions, class, and ethnicity. Traditional social mores were unraveling. Churches were experiencing new and deep tensions. The decade may have been a lark for a suburban White teenager, but the memories of those days for many others are more unsettled.

The 1963 March on Washington, for example, was an interesting item on the evening news for a large portion of the nation. But for others, it was a lived reality. A hundred years after Lincoln issued the Emancipation Proclamation, a whole lot of children in the nation were still being judged by the color of their skin rather than the content of their character.

While I had the luxury of sitting in my small, insulated world, others my age couldn't walk down the street at night without fear, or ride in a car through a White neighborhood without being stopped, or walk through the front door of the restaurant on Main Street without being kicked out. Or walk into a White church without discomfort—or, in some cases, an escort out the back door.

In the community around the church that A. L. Cassius built in South Los Angeles, not far from where the Pepperdine College campus was then located, the neighbors felt excluded from good schools, decent paying jobs, and adequate housing. Anger simmered just below full boil. There in Watts, on August 11, 1965, two years after Martin Luther King's speech in front of the Lincoln Memorial in Washington, a Black man was arrested by a White patrolman, and the neighborhood erupted. The riots lasted six days.

Less than three years later, on April 4, 1968, King was assassinated just outside Room 306 on the balcony of the Lorraine Motel in Memphis. In the days that followed, after decades of pent-up frustration at the racism and discrimination long experienced by the nation's Black communities, cities exploded into violence.

That June, a group of African American and White leaders from Churches of Christ met in Atlanta for the purpose of addressing the racial issues that divided the nation and their churches. At the end of the meeting, a statement was prepared confessing the wrongs of discrimination in the churches and church-related institutions. While many of those in attendance signed the document, some did not, including several Christian college presidents who apparently believed there was no wrong to confess. I know more than a few Christians today who still believe that.

In the months afterward the violence mostly subsided, the headlines moved on to other things, and most people across the country just returned to their normal world. But some could not. Whatever one's race or age, from whatever vantage point one experienced the decade, it was clear that something serious was going on. Massive cultural transformation seemed to be occurring.

The times, we were told, they were a-changin', but the world did not seem to be getting better. Not for everyone. For each of us who experienced those days as carefree, there were others who saw them as disturbing and even dangerous. The good old days for some are rarely the good old days for all. Every era reflects both hope and uncertainty. And beneath the uncertainty is the recognition that something is broken.

Several years ago, Neal Plantinga wrote a penetrating book about the nature of sin entitled *Not the Way It's Supposed to Be.*[2] The theme of the book is a self-evident truth. Things are not right in the world. God's *shalom*—the world as God created it and desires it—has been disrupted. Things are broken. Better said, we are broken. I am broken.

At the heart of human yearning for a golden age is the sense that our own world is not as it should be. Surely, there was a day when things were good and right, when streams flowed of milk and green oaks dripped of honey. But not today.

All movements of church renewal or restoration, boiled down to their essence, are driven by a keen sense that things today are not okay but that there was a time when the church was the way it was supposed to be. Or at least, back then, God's original intention for the church was clear and true.

If only we could find our way back, then everything would be all right.

Heavy Burdens

The problem with golden ages, of course, is that the reality on the ground rarely matches the memories in the brain. Which is why nostalgia can be such an insidious disease. In fact, it is sometimes incurable.

For many folks in mid-twentieth-century Churches of Christ, the 1920s–40s were the golden years of the church. After the division at the turn of the century, these were the years in which the self-identity of these churches solidified. They were days when great new buildings were being built and new churches planted, when church membership grew, and when there seemed to be a common understanding about truth.

"There were giants in those days,"[3] Foy Wallace said in 1935, reflecting on the preaching in the years just after the Great War. Tent meetings often lasted for weeks as dozens, sometimes hundreds, "came forward" to be baptized or restored.

But again, years that were great for some were not so great for others. Whole groups were marginalized in the years between the world wars, many of them at the hands of Foy Wallace himself. Pacifists such as J. N. Armstrong, the first president of Harding College, were written up in the journals, pushed to the margins, and publicly shamed. Premillennialists were told they were not welcome. What constituted the new orthodoxy was crystallizing.

But few experienced the marginalization in those years quite like those who were not members of the majority race. Whites in America, no matter what their religious inclinations, had opportunities that brought them relative power and advantage, even though they were—and still are—largely unaware of the nature and extent of their privilege. They could afford to look back to earlier decades with nostalgia. For many African Americans, however, those years could hardly be remembered without pain.

Annie C. Tuggle was the granddaughter of slaves on both sides of her family. Her surname came from the master of her paternal grandfather, Charles. Her grandmother on her mother's side was the offspring of a house slave and her master.

Edward Robinson, in his compelling book *I Was Under a Heavy Burden*, describes Tuggle's triple load: "White people devalued her because of her race, Black men distrusted her because of her gender, and many outside Churches of Christ spurned Tuggle because of her sectarian stance."[4]

In 1908, when she was eighteen, Tuggle organized a congregation of women in Germantown, Tennessee, near Memphis, where she often taught and led worship. She describes what happened when a White preacher was invited to hold a gospel meeting among Black and White churches in the area. After one of the services, the preacher "touched a string of beads I was wearing without thinking of anything but the good work that was in progress."

But when she went home afterward, her mother was furious. "Something went on under the tent tonight that I certainly did not like. . . . I saw that white preacher with his hands on the beads you were wearing around your neck and before you know anything, there will be a lynching scrape right here in Germantown and you will be the one lynched."[5]

Such a conversation between White daughters and their mothers would not just have been unnecessary, it would have been unimaginable. That's part of White privilege, then and now, that many Whites seem unable to grasp. For many African Americans, in one form or another, Annie Tuggle's experience was and still is an everyday occurrence.

In 1920, Tuggle was invited to teach sixth grade at a new school in Nashville for African American students, the Southern Practical Institute. The principal was the great preacher G. P. Bowser. The White superintendent, C. E. W. Dorris, insisted that the Black students—which is to say, the entire student body—enter the school through the back door, since this was the custom throughout the South.

Let that sink in for a minute. The White superintendent issued a rule that students and faculty could not come through the front door of their own school.

Bowser refused, believing it would be an unnecessary humiliation of the students and their teachers. He would not budge, but neither would Superintendent Dorris. The impasse was never overcome. The school closed in six weeks.[6]

Some days it is clearer than others that things are not the way they are supposed to be.

In March of 1941, in an article that is now almost too disturbing to quote, Foy Wallace castigated White Christians for mixing too much with Blacks in church. He spoke of several White women so excited about a sermon from a "colored preacher," they went up to him afterwards, shaking his hand "and holding his hand in both of theirs." Commenting on this behavior, Wallace said,

> That kind of thing will turn the head of most white preachers, and sometimes affect their conduct, and anybody ought to know that it will make fools out of the negroes. For any woman in the church to so far forget her dignity, and lower herself so, just because a negro has learned enough about the gospel to preach it to his race, is pitiable indeed.[7]

He spoke of a young Black preacher who had been employed by a White church as their janitor. When Wallace held a gospel meeting at the church, the young Black man

> made it a point to stand out in the vestibule of the church-building to shake hands with the white people. When I insisted that it be discontinued, some of the white brethren were offended. Such as this proves that the white brethren are ruining the negroes and defeating the very work that they should be sent to do, that is, preach the gospel to the negroes, their own people.

As difficult as these words are now to read—and they are not the hardest words in Wallace's scandalous article—our pain in reading them cannot compare to the experiences or the memories of those who actually lived them. For minorities in America, certainly for African Americans, the 1920s and 30s, when "giants" were supposed to have walked among us, were no golden years. And yet, in spite of the almost unimaginable hardships, an indomitable spirit often emerged.

Annie Tuggle eventually served as a school principal, led churches and advised church leaders, wrote numerous articles for several journals including the White church paper the *Gospel Advocate*, raised money and awareness for missions, and taught countless children, some of whom became among the most influential church and national leaders, including Fred Gray—the prominent American Civil Rights leader, who was Martin Luther King's and Rosa Parks's attorney, who argued before the US Supreme Court to end racial segregation on public transportation in the state of Alabama, who fought to achieve justice on behalf of those who had been wronged in the infamous Tuskegee syphilis study, and who was (and still remains at the writing of this book) a pivotal leader and preacher among Churches of Christ.

The notion that the world today is not as it should be helped shape the collective imagination of an entire culture. Surely there was a day when things were better. Or at least when the ideals of a just world prevailed.

Within Western civilization, the memory of a once golden age played a crucial role in the creation of the modern world as we know it. In the early nineteenth century, it fueled the rise of what would come to be called the Restoration Movement.

Being Wrong

It's one thing to recognize that the world is not the way it's supposed to be. It's another to say, that's on me; I helped bring that about.

It's one thing to acknowledge that all of us have sinned. It's another to say that sinner is me. It's tough to confess we are wrong. But until we are able to come to grips with being wrong, our churches are never going to get better.

Kathryn Schulz, in her remarkable book *Being Wrong: Adventures in the Margin of Error*, explores why most humans assume and often insist they are right and find it so disconcerting to discover they are not.[8] We hate being wrong. We often go to great efforts to justify wrong actions or explain away wrong opinions rather than just admitting it—we were wrong; I was wrong.

Schulz asks a particularly revealing question: What does it feel like to be wrong? Well, that's easy. We feel bad about it, of course. We feel embarrassed or horrified or ashamed. But these are not answers to her question. They are answers to a different question: What does it feel like when we *discover* we are wrong? *Being* wrong, Schulz says, feels exactly like being right.

In the moment, when I am wrong, inside my head it feels like I am right. What it feels like to be wrong is to feel confident and certain. I am convinced I am right. I know I am right. If I thought I were wrong, I wouldn't have said what I said. It is only later that I have to come to grips with the foul truth, I was wrong.

It turns out, I have been wrong about many things. As a young man, my ministry was marked by a high degree of certainty. I knew the answers to most of life's questions only to discover in later years I was wrong. I was wrong about many things, important things.

Now that I am no longer young, I continue to be wrong. I am often wrong, sometimes shamefully wrong. I am finding, however, the older I get that it is becoming a little easier to admit I am wrong. Which does not mean, however, I have become patient with other people when I believe they are wrong. God still has work to do in my heart.

Reading, for example, about the treatment of African Americans—in our country, in our churches—is excruciating. Most Americans in the nineteenth century believed Blacks were intellectually and morally inferior to Whites. Even leading citizens—scientists, intellectuals, church leaders, politicians—believed it. Even those who wanted to emancipate the slaves believed it. Abraham Lincoln believed it. Barton Stone believed it. They were wrong.

So how should I feel about that? What should I do? What should I think when I read about a White superintendent who would rather shut down the school than let Black students and teachers enter their own school through the front door? Or Foy Wallace chastising a Black man for shaking hands with White people since, you know, those people should stick to themselves and preach the gospel to their own people?

I'm not willing to simply overlook what happened, to claim, well, they just didn't know better. Their beliefs had real consequences. Their actions damage us still. They could have chosen differently. They should have. They were wrong.

But if we are willing to be hard on these people from the past, where recognizing their blindnesses is relatively easy in retrospect, we've got to be willing to be tough on ourselves, to be clear-eyed about our own blindnesses and mistakes, to see those areas where we have been wrong, to discern ways we may be wrong even now. We still haven't dealt with the racial divide in our churches. We still struggle to recognize our own failures. Most of us still haven't grasped the likelihood, the inevitability, of our being wrong, even about some things we most strongly believe.

But being wrong is not just inevitable. It is, in part, what makes us human. Centuries before René Descartes said, *Cogito, ergo sum*: "I think, therefore I am," Augustine asserted, *Fallor, ergo sum*: "I err, therefore I am." When I am wrong, Augustine is saying, I recognize that there is a measuring stick within me against which I must be compared, the very image of God, and I know I don't measure up. In other words, when I discover I am wrong, I am forced to acknowledge not only my own existence but God's. Said differently, because of the God who is in me, I see that I am wrong and therefore know I am human.

Such a confession—because I am human, I will be wrong about things—ought to unlock opportunities and relationships. But for some of us, acknowledging we are human—well, after all, I'm only human—has become an excuse rather than a doorway to understanding God and ourselves. Asserting that we are all human should not be a justification for ignoring bad choices and perpetuating our failures. It is a call, rather, to admit the truth about ourselves and to do something about it.

Imagine what it would be like to have a conversation today with someone on the opposite side of the political spectrum, a staunch Republican or a lifelong Democrat, in which you both confessed up front, "I might be wrong."

What if the elders of our congregations spoke that way? What if all our conversations about disputable matters, about the things that can tear up a church, began by everyone in the room admitting up front, I might be wrong? Would anything be different? Would we be different?

We live in a highly polarized culture today, in a political climate where compromise is virtually impossible, where admitting we may be wrong is almost inconceivable. This disease is infecting our churches. The world is the worse for it. It doesn't have to be this way.

Rebirth

About five hundred years ago, the notion of an ideal time in the past became part of the common vocabulary of Europe. But the golden age these Europeans imagined was not the one Ovid originally had in mind.

Ovid had written about a mythical age in the distant past. The fourteenth- and fifteenth-century Europeans pointed to a different period, one that was well documented in history, of extraordinary human achievement like the world had never seen—the height of the Roman Empire, the days of Ovid himself.

The idea of a new Western culture that was fashioned in the image of this splendid past took root and began to flourish. Western Europe was slowly coming awake after a thousand years of slumber.

A few hundred years before, at the turn of the first millennium, Christianity in Europe had been hanging on by a thread. By the year 950, it was on the verge of collapse. The prospects for Christianity, and for civilization as we know it today, were dim. This was the lowest point in what would later be referred to as the Dark Ages.

The Roman Empire, or at least the western half of it, had crumbled in the early fifth century. In the centuries after Rome fell, the West essentially died. Over time, the memory of it—of the old republic, of the emperors, of great victories and world domination, of philosophy and science, of literature, art, and the rule of law—was largely forgotten.

For centuries after civilization's collapse, nameless people lived in nameless villages, without knowledge of what year or even what century it was, without awareness of what was happening in the next village much less in another part of the world. Literacy died, except for a few monks who day after tedious day copied and stored documents from ancient Greek and Roman civilization.

But slowly, haltingly, beginning in the 1400s, Europe began to revive. The causes of the reawakening were many and complex, few of which could compare in significance to the discovery (or better said, the recovery) of the important documents of ancient Greece and Rome that the Christian monks had preserved, and that the Muslim scholars of North Africa and Mesopotamia had built their societies on, now gradually being read by the Europeans.

With these documents came the stories, the philosophies, the mathematics and astronomy, the art, and the culture of ancient Greece and Rome. With them also came an awareness that the world they lived in, the world they had always known, had not always been that way. Things were not as they should be. They used to be better. They could be again.

In this cultural and intellectual reawakening, Europeans looked not so much at creating something new. Rather, they envisioned a future by looking to their past. They began to imagine a rebirth—a Renaissance—of a once golden age. The quest for its rebirth captured their imaginations as their world, slowly but dramatically, morphed into modernity. This is the golden age that fueled the imagination of the founders of the new American nation.

And this idea of a golden age long past is what inspired early Restoration Movement leaders, who drank deeply of the American spirit, who sought to restore in their own day the ancient order of things. But the world they wanted to restore was not so much the glories of ancient Greece and Rome, but the church of the first century. That world and those churches were the way things were supposed to be.

By 1973, the vision of what the church should look like had been poured and hardened into the minds of many of the ministers who gathered in Memphis for this long-expected confrontation. They were fighting against those who would undermine this vision. They were fighting for a church fully restored, as God surely had intended.

O Canada

During the Second World War, in anticipation of the inevitable wounds and injuries of battle, the US War Department planned the construction of several dozen new hospitals across the country. The hospital built in Memphis, named after World War I army surgeon and brigadier general James M. Kennedy, was completed on January 26, 1943. It was located on Shotwell Road at Park Avenue.

But soon after the hospital was completed, Mrs. M. E. Brown of Marvell, Arkansas, wrote a local Memphis paper saying she thought the street name was inappropriate for a hospital, whose purpose was to treat wounded soldiers. The city agreed and changed the name from Shotwell to Getwell.

Seven years later, in 1950, the Getwell Road Church of Christ began to meet, just a few blocks south of the hospital. The redbrick, white-columned building faces east. A large concrete drainage ditch separates the church property from the road, carrying floodwaters as well as various sorts of urban flotsam and jetsam when it rains.

There, on a hot September afternoon in 1973, after a crowded lunch at Robilio's, more than two hundred preachers gathered. They had questions for the four visitors. The meeting lasted until after midnight.

Lynn Anderson was thirty-seven. By then, he had been the preaching minister at the Highland Church of Christ in Abilene, Texas, for two years. Memphis was not unfamiliar to him, having completed a master's degree at what was then called the Harding University Graduate School of Religion, whose campus is just a few blocks away from the Getwell Church of Christ building.

Anderson had grown up among ranchers and cowboys, merchants and schoolteachers, the hard-hewn, plain-talking, generous folks of Southwestern Saskatchewan, about a hundred miles south of Moose Jaw in central Canada, just north of the American border. Anderson was the great grandson of Swedish immigrants on his father's side and the grandson of German immigrants on his mother's.

His parents, Lawrence and Mary, had been converted by the missionary J. C. Bailey shortly before Lynn was born. Bailey had told them, "A church is not a building, not a denomination, but a circle of people gathered around Jesus." That's the kind of church they wanted to be a part of. That's how they raised their kids.

In 1965, as a young minister in Kelowna, British Columbia, Anderson had to make decisions about what was important and what was not. The town was a tourist paradise, with mountains and ski slopes, lakes and beaches. In those years, in addition to the tourists, a lot of hippies from the American West Coast found their way there.

Anderson would often go to their hootenannies on the beaches of Lake Okanagan and visit with them in their pads, sometimes setting up Bible studies. It didn't take long for him to figure out that his starched-dress-shirt-and-tie attire, quoting the King James Bible, and preaching about all the insider Church of Christ issues might not be the best gospel strategy for the hippies of Kelowna.

In 1971, when Anderson was appointed Highland's preacher, he was relatively unknown in the United States. That obscurity would not last long. For one thing, the Highland Church of Christ was one of the most influential congregations in this fellowship. Whoever preached there would likely be well known, no matter what. That Anderson's preaching was utterly captivating did not hurt, of course.

Highland's influence over the years had come, among other reasons, because it was the primary supporting church for the most prominent parachurch organization among Churches of Christ at the time, the Herald of Truth, whose main focus was mass-media evangelism. This organization received financial support from Churches of Christ all over the world. It had global impact and, therefore, it bore global scrutiny.

But Anderson's growing reputation emerged not so much because of where he preached, but how. I was a college student in Abilene when he first arrived. My classmates and I were electrified by what we experienced. We had never heard expository preaching before, not like this. He worked out of single texts each week, examining entire books of Scripture in context. More than that, his language was accessible, his stories engaging, his manner charming, his humor wry, his effect powerful.

Anderson seemed to be a preacher from a new era, emerging from the new cultural expressions of the sixties. The form of his sermons, his idioms and phrasing, his candor and panache, his way of interacting with people, even his clothes and hairstyle were unlike anything we had seen before from the pulpit. He had crossed a generational and cultural chasm with stunning effectiveness.

But he was not alone. One of the new spokespersons for Herald of Truth and representing the organization at the Memphis meeting was one of Anderson's college classmates, though his style of preaching was very different. When Landon Saunders spoke, his words had an almost mystical edge—intense, deliberate, probing, piercing, poignant, moving. His sermons had an emotional resonance that came not only from his close relationship with God but also his willingness to lean hard into the emerging culture. I had never before heard a preacher quote Dylan Thomas and Bob Dylan as well as Luke and Paul. And in the same sermon. Few people spoke to the rising Boomer generation with such relevance and power. To this day, when I preach, Landon's mystical presence and Lynn's expository style are never far from my consciousness.

In the early 1970s—culturally speaking, the final years of the sixties—Anderson and Saunders were a part of a budding group of preachers whose effect on a younger generation among Churches of Christ was profound. Drawing from their study of Scripture, they preached a gospel of grace, a gospel of inclusion, and a call to costly discipleship.

Saunders, representing the Herald of Truth, and Anderson, as the preaching minister of its primary supporting church, were prepared to make opening statements and respond to the questions several churches had begun to ask. These two young preachers had especially been criticized by several of the church leaders who gathered in Memphis that day, some of whom had flown in from halfway across the continent to make their case, to confront their supposed adversaries.

In addition to Anderson and Saunders and a couple of Highland elders, two other ministers were present, representing Herald of Truth. Harold Hazelip was a calm, thoughtful, focused presence. He taught theology and was the dean at the Harding Graduate School of Religion, and he preached at the Highland Street Church of Christ in Memphis. Hazelip would later become the president of Lipscomb University. But on this occasion, it was his role as a writer and spokesperson for Herald of Truth that called him there.

Batsell Barrett Baxter was also present. Surely no preacher of this era carried as much credibility or personal influence within Churches of Christ as did Dr. Baxter. Baxter was from an older generation, the World War II generation. He was a calm, reasoned, eloquent, gentle-spirited man whose ministry over the years had rarely evoked criticism. He preached at the Hillsboro Church of Christ in Nashville and taught at David Lipscomb College. More importantly for this meeting, Baxter had been the main face and voice of Herald of Truth since 1959.

It was primarily these four men who faced the gathered crowd. But the focal point, more often than not, was Anderson, whose recent sermons seemed to have created the greatest distress. Understanding why the concerns that day were so substantial may provide a clue into the nature of the movement itself.

Throughout the sixties, an environment conducive to fear had grown among Churches of Christ, as it had in the larger culture. Opinions that used to be marginal in the movement now appeared in the mainstream, including views about the Holy Spirit. Most thought the issues had been settled a long time ago. Most members of Churches of Christ in the first half of the twentieth century believed what Alexander Campbell believed a century before, that the gift of the Holy Spirit was the Bible itself.

But by 1973, more and more people in Churches of Christ seemed to believe the Spirit actually worked within Christians today. A few even thought modern miracles, such as healing and speaking in tongues, were possible. Certainly, several people at the Highland Church in Abilene did at the time. These believers in modern-day miracles at the Highland Church numbered only a handful, but they had not been kicked out of the church. In fact, these members appeared to be loved and honored there, to the frustration of the church's opponents.

Viewed in the best possible light, the concern most of the questioners brought to the Memphis meeting was to seek and defend truth. And for them, truth grew directly from a commitment to the restoration of the church. They saw themselves as part of a movement whose goal was not to reform an existing denomination but to restore the church as it had been in the beginning.

Frankly, most in the room would not have viewed anything that Stone or Campbell had said as being particularly relevant. Or anything else in Christian history since the first century. Most cared little, and knew even less, about Stone and Campbell. They were just restoring—or, as some believed, they had already restored—the New Testament church. Any intervening history was irrelevant.

Nonetheless, the conscious involvement of these preachers in a movement whose purpose was to restore the early church had been passed on to them by those who had gone before, accompanied by a common vocabulary and set of distinctive doctrines and practices, shared by most mid-twentieth-century Churches of Christ.

It is not difficult, in fact, to trace the historical connections from the present to the past, generation by generation, congregation by congregation, students from their teachers, churches from their preachers, preacher by preacher, back to the first congregations in each community, to the turn of the twentieth century when the split with Christian Churches and Disciples of Christ occurred, to the late nineteenth century when the conflicts were escalating, to the crisis of the Civil War, back to the union of two movements in the 1830s, and to the years just before that union when a Reforming Baptist, in a series of defining articles, made the case for restoration.

He was not the first, nor was he the only one. But it would be difficult to understand the heart and nature of the modern Restoration Movement apart from the groundwork laid by the Reforming Baptist, Alexander Campbell.

Campbell's words, spoken again and again by the succeeding generations, often without awareness of their origins, shaped the grammar of the movement, from church to church, preacher to preacher, generation after generation. All the way to a meeting in Memphis in 1973. All the way to today. For five years, beginning in 1825 and ending in 1829, Campbell wrote thirty-two articles in his journal the *Christian Baptist* under a common title: "A Restoration of the Ancient Order of Things."

Campbell soon moved on to other concerns; his opinions on restoration and other issues evolved over the years. But Campbell's 1820s articles profoundly affected what became Churches of Christ. They set the stage for the often-heated discussion among two hundred preachers on an already hot September day in Memphis.

The issue at hand during the tense confrontation was nothing less than the truth. Was the Herald of Truth, in fact, heralding truth? Was the Highland Church? Was Anderson? What is the truth about congregational cooperation? What is the truth about the nature of the Holy Spirit? Can the New Testament church be truly restored? More significantly, borrowing a phrase from a not-so-beloved Bible character, "What is truth?"

Truth and Truthiness

The great American philosopher Yogi Berra once said, "You can observe a lot by watching." When I was a kid, I watched Mr. Berra often, though apparently I did not see him well. There was much about him I missed. I didn't grasp that many of the things Yogi said didn't actually make sense. I hardly remember him saying anything at all, really, except perhaps in some post-game interviews.

I now know that people used to chuckle about what Yogi said. His sentences got all jumbled up or his syntax was mangled, creating looks of confusion or amusement on the faces of his interviewers. "When you come to a fork in the road, take it," he would say. Or, "We made too many wrong mistakes." Or, "You can observe a lot by watching." But after a while his little expressions began to make a certain kind of sense until, over time, they became, well, wise.

But I didn't know that then. I was just a kid, and I thought Yogi was just a baseball player, a great baseball player, the catcher for the New York Yankees, the greatest baseball team in the world.

I watched the Yankees almost every Saturday, so I saw Yogi almost every week. I watched them for two reasons. First, because CBS televised the Yankees every Saturday during baseball season. It wasn't the Phillies or the Red Sox or the Giants in the Game of the Week broadcasts. It was always the Yankees, so that's what I watched. Dizzy Dean and Pee Wee Reese called the games, of course. The inimitable and sometimes outrageous Dizzy, and the calm, smooth-talking Pee Wee. Pee Wee, the perennial All-Star infielder for the Dodgers, was a sort of hero to me because he was a relative of mine, which I bragged about to my friends.

But the main reason I watched those games is because that's what the Reese boys did. My brothers and I. And my dad. And usually my mom, who could tell you the ERAs of most of the Major League pitchers and the batting averages of most of the hitters, and why the Cubs would never win the World Series in spite of having the great Ernie Banks. The Cubs' pitching staff was too weak, you see, and Ron Santo, as good as he was, was no Eddie Mathews, and certainly Randy Hundley couldn't hold a candle to Yogi, and basically you just knew they were going to choke at the end of the season. Mom knew all that, of course, like all mothers everywhere surely knew. She was my mother and so she was my picture of what mothers were like.

I watched Yogi play each week during the regular Major League season and on into the World Series. Because they were always in the World Series. Because they were the greatest baseball team in the world. Which is why I hated them. I rooted for whoever was playing the Yankees. Or said differently, whoever was losing the World Series to the Yankees. Dad was for the Yankees. He had been since he was a boy, rooting for Ruth and Gehrig and later DiMaggio. But the Reese sons were against them. We were for the National League. That was set. That was who we were.

My family, like every family—and every organization, every church, every tradition—has a story. Over time, as we keep telling our stories, we come to see ourselves in certain ways. We create for ourselves—unconsciously, for the most part, but truly—a sense of our self-identity, our particular myth.

I don't mean myth as if our story were a lie, but myth in the sense of a defining narrative for our lives, for our people. There's a certain way we have come to understand ourselves, where we come from, what our people are like, who we are. Perhaps more importantly, there's an image of ourselves that we want to show others, how we want them to see us, who we want them to believe we are. Whether that self-narrative is true is another matter entirely.

Lawrence Wright, in his bestselling book *God Save Texas*, talks about the Texas myth, the self-identity of this people, where their self-understanding came from, the insecurities and arrogances, the truths and fictions that perpetuate the myth. "Texans see themselves as confident, hardworking, and neurosis-free—a distillation of the best qualities of America," he says. Non-Texans often tell another story, that Texans are "braggarts; careless with money and our personal lives; a little gullible but dangerous if crossed; insecure but obsessed with power and prestige."[9]

So which version of the story is true? Is the Texas myth true? Yes. No. Probably. For some. In part. But it's also more than true. And less. It feels true. It's true in the imagination, beyond what the facts may support. It is true in a general sense. The Texas myth, like all defining narratives, smacks of "truthiness," as Stephen Colbert used to say, or at least as the TV character Stephen Colbert played by the comedian Stephen Colbert used to say. It's hard to nail all that down, because truth doesn't always nail down easily.

Truth is a squirmy little thing. You try to hammer it to the wall, but it slips out of your fingers and scurries along the baseboard just out of your grasp, into a crack you had never seen before, behind the drywall in the open space between the studs where the cockroaches live. Truth is sometimes hard to find, but when it scurries out from behind the wall and crawls across your foot, you might surprise yourself with the scream you hear rattling around the back of your throat.

Because coming face to face with the truth, when you have always believed something else, can be disconcerting and even a little scary. It's easier just to never look.

We each have a story, a sort of movie playing inside our heads, where we are the center of the action. Our story feels true because we are living it. Growing up, we inherit, or simply acquire through social osmosis, certain values from the generations before us—instincts about people and things, ways of seeing the world. Over time, our particular families form a self-understanding that shapes and defines who we are.

Many a child has found success or ruin trying to live up to the family story. Or live it down. But when you get older, or when life happens and your story is blown up, then you may have to stand back and will yourself to look at your stories, the beliefs and values that formed you.

The problem is, over time we come to believe our own myths, to assume that how we see ourselves is, in fact, true. Often it is not. Not completely. Our eyesight isn't always accurate. Our story may be truthy, it may be true in general, but that's not the same as being true. Our eyes miss some things and distort others.

There are a lot of reasons for this faulty vision. In part, our memories can't be trusted. They are notoriously unreliable. In one well-known study, a team of researchers interviewed several thousand people about what they remembered on 9/11, at three intervals after the event: one week later, after three years, and then after ten years. While the people were absolutely confident of their recollections of that awful day, their memories, at least for most of them, were different at each juncture, sometimes substantially so.[10] Our sense of the way things used to be often becomes distorted over time by our unreliable memories.

But not only are our memories not entirely trustworthy, our perspectives are limited. We don't see the-truth-the-whole-truth-and-nothing-but-the-truth but rather a piece of the truth, a particular angle of the truth at a certain point in time filtered through our unique experiences. Over time, our personal and family stories are created out of these limited perspectives and fallible memories. And when our personal story is the primary or even exclusive source from which our opinions about the world are formed, then we have problems. Inevitably.

But mostly we don't stop long enough to examine our stories. We don't look at them hard enough, penetrate them deeply enough, or discern them wisely enough. It is easier to observe the stories without actually watching, and so we miss stuff, we misremember, we leave things out. Sometimes we are flat-out wrong.

It turns out I'm not related to Pee Wee at all. Not remotely. I fudged that story to my childhood friends. And my brothers and I usually had to work in the yard on Saturdays, or play our own ballgames, so we actually missed most of the televised games, whoever was playing, which was often not the Yankees. And most moms don't know pitching rotations and ERAs. It turns out other moms were not like my mom.

And, to tell you the truth, my mom in real life was not exactly the mom of my memories. In retrospect, she hardly ever watched the Saturday baseball games. She actually had a life. And she was ultimately wrong about the Cubs, though no one should hold that against her since their 2016 World Series victory occurred four years after she walked off the mound and hung up her cleats.

You can observe a lot by watching. The meaning of Yogi's adage is obvious enough, in an it-goes-without-saying sort of way. But it is also profound and maybe not so obvious, since a lot of people watch but don't actually see. Which is the whole point, of course.

For most of us, our understanding of church has been shaped by our experiences with church over the years. Stories were passed down from generation to generation about where our people came from, about what is true and what is not, about how our church fits into God's eternal plan. The teachings that made our churches distinct are emphasized. The teachings of other groups are often caricatured and condemned.

Over time, imperceptibly, this picture of who we are becomes the truth in our minds: it is just the way things are, the way things should be, not just for ourselves but also for others—what we think they should believe, how we think they should do church.

What has been handed down to us, however, is often distorted, like the old Telephone Game where each player whispers a sentence to the next person, who whispers it to the next, down the line to the last player. What is said at the end of the game is often funny because it is almost always wrong. Terribly wrong. But when the game takes a couple of centuries to play and the original whisperers are dead and gone, and when what is passed down is not a sentence but an entire belief system that influences, if not governs, the decisions we make about church, then we better stop and look at it.

A particular version of the restoration ideal was first articulated about two centuries ago in articles by a young Alexander Campbell. But Campbell was not attempting to describe everything that should be restored. The central tenets of the faith, like the nature of God and the atoning work of Christ, like grace and discipleship, were not included in those articles, not because they weren't important to Campbell but because he assumed them. And because he was attempting to do something else. He was focusing on certain externals of the faith as a means of creating the possibility for Christian unity.

Generation after generation, these principles of restoration were passed down, largely divorced from their original setting and missing the theological core that Campbell had left unexpressed. They came to have a life of their own, significantly filtered and shaped by twentieth-century concerns and the personalities of powerful preachers. Like whisperings of a multi-generation Telephone Game, these restoration ideals morphed into something they had not been when Campbell first articulated them. The movement's sense of the way things were became distorted by an imperfect institutional memory and was finally codified into something else, something that came to feel like gospel.

We can observe a lot by watching. But first we have to actually look. We have to be suspicious of our memories, of our own sense of certainty. We have to be alert to oversimplification and to changing contexts. Otherwise, we end up observing without actually seeing. We miss how our view of things has been filtered through our own experiences. We overlook how our understanding of things changes over time, misremembering all the dead ends and detours in our own search for truth.

In *The Importance of Being Earnest*, Oscar Wilde's character Algernon tells Jack, "The truth is never pure and rarely simple." Truth is hard. It's easily distorted or obscured. Over time, we come to believe our own story. But sometimes our story is more truthy than true. It seems true. Or we want it to be true. Which is why humility is a crucial Christian virtue and why grace lies at the heart of the gospel.

Freedom and Conformity

Most efforts at religious renewal begin in freedom but mutate into conformity.[11] It happens so often, it feels almost inevitable.

Take the English Puritans. They were committed to transforming the Church of England. They believed their only model was the church of the Bible. They believed Scripture was their sole authority.

But what they were most interested in was freedom. They wanted freedom from laws they believed were unjust or unchristian, freedom from the heavy-handedness of many priests, freedom from paralyzing ritual.

But it was not just a freedom *from* but also a freedom *to*. They desired freedom to think for themselves, freedom to read the Bible without the mediation of priests, freedom to worship as they believed, freedom to create the kind of church they believed the Bible taught.

But here's what happened. As the Puritans gained a measure of freedom, they created new boundaries, established new institutions, and set doctrines and practices that required conformity. Later generations, then, would seek their own freedom from the now oppressive system that, ironically, had been established in freedom.

It happened over and over again. Not just with the Puritans but also with their spiritual children, the various movements they influenced.

The Presbyterians of Scotland, for example, like their Puritan cousins, sought freedom from the Church of England. In so doing, they established particular patterns and rules that had to be followed. Then many of their congregations, in the exercise of their freedom, decided to walk away—to secede. But Seceder Presbyterians soon established their own patterns and rules against which the Pro-Burghers rebelled and the New Lights protested. So, Anti-Burgher, Old Light, Seceder churches were begun, conforming to new patterns and rules. Thomas Campbell and his group, then, sought freedom from the Seceders. To do so, of course, they had to walk away from them. On and on, generation after generation, world without end.

This cycle of freedom and conformity, which occurred so frequently among the Presbyterians, made its way into the DNA of Churches of Christ. But of all the groups with roots in the Puritan churches, the Baptists were the ones whose move from freedom to conformity most directly impacted the early Stone and Campbell churches. It will be helpful to understand why.

The so-called Regular Baptists that Barton Stone and Alexander Campbell encountered in Kentucky came from two streams. One grew out of a Baptist movement in England steeped in Calvinism. They believed God saves only the elect, the particular ones God predestined for salvation. Thus they were called Particular Baptists.

The other Baptist stream came from America, growing out of the Great Awakening of the 1730s and '40s. During this religious revival, many Christians came to believe that the established churches in America were dead or dying and could not be reformed. So a number of them separated themselves from the established churches. They called themselves Separate Baptists. They advocated Spirit-filled revivalism and aggressive evangelism in order to reach out beyond those churches.

Through the opening decades of the 1800s, these two Baptist streams intermingled out on the American frontier and began to form a common thrust and identity—the strong Calvinists with English Baptist roots and the aggressive revivalists out of the American Great Awakening, all seeking freedom.

These Baptists in Kentucky spoke passionately about freedom in the Spirit. They advocated mutual forbearance. They desired freedom from oppressive laws, freedom from the kind of persecution Baptists and other dissenters had experienced in Europe and the colonies, freedom to think and be what they believed the Bible taught.

But soon their language of liberty began to shift. As they found themselves competing alongside other groups on the American frontier—such as Methodists and the growing number of Stone and Campbell churches—many Baptists began to insist that theirs was the only true church.[12]

By the 1820s, many Baptists had come to see themselves as the church of the New Testament. For these Baptists, the road from freedom to conformity was a short one.

Soon a number of Baptist leaders took these claims to their logical conclusions. Landmark Baptists, as they were called, set clear boundaries between the one true church, the Baptist Church, and all others. They claimed there had been Baptist churches throughout Christian history—there must have been since Jesus had said the gates of Hell would not prevail against his church, and they, the Baptists, were that church. One Baptist leader claimed, "all Christian communities during the first three centuries were of the Baptist denomination, in constitution and practice."[13]

Not surprisingly, the arguments between Baptists and the churches associated with Campbell and Stone became especially heated. This happened, in part, because these churches competed for members in the same communities. But in no small measure, the friction between Baptists and early Churches of Christ occurred because many of these latter churches had come to the conclusion that they, rather than the Baptists, were the church of the New Testament.

And so, Stone-Campbell churches began to leave the Baptist fold. And Baptists pushed out Stone-Campbell members. The lines between Baptists and Churches of Christ, which had once been blurred, now hardened.

The rhetoric of early Churches of Christ, then, was rooted in freedom. They yearned to be free in Christ, free from creeds, free to study the Bible on their own. But sometimes what that meant was that they wanted to be free from the Baptists. And like Baptists and most other groups who had Puritan roots, Churches of Christ soon found themselves on their own road from freedom to conformity.

By the time of the 1973 Memphis meeting, the lines between right and wrong were clear and the consequences for crossing them grave.

Means and End

Freedom was what Campbell was arguing for. Nothing short of freedom.

At the launch of his newpaper, the *Christian Baptist*, in 1824, Alexander Campbell made clear that it would be direct and hard hitting. He recognized that he sometimes was, in his own words, "tart and severe,"[14] especially to other preachers. But he believed being so harsh was sometimes needed to bring freedom to people being held in spiritual bondage.

In those years, Campbell still considered himself a Reforming Baptist. He wanted Baptists and other Christian traditions to be free from creeds and confessions. He believed these traditions had hemmed in the people of God and limited their ability to think and act for themselves.

But he also wanted freedom from the power of clergy. It was the clergy, he believed, who were responsible for most of the problems in the church. He denounced priests and pastors who were overly concerned about their salaries and their titles, who flaunted their education and fleeced their own churches while making the people think that they actually cared for their souls.

At its heart, the freedom he sought was nothing less than the restoration of the primitive church. That was the purpose of his series of articles in the *Christian Baptist* on "A Restoration of the Ancient Order of Things."

Campbell opened with an extract from the minutes of the Baptist Missionary Association of Kentucky, held September 11, 1824. In his remarks about the meeting, Campbell said that the churches of his day were wanting, lacking, and needed to be brought up to the "standard of the New Testament."[15]

In this and the articles that followed, Campbell argued for a restoration of the first-century church. He urged every Christian and every congregation to "discard from their faith and their practice everything that is not found written in the New Testament" and to "believe and practice whatever is there enjoined."[16]

For the next five years, in a total of thirty-two articles and essays, Campbell addressed a number of issues regarding the restoration of the church, such as the Lord's Supper, Christian fellowship, congregational giving, the qualifications of bishops and deacons, love feasts, hymn singing, the church, and Christian discipline. The focus of the articles was on the organization, form, and structure of the church.

Campbell's strong, clear call for the restoration of the ancient order had a powerful impact on many of his readers, certainly on a lot of Baptists, particularly among those who had become skeptical of the necessity of an emotional religious experience. His language was simple, clear, and logical. Thousands of these Baptists were convinced.

And yet, Campbell's desire was not to pull folks away from their churches into some new sect or denomination. The very basis of his arguments was to call Christians to unite, not to further divide. Unity was the heart of it all. Christian unity was a command of Jesus that must be obeyed.

But it was also more than that. For Campbell, unity among Christians would be nothing less than the means by which the second coming of Jesus would begin, which Campbell believed would be the culmination of God's thousand-year reign on earth—the millennium.

It may be difficult for modern Christians to grasp the extent of the millennial fever that swept across America in the first half of the nineteenth century. Their millennial hopes, however, were of a different sort than what many believers talk about today.

Modern premillennialists believe that Christ will come to earth and reign over God's kingdom for a thousand years. Campbell and many other nineteenth-century Christians believed what today is called postmillennialism. They believed that Christians, through the accomplishments of human progress, would themselves usher in the thousand-year reign of God on earth, at the end of which Christ would return.

Campbell, and many others in America at the time, believed that the extraordinary accomplishments of human knowledge and progress were abundantly evident. What was still needed was for Christians to be united. Only then would the kingdom of God on earth begin.

And Campbell believed the unity of Christians was within reach.

We should pause to note that Campbell's restorationist views alongside his millennial expectations concealed a problem, an inconsistency, that wedged its way into the DNA of the movement and helped pave the road for the division to come. Campbell's commitment to the "restoration of the ancient order" pointed back to the golden age of the first century. But his millennial hopes pointed to a new golden age, not in the past but sometime in the future, sometime soon, when the kingdom of God would prevail on earth for a thousand years.

Campbell's millennial hopes were rooted not so much in pessimism about a world that's not the way it's supposed to be but in optimism that people were turning to God and that God was creating the kingdom through the remarkable progress of humans.

Further, Campbell was convinced that Christian unity would never come about as long as people followed denominational creeds and confessions. He believed creeds divided Christians rather than uniting them. So, he urged them to discard their creeds and come together using the Bible alone.

It was in this context that Churches of Christ first began to claim that they were not part of any denomination. Their nondenominational Christianity was not a claim that they were the only Christians, as if the believers in all the other Christian groups were not actually Christians. Rather, early Churches of Christ believed there were Christians scattered throughout the various denominations.

And so, Churches of Christ urged Christians everywhere to drop their particular denominational loyalties—in other words, to be nondenominational—and simply become part of the great communion of believers, following the Bible alone. Then, when the New Testament church was finally restored and Christians were united, the long-expected millennium would begin.

Churches of Christ, then, began in freedom founded upon the vision of a golden age, both in the past and yet to come. But what began as a revolution of freedom soon became a restoration of conformity. What began as a movement devoted to unity became a church marked by division. Many things contributed to this shift.

First, Campbell's harsh language did not help. His "tart and severe" treatment of others, while couched in the language of freedom, did not make uniting with them easy. At one point, several young readers cancelled their subscriptions to the *Christian Baptist* because Campbell was on "a firm course of ridicule and sarcasm."[17] Another reader said that Campbell had forgotten the Christian virtues of gentleness and kindness.

Campbell's pugnacious rhetoric toned down a little in later years, but he never apologized for it. He was happy to engage in the give-and-take for the sake of his ideas, and he took as much as he gave. He believed he was fair. He always allowed letters of disagreement to be published in his journals, and he was willing to listen for hours to those who disagreed with him.

But his often-combative style became part of the tenor of the movement, not just in the first generation but also in the generations to come. It is hard to escape the fact that Campbell's hard words and tone, used in advocacy of Christian freedom and Christian unity, contributed substantially to the transition of the movement away from freedom and toward conformity and division.

Second, in his description of the restored New Testament church, Campbell made clear he was not attempting to determine who was saved and who was not. That was God's job. Rather, he was describing the church he believed God wanted. As he said in his very first article on restoration, his goal was to bring the church up to the standard of the New Testament.

When one reader asked Campbell if he was guilty of creating a new creed like the ones he so strongly criticized, he replied that he was not. His essays on the restoration of the ancient order, he said, were never "a test of christian character or terms of christian communion."[18] In other words, a person may not get everything right and still be saved.

But his distinction between laying out the "standard of the church," on one hand, and using that standard to define the "terms of Christian communion" (that is, who was an authentic Christian and who was not) was not readily apparent to many of his followers, then or now. And with Campbell's often-domineering manner, it is not surprising that many of his associates themselves acted in a domineering way, criticizing any kind of church other than their own.

Third, restoration moved from freedom to conformity when it became clear that the millennium was not coming soon. The hard, rancorous years leading up to the Civil War made that abundantly clear. If the kingdom of God on earth depended on the unity of Christians, then no millennial reign was at hand. Clearly, Protestant denominations were not dissolving into union with the body of Christ at large.

This point is critical. If the logic behind the original "restoration plea" is missed, then the original purpose of restoration will be misapplied. And Churches of Christ have almost always misapplied it.

For Campbell and churches in the early years of the movement, the restoration of the ancient order was a *means to a means to an end*. Restoration was the means to create unity, and unity was the means to bring about the ultimate end—the thousand-year kingdom of God on earth.

When it became clear that the end was not near since Christians were not being united, the desire of some of Campbell's followers to restore the New Testament church became an end unto itself. This was a radical shift.

The freedom that they originally sought through the restoration of the early church eventually became conformity to a young Campbell's early articles about the restoration of the ancient order, and these focused almost exclusively on the church's form—its organization, practices, and polity.

In the coming decades this restoration impulse, when it was divorced from its original commitment to unity, began to drive a wedge into these churches. For many, the original unity movement had now become a restoration movement instead. As the nation increasingly divided, the churches increasingly fragmented. Each group grew more concerned about their distinctives—what made them different rather than what drew them together.

Over time, as each issue was debated and each doctrine more clearly defined, the language of freedom diminished. Conformity took its place. Conformity on every issue. Restoration, then, changed from emphasizing Christian freedom to focusing on the nature of the one true church. Not Baptist churches. Nor any other. Our church. Only ours.

Persistence

How has the self-identity of Churches of Christ remained so constant over the years when there is no denominational office to sustain it? How does any group's understanding of itself stay pretty much the same generation after generation?

Some things about people change over time, whether family, organization, nation, or church. In fact, some things can change quickly, with little impact on us. But some traits, whether helpful or destructive, remain part of a group's identity for years, even centuries, often without much conscious awareness or scrutiny. To change them would be to fundamentally change who we are.

Social scientists often refer to this phenomenon as *cultural persistence*.[19] Certain self-descriptions of the group, certain self-understandings, remain constant over time. In other words, they persist.

Why some group characteristics remain constant over the years while others do not can be difficult to determine. But here are some common themes:

- *Clear and repeatable vocabulary*. A group's behaviors or beliefs can be easily named and are repeatable over time with little or no change of meaning.
- *A verbal shorthand for group beliefs*. A group vocabulary develops, a type of verbal shorthand where specific words and texts come to represent the group's beliefs or doctrines.
- *The vocabulary becomes authoritative*. The verbal shorthand, passed down from generation to generation, evolves into a command, eventually becoming the essential identity of the group.
- *Reinforced when challenged*. If this emerging identity is ever publicly challenged and the group stays together anyway, their verbal shorthand is reinforced and their identity persists.

Cultural persistence happens to many groups. It happened to Churches of Christ in spades.

Beginning in the 1820s, largely inspired by Campbell's articles in the *Christian Baptist* on the "Restoration of the Ancient Order of Things," a growing group of people on the American frontier, especially in Kentucky and Middle Tennessee, came to believe that not only could the first-century church be restored but that they had restored it.

They were not the first ones to make such a claim, nor would they be the last. But within a few years, this particular notion of restoration, the restoration of the New Testament church itself, became a defining characteristic of these Christians. Their primary focus, based on Alexander Campbell's influential articles, was the restoration of the forms, practices, and external patterns of first-century churches to their own time and place.

This self-understanding did not simply emerge at the turn of the twentieth century when Churches of Christ began to be recognized as a group separate from Christian Churches and Disciples of Christ. Its roots were much earlier, close to eighty years earlier, even before the union of the Stone and Campbell churches.

In the wake of Campbell's restoration articles, a self-identity was created for a growing group of Christians, that they and only they were the church of the New Testament. In the decades that followed, this identity would grow into full flower.

But as we have seen, the group's original vision of restoration was different. Beginning in 1824 in his first restoration article, Campbell said he was not attempting to determine who was authentically Christian and who was not. Rather, he was trying to create an opportunity for Christian unity by means of a recovery of New Testament norms and practices. The restoration of the ancient order was not the ultimate goal but a means to a means to an end. Restoring the church would bring about unity, and unity would usher in the kingdom of God on earth.

However, as Campbell's restoration articles were published, some churches began to adopt a narrower vision and vocabulary about the nature of restoration. And later, when the situation changed, when broad Christian unity and the millennial reign did not occur, when the language of restoration lost its original context and therefore its original meaning and purpose, these churches' vision for restoration nevertheless persisted. These were the churches who saw themselves as the Restoration Movement.

In many ways, here is the cultural starting place of Churches of Christ. Beginning in the 1820s, this self-identity as the restored church of the Bible became increasingly persistent. In Richard Hughes's words, "With neither postmillennial optimism nor ecumenical vision to sustain them, these people increasingly identified the primitive church of the New Testament age with the Church of Christ movement to which they belonged, and they defended that church against all comers. In this way, ironically, they built a sect on the foundation of the original vision of 'nondenominational' Christianity."[20]

Over time, differences within the movement grew, especially in the face of opposition to this narrowly focused understanding of restoration. In fact,

Campbell himself publicly opposed these early churches that insisted they had restored New Testament Christianity. The more opposition these churches faced, the stronger their sense of identity. The greater the pushback, the more cohesive the movement.

By the late 1880s, Daniel Sommer had led several of these restoration-ist congregations away from the movement. Through the 1890s, many of the remaining restoration churches chose to affiliate only with other like-minded congregations until, by the early twentieth century, everyone recognized that the group had broken away.

What began as an undercurrent had become a full-fledged undertow. And a new, separate fellowship of churches had begun. They called themselves almost exclusively Churches of Christ.

But in the 1820s, all of that lay in the future. In those early days, the movement was still embryonic. Its future shapes had not yet congealed. Before the identifying characteristics of Churches of Christ could persist over time, they would need a clear and distinctive vocabulary, repeatable over time, a type of verbal shorthand where specific words would represent the group's beliefs and would become authoritative within the group.

This vocabulary would soon emerge, but not simply because of Campbell's restoration articles. It arose because of a new preacher, a Scotsman who wasn't even a member of their group when he started preaching among them, whose clear and memorable explanations of how a person became a Christian would soon be a hallmark of these churches and a critical piece of their growing self-identity.

First Foot

The narrow streets were thick with revelers. In the early morning hours, the old city was normally dark, the roads and lanes empty. But not this day. Two brothers had to slog their way through crowds every bit as dense as at midday, but at this hour the residents were noisy and festive, and not altogether sober. It was New

Year's in Edinburgh, and the young men were intent on being *qualtagh*, or "first foot," in the house of a friend.

Earlier in the evening, the brothers had been at a celebration in a nearby home, exchanging stories, songs, and traditional blessings with the other guests. But after midnight, following the ancient tradition, they left for the house of a friend, bearing gifts and a good word. The Scots placed great significance on the individual who put the first foot across their threshold on New Year's Day. The right person and the right blessing were supposed to bring good luck.

James and Walter crossed over the Old Edinburgh Bridge, a few blocks south of St. Giles Church (the church of John Knox and the Scottish Reformation), and continued on their errand of hospitality. Afterwards, as James made his way back through the crowds and across the bridge, he looked around and saw that his brother was not with him. He hurried on to the house they shared, thinking Walter would join him soon. But when his brother did not arrive, he headed back to the bridge.

There he found a crowd gathered. James heard from among them the clear, resonant voice of his brother singing a song of Old Scotia to the delight of his hearers. When James pushed his way through, he saw Walter standing on stone steps leading up to a shop nearby. Just below him stood a blind man holding out his hat to receive coins from the crowd.

Throughout the day, the man apparently had sat on these steps, imploring passersby for a little generosity, but they were focused instead on the tasks and pleasantries of the day. By the evening, his begging had accomplished little.

When Walter was on his way home from his "first foot" journey, he had noticed the beggar and was touched by his need. But he had had no coins to give him. Seeing how little the man had accumulated during the day, Walter quickly formulated a plan.

Two years earlier, in the fall of 1809, Walter had been enrolled in the University of Edinburgh at the age of fourteen, which was not uncommonly young for that era. He was already an excellent musician, having been trained well by his father. Not only did he sing beautifully, but he also played the flute. Shortly after his arrival in Edinburgh, one of the city's most eminent musicians, having heard Walter play, offered to give him advanced lessons. Soon his skills surpassed those of the master. Though he was still a teenager, many recognized Walter as the finest flutist in the city.

And now in the early hours of this New Year, even though the sixteen-year-old was painfully shy, he began to sing. As people stopped, drawn to the sweet and haunting melodies, Walter gestured to them to be generous to the beggar. He sang well into the night, the blind man leaving with enough support to sustain him for quite a few days.

Many years later, James often told this story about his brother, Walter Scott, the evangelist and friend of Alexander Campbell, who did as much as any individual in helping launch what would become Churches of Christ, Christian Churches, and Disciples of Christ.

But it was a single sermon, preached years later, that opened up the future for Walter. That sermon changed his life. Not because what he said was so memorable, though I'm sure it was fine. It was just so well received that he was asked to head a mission to the Western Reserve of Ohio. That two-year mission transformed Campbell's churches.

So, what does any of this have to do with a 1973 Memphis meeting, you ask? Or with modern Churches of Christ? Much, as it turns out. Scott's Ohio sermons indelibly stamped Churches of Christ with a key piece of their self-identity. Scott gave them a defining vocabulary, which explains to a great extent why they came together so vigorously and why they stayed together so doggedly.

As we have seen, some ideas and groups come together and remain together because they exhibit elements of cultural persistence: they develop a clear and repeatable vocabulary that is easily reduced to a verbal shorthand, which becomes authoritative over time and is deeply reinforced when challenged. Scott gave them their clear, repeatable, and authoritative verbal shorthand.

It was after Scott's death when many of the challenges came—the struggle between North and South, the battles over societies and organs, a fight between Texas and Tennessee Christians. By 1973, the issues were long decided. You were either right or you were wrong. You were either in or you were out. A commitment to freedom, which was conspicuous early in the movement, had become locked down into conformity.

But here's the rest of the story. At some point, conformity always seems to break down. And freedom finds a way of breaking loose.

The Sermon That Changed the Movement

Walter Scott attended his first Mahoning Baptist Association meeting in 1826. In the six years since the association had been founded, the number of congregations had remained stagnant—around ten churches and less than four hundred members. Year after year the number of baptisms barely exceeded the number of dropouts and deaths. This was the core of Campbell's movement. It was hard for them not to be discouraged.

This lack of growth created the crisis that introduced the man whose abilities eventually revolutionized the movement. The opportunity came when Scott preached during the Sunday morning service at that year's annual meeting. That he was preaching that day was a surprise, not because Scott was new but because he was not a Baptist.

As one might imagine, the name Walter Scott was common in the Old Country. The year Scott became a student at the University of Edinburgh, another Walter Scott was a classmate. Two others had come the year before. The famous poet and novelist by this name had been a student there twenty years earlier and was in Edinburgh during the six years Walter studied at the university.

After finishing his work at the University of Edinburgh, Scott had come to America. He immediately found work at a school on Long Island teaching English, Latin, and Greek, which was not surprising. He was Scottish, after all. Everything in Scott's life had prepared him to teach.

Scott had been nurtured in Scotland's bosom, graced with a keen mind, instilled with a passion to learn, equipped from his earliest days with languages and tools, and challenged by some of the greatest scholars of the age. From the time he arrived in the United States as a young man until he died at the age of sixty-five, Scott was engaged in teaching. Even when he preached, he taught. His preaching was intellectually rather than emotionally driven—clearly organized and logically compelling.

There would be times in Scott's life that he would be debilitated by dark periods of crushing sadness. He would move from periods of unmatched energy and productivity, sometimes lasting for several years, to long stretches of fatigue and depression. He would likely be diagnosed today as having bipolar disorder. But in spite of it, he never lost his passion or his mission. He knew who he was. He was a teacher gifted by God, prepared by God's hand, for God's good purpose.

So, when Scott moved to Pittsburgh in 1819, he looked for a place to teach. George Forrester, the headmaster of a school and fellow Scotsman, invited Scott to join him in his work. As it turned out, Forrester had been influenced by some of the same independent church leaders who had so deeply affected Thomas and Alexander Campbell in Scotland and Ireland. Consequently, like the Campbells,

Forrester had come to reject creeds, question traditional Calvinism, and practice baptism by immersion and weekly communion.

From the moment Scott arrived in Pittsburgh, he threw himself into teaching at Forrester's school, working at the church, and studying for the sake of his own intellectual growth, which he pursued with considerable discipline. Under Forrester's tutelage, Scott began to see church, faith, and the Bible in new ways. He used his own classical training to study the New Testament in Greek. Soon, he asked Forrester to baptize him by immersion.

Shortly afterward, Forrester died and everything fell into Scott's hands—the school, the church, and, not unimportantly, Forrester's vast library. There in the library, and through the books, pamphlets, and articles Scott acquired, many of the intellectual pieces began to come together for him.

He came across a pamphlet entitled *On Baptism* written by Henry Errett from New York City. In the little book, Errett argued not primarily about baptism's mode, which he assumed to be immersion, but about its purpose: the forgiveness of sins.[21]

This was a revelation to Scott. He had come to believe that baptism should be by immersion. But its connection to forgiveness of sins was a new idea to him. He pursued this idea with singular focus. It was a crucial piece of what would come.

Through one of his students, a thirteen-year-old boy named Robert Richardson, Scott was introduced to Thomas and Alexander Campbell, who were friends of his family. In a few years, Richardson—as a medical doctor, professor of chemistry at Bethany College, author of well-reasoned journal articles and evocative devotional pieces, and as the biographer of Alexander Campbell—would himself become an individual of powerful influence in the Stone-Campbell Movement.

The bond between Walter Scott and Alexander Campbell was almost immediate. Scott saw in Campbell unusual drive and vision. Campbell found in Scott a well-trained mind, a heart for evangelism, and an ability to make complex ideas clear and accessible.

Over the next few years, they were constant companions. In the early summer of 1826, Scott and his young family moved to Steubenville, Ohio, not far from Campbell's home across the Ohio River. A couple of months later, Campbell invited him to the annual meeting of the Mahoning Baptist Association.

The meeting began on Saturday, August 26, in David Hays's barn. Campbell was given the position of honor and preached the opening sermon. On Sunday morning the meeting opened with sermons by two former preachers from Pittsburgh.

Sidney Rigdon preached first. Rigdon saw himself as Campbell's closest associate and heir to the leadership of the movement. But Campbell would soon push Rigdon to the margins, as he commonly did to rising stars, leading Rigdon to soon walk away from Campbell and his churches.

Rigdon and his entire congregation near Cleveland would eventually join Joseph Smith's Latter-Day Saints, with Rigdon bringing more than a few of Campbell's teachings into the heart of the Mormon Church. Later, when Joseph Smith was killed, Rigdon was pushed aside again, when the leadership of the Mormons fell into the hands of Brigham Young. None of these developments, however, could have been envisioned by anyone listening to Rigdon's strong sermon at the 1826 Mahoning meeting.

Immediately after Rigdon finished, Walter Scott stepped to the pulpit. It was likely because of Campbell's urging that Scott had been chosen to preach that day. It was an inspired choice. Scott's sermon was so powerful, so well presented, that it was still being talked about at the following year's meeting. Because of it, a decision was made that would turn the movement upside down.

Five Easy Fingers

"Did you ever play toad sky-high?" Scott's brogue was thick as he began to play to the boys in the crowd. His long, clean-shaven face had suddenly become animated. His eyes scrutinized the room intently. His unruly hair, still noticeable behind a receding hairline, danced with every gesture.

He had almost lost his audience, and he knew it. More than a few of them had come that night for sport, ready to make fun of the crazy man who had lured them there. But the anticipated merriment had been replaced by drowsy inattention. Up to this point, the sermon had been clear and logical. And boring. Scott sensed he had to change pace before they fell asleep or walked out.

"Boys," he said, "did you ever play toad sky-high?" The children leaned forward, their eyebrows cocked in amusement.

"Well, boys, I'll tell you how we played it in Scotland. First, we caught a toad and went out into a clear open place, and got a log or big stone, and across this we laid a plank or board, one end of which rested on the ground and the other stuck up in the air."

The adults now began to stir, sorting through the rrr's of the preacher's strong Scottish burr.

"We then placed the toad on the lower end and took a big stick and struck the upper part of the board with all our might."

He was almost shouting now.

"The other end flew up, and away went the toad, sky-high."

The boys howled with laughter at the thought of the toad, launched by the board, now arching upward toward the sky. That the boys were in the audience was no accident, of course. Scott had done everything he could to get them there. Better said, he had done everything he could to get them to bring their parents there. He now had their attention and did not hesitate to spring the trap.

When he had first entered the village that morning, he had spotted the boys and immediately began to engage them. "Hold up your left hands," he said to them. They did so enthusiastically. "Now, beginning with your thumb, repeat what I say to you."

He began to tick through his list, one by one, from thumb to little finger.

"Faith, repentance, baptism, remission of sins, gift of the Holy Spirit—that takes up all your fingers. Now again! Faith, repentance, baptism, remission of sins, gift of the Holy Spirit."

They repeated it with him over and over.

"Now, run home. Don't forget what is on your fingers, and tell your parents that a man will preach the gospel tonight at the schoolhouse as you have it on the five fingers of your hands."

Throughout the day, the story of this strange man had been repeated in home after home, the children emphasizing with their fingers the list they had memorized. Long before the service was scheduled to begin, the room had filled to overflowing and was buzzing with expectation, teetering between curiosity and mockery.

It had been a tough beginning, but the toad story had finally drawn them in. But Scott had a point to make, and he made it forcefully.

"But boys, what we did to that toad was not right. That toad was one of God's creatures and could feel pain as well as any of you. It was a poor, harmless thing, and it was wicked of us boys to send it flying through the air, for in most cases, when the toad came down, the poor thing would be dead."

The room was hushed. He had them now.

"And, boys, we felt very badly when we saw the blood staining its brown skin and its body bruised and its limbs broken and lying motionless in the grass through which it had hopped so merrily a few minutes before."

He continued to describe this cruelty to the toad until some of the boys in the crowd were in tears. Even the grown-ups were affected, and he addressed them pointedly. Their children, he said, were in tears about a toad, and they had been asleep when he had told them about the suffering and death of their Lord. He didn't lose their attention again.

That night, as in all of the sermons Scott preached throughout Ohio's Western Reserve, he did not call his listeners to wait until they felt some urging from God that indicated they were among the elect whom God had chosen to be saved. Rather, Scott insisted, salvation was for everyone. The time to respond to God's saving acts was now.

God had made promises, and they were all free to act. There were things they should do, and things God would do: they should believe, repent, and be baptized; God would grant forgiveness of sins along with the gift of the Holy Spirit and eternal life.

Night after night in community after community, Scott preached. His messages were simple, his call to action clear. His sermons resonated with the independent-minded, hard-work oriented, common-sense folks in eastern Ohio.

Scott's reputation increased, as did his crowds. In almost every town and village, people were baptized, sometimes by the dozens. For the first time, the churches in Campbell's movement began to grow. Within a few years, joining with Stone's Christians, the movement would become one of the largest in the expanding American West.

It was because of the churches' lack of growth that Scott was on his evangelistic campaign in the first place. At the 1827 meeting of the Mahoning Baptist Association, after years of dithering about their low growth, they did something about it. They acted in concert, deciding as a group to support a minister who could devote full time to evangelism in the area. They could not have predicted how effective his preaching would be.

Over the next few decades, Scott devoted his life to writing and teaching. He was widely loved and carried considerable influence. But he found it increasingly difficult to embrace the churches he thought were overly sectarian, these emerging churches—Churches of Christ in embryo—that focused on restoration rather than unity. The irony, however, was that it was Scott himself who had provided these churches some of their defining vocabulary.

Scott spent much of his later years in anticipation of God's thousand-year reign. He believed that Protestant values and American greatness would usher in the kingdom on earth. But the national strife leading up to the Civil War crushed those hopes. Scott died ten days after the Union surrender at Ft. Sumter, racked by pneumonia and heartbroken by the divisions that were tearing the country and the churches apart.

From Five Fingers to Five Steps

Scott accomplished much in his life. His books and articles had a significant impact in his day. He served as the president of a college. He advocated for the education of women, a rare concern in those days.

Moreover, he cared about the arts, especially music. It is not surprising, then, that he promoted excellence in church hymnody. In 1835, Scott, along with Stone, Campbell, and John T. Johnson, published the first hymnal of the combined Stone-Campbell Movement.

But with all he had accomplished, it turns out that Scott's most lasting legacy may have been the power of his early preaching and his mnemonic framework for the gospel, easily ticked off with five fingers, which even a child could recall.

Scott expressed concern early on that his plea for the restored gospel of the first century had become, for too many preachers, a simplistic formula. He was afraid the five-finger exercise had made it too easy for hearers to miss what the gospel rested on—faith in Jesus Christ as the Son of God, not human works.

In his book *The Gospel Restored*, published less than a decade after his mission in Ohio, Scott insisted that God's work preceded human salvation. Always. God alone did the saving. Here, Scott laid out not five fingers but a six-fold formula—faith, repentance, baptism, remission of sins, Holy Spirit, eternal life.

Scott believed these six acts should not be seen in light of what humans do but in light of the work of God. God is the one who accomplishes our salvation.

God's saving work awakens sinners, which leads to a trusting faith, a heart for repentance, and surrender to Christ in baptism.

But the power of Scott's simple memory hook in his early preaching was hard to overcome. It was just too good a rhetorical device. In other words, it worked. It led to thousands of conversions.

By the twentieth century, Churches of Christ had taken Scott's five-finger exercise and transformed it into the Five Steps of Salvation, now with an almost complete emphasis on human actions. To be saved a person had to (1) hear, (2) believe, (3) repent, (4) confess, and (5) be baptized for the remission of sins. After these five steps were taken, God would grant salvation. The implication was that God owed us salvation after we performed the right works in the right way for the right reasons and in the right order.

By the twentieth century, Scott's emphases on the Holy Spirit and eternal life dropped off of the list entirely. And remission of sins became part of a command that required obedience rather than thanksgiving for the work of God. This was not what Scott had intended. His original memory device had mutated into a human-centered formula. It had begun in freedom but had ended up a tool for conformity.

I should be clear. It is not that hearing, believing, confessing, repenting, and being baptized are not important, mind you. They are. They are just not steps. They are not human works.

When conceived of as one of several steps, faith appears to be a human act, an exertion of self. But that's not what faith is. Faith is a relinquishing of self, an excruciatingly passive act, a giving over of one's life to God's control, a surrender of one's own power to God's power, of one's own future to God's future.

To repent and confess is to say, I can't do it. I have no power to accomplish my own salvation. I am a sinner, broken and unworthy. God has to do it. The very image of baptism is profoundly passive—being laid into a watery grave, "buried with Christ in baptism," the picture of dying, of self-emptying, of surrender to a sovereign God.

The work of salvation is God's entirely. "For by grace you have been saved through faith, and this is not your own doing; it is the gift of God—not the result of works" (Eph. 2:8–9) Not that human works are not important. They are. But they emerge *from* salvation rather than serving as salvation's *cause*. "For we are what he made us, created in Christ Jesus for good works, which God prepared beforehand to be our way of life" (Eph. 2:10).

Seeing salvation as a series of human steps not only misses what Scott had said, it misses what Scripture teaches. Faith, repentance, baptism, Holy Spirit, forgiveness of sins, and eternal salvation are all gifts of God, not human actions meriting God's reward.

But to be honest, Scott's own preaching and writing contributed to certain understandings that have continued to impact this movement. When Scott devised his six-fold formula, he claimed that he had restored the *ordo salutis*, the ancient order of salvation, and that by so doing he had restored the gospel itself.

Not surprisingly, many of those who followed him focused on getting gospel matters done in the right order. If the order was not properly kept, could a person be truly saved?

This is not an idle question. Could people be saved if the order of their responses to Jesus were different than Scott's understanding? What if one were to understand salvation in the following order: faith, repentance, forgiveness of sins, Holy Spirit, baptism, and eternal life? Could that person be saved?

In other words, if a person, trying to follow God's will, believed that God granted salvation at the point of faith and repentance, and then was baptized afterwards as an act of obedience to God, trusting God, as a public declaration of God's saving grace, would that person be saved? Would God bestow eternal salvation on anyone who, in faith and obedience, got all the pieces right but did them in the wrong order?

This is not an academic question. By the 1880s, twenty years after Scott's death, a firebrand from Texas would challenge and publicly ridicule a gentleman editor from Tennessee over this very matter. But that divisive issue was years away from Scott's life and ministry. Scott lived in a different time. He faced different issues.

Beginning in the mid-1820s, Walter Scott's preaching was a turning point in the movement. His early evangelistic efforts in Ohio resulted in over a thousand baptisms. He averaged a thousand baptisms every year for the next thirty years. Entire congregations often converted after hearing Scott preach. That preaching, in many ways, defined the movement and set the future.

By the end of his life, in April of 1861, the movement had become a substantial presence in American life, especially in the states along the Ohio River. Which meant that by that point, as the nation began to split in two, churches in Pennsylvania, Virginia, Ohio, Indiana, Illinois, and Kentucky had decisions to make. But that was also true for churches in Tennessee, Missouri, Arkansas, and Texas.

In the fall of 1861, thirty-five years after Scott's stirring sermon at his first Mahoning Baptist Association meeting and less than six months after Scott's death, hundreds of Christians convened in Cincinnati for the American Christian Missionary Society meeting. The gathering was sober. There seemed to be more pressing matters at hand than stories about toad sky-high and five-finger exercises. The war had begun, and Christians had to make decisions about the nature of their loyalties.

The Colonel's Speech

By the time the delegates to the convention gathered in Cincinnati, the world had turned upside down. It was October 1861. The Confederate States had established a new government, Lincoln had been inaugurated, Fort Sumter had fallen, residents of western Virginia had voted not to join the rest of the state in secession, and the Union Army had been routed at the First Battle of Bull Run. To say the least, tensions were high.

No Christian Church (in other words, Church of Christ) leaders from the Deep South were at the meeting, though many of them had been at past meetings. However, several church leaders from the border states, especially Kentucky and Missouri, were present. More than eight hundred had come, the largest gathering of the American Christian Missionary Society in its twelve-year history.

Alexander Campbell, the society's president, was there, but he was seventy-three and no longer able to function as he once had. Isaac Errett presided in his place. Several of the men wore the uniforms of Union Army officers, including Colonel James Garfield.

It was the age of societies, both in the United States and in Europe. From the late eighteenth century and throughout the nineteenth, thousands of national, regional, and local societies were established, connecting interested people with single-issue causes. They were everywhere.

There were anti-slavery societies, temperance societies, women's suffrage societies, literary societies, agricultural societies, societies for artists, societies for musicians, societies of various ethnic groups, and academic societies. Methodists started religious societies in most states. Baptists established several national societies, including the Baptist General Tract Society and the Home Mission Society.

The historical movement begun by the Campbells decades earlier had itself been a product of a kind of society, a British missionary movement, which emphasized interdenominational cooperation and minimized denominational differences.[22] In other words, the Campbells' quest for unity was not created out of whole cloth. Thomas and Alexander had each come to the New World with certain values generated by a substantial British evangelical missionary movement. Which is to say, Churches of Christ in America were forged from the very beginning through the efforts of a missionary society. Without British evangelistic societies and their mission efforts in America, there would be no Churches of Christ as we know them today. It should not be surprising that in the next several decades this growing network of churches would launch its own missionary society.

Before the Civil War, three national societies were established among Christian Churches, Churches of Christ, and Disciples of Christ. David S. Burnet played a role in the establishment of all of them. In 1845, he established the American Christian Bible Society, whose purpose was to "put into the hands of every human being the Bible, without note or comment." The next year he established the Sunday School and Tract Society, later renamed the American Christian Publication Society.

In 1849, Burnet presided over 156 individuals from a hundred congregations in eleven states, North and South, to discuss how they could better support missions. A number of state missionary societies had already been established, both in the North and the South. By the end of their meeting, the group had formed the American Christian Missionary Society.

Not everyone thought a national missionary society was a good idea. Campbell opposed it at first, among other reasons because it competed against fundraising for his own Bethany College. However, Campbell's involvement was considered crucial to the organization, and he was asked to serve as president, which he eventually accepted. The title was essentially honorary. Burnet guided the organization as a vice president.

One of the other vice presidents of the national missionary society that first year was Tolbert Fanning, the Tennessee church leader, founder and editor of the *Gospel Advocate*, and founder of Franklin College near Nashville. In 1852, Fanning had helped organize the Tennessee Evangelizing Association, a state missionary society. In a few years, Fanning would oppose such societies, deeply shaping the Churches of Christ under his influence. But that was later, as the fault line in national politics began to take its toll. In the early days, Fanning was a leader in the missionary society movement.

From the beginning, the American Christian Missionary Society struggled with its identity and purpose. Some questioned its legitimacy. Since, as most leaders in the movement believed, the local church was the primary sending organization for missionaries, what were the appropriate responsibilities for such an organization, which was not the church but which came alongside the church?

Some concluded that, since the Bible did not specifically authorize such an organization, it was unscriptural. Others believed it was in the realm of human expedience and was, therefore, permissible. Though Fanning eventually came to argue against the missionary society, he continued to attend the annual meetings. As late as 1859, Fanning addressed the national convention, stating that while Tennessee churches opposed the society, the members of the American Christian Missionary Society were still his brothers in Christ. "We are one people," he told them.[23]

There was no other national forum for discussion, so the meetings of the society often became opportunities to address the pressing concerns of the day. And there were few concerns that could compare to the war that had broken out, which, one way or another, affected all of the churches.

Many moderate Northerners in the 1861 meeting wanted the society to take a pro-Union stand, but they knew doing so was fraught with difficulties. They wanted to keep the radical abolitionists from bolting from the society.

Christian Church abolitionists, in fact, had already formed an alternative society. Perhaps, if the moderates played their cards right, the abolitionists could be persuaded to remain with the others. On the other hand, if the abolitionists were appeased, then the Southerners, even moderate ones, would be repulsed, and the unity of the church would be destroyed. Success depended on threading the proverbial needle. Much was at stake.

In an action of considerable consequence, John P. Robison of Bedford, Ohio, presented a resolution, seconded by Lewis L. Pinkerton, that generated an uproar in the crowd. It essentially called for them to take sides in the war:

> *Resolved*: That we deeply sympathize with the loyal and patriotic in our country, in the present efforts to sustain the Government of the United States. And

we feel it our duty as Christians, to ask our brethren everywhere to do all in their power to sustain the proper and constitutional authorities of the Union.

David Burnet, whose efforts had largely launched the organization more than a decade earlier, questioned whether the society had a right to consider such a resolution. But presiding president Isaac Errett ruled Robison's motion in order.

However, Raccoon John Smith, who thirty years earlier had played a major role in the uniting of the Stone and Campbell movements, appealed the decision. After a long and sometimes angry discussion, the convention voted to sustain the appeal. In other words, there would be no vote on the resolution.

In what may have been a prearranged strategy, Pinkerton called for a recess. Then, while the conference was not in official session, Robison's resolution was presented again.

Colonel Garfield, dressed in his new blue officer's uniform, strode to the podium. Though still a month shy of his thirtieth birthday, barely ten years after he had been baptized as a teenager in the Chagrin River, Garfield had become a significant leader among these churches. He was a preacher of considerable renown. A few years earlier, Garfield and Alexander Campbell had held a two-week gospel meeting together in Alliance, Ohio, baptizing fifty people. Garfield visited Campbell's home often, usually sitting in his favorite chair in Campbell's living room. His anti-slavery sentiments had grown more pronounced over the years, and he was more frequently speaking out against slavery.

As a preacher, professor, college president, lawyer, state congressman, and now Union Army officer, Garfield had influence that few people in the room could match. His uniform reinforced his gravitas. The hushed crowd listened to Garfield's short but compelling speech. Garfield strongly endorsed the resolution and advocated the support of these Christian leaders for the Union cause.

How significant Garfield's speech was in the final analysis is hard to say. But something had changed. The resolution now passed overwhelmingly. Since the vote had been taken out of session, the result was not official. Nevertheless, most of the delegates at the missionary society had voiced support for the Union.

Few seemed pleased by the outcome. The radical abolitionists thought the motion was too tepid. Moderate pro-Southerners were outraged. The radical pro-slavery leaders among Churches of Christ, who were not even present, would never support the society again. In a few years, the very existence of mission societies would be considered by the mostly Southern Churches of Christ as sufficient reason to divide from their Northern brethren. This momentous society meeting of 1861 ended in confusion, if not chaos.

Things got worse. Two years later, in 1863, during the darkest days of the war, the missionary society passed an even stronger resolution:

> *Resolved*: That we tender our sympathies to our brave soldiers in the fields, who are defending us from the attempts of armed traitors to overthrow our Government, and also to those bereaved, and rendered desolate by the ravages of war.

Churches of Christ in the South never got over their resentment. Fellow Christians had called them traitors. In 1866, the normally peace-minded David Lipscomb, serving as the editor of the *Gospel Advocate*, wrote about the 1863 resolution, "The society committed a great wrong against the church and the cause of God."[24]

The American Christian Missionary Society had cracked in two. And so had the movement, though it would take another thirty years before the drama would ultimately play out. Within a generation, churches in the South would be one fellowship, churches in the North would be another. The movement, established in unity, was rupturing.

Societies and Organs, Region and Division

The conflict and ultimate division among Stone-Campbell churches clearly reflected the national division of the Civil War, but it would be an overstatement to claim the differences were only regional. Early on, the door had been opened for people to express themselves freely and to disagree with one another. And they did, often profoundly.

Many of the differences were about substantive issues, and these did not always fall along geographical lines. Concerns had been expressed about mission societies and instrumental music before the war and certainly before the division at the turn of the twentieth century. Stone of Kentucky and Campbell of (West) Virginia disagreed about many issues, yet they lived in similar geographical areas—both of them in what was then the West, both in border states along the Ohio River.

That being said, it is hard to miss the power of location. Churches in rural communities, for example, often fell on a different side of certain doctrinal disputes than churches in urban areas. Most dramatically, however, the churches that were part of the Confederacy were mostly the ones who opposed missionary societies and instrumental music. Those who were part of the Union most often did not.

This geographic divide included Northern states and the parts of Southern states that sided with the North. Churches of Christ in Kentucky (a Union state), as well as East Tennessee (whose citizens were mostly pro-Union), and West Virginia (which became a Union state), generally chose to participate in mission societies and allow instruments of music in worship. To say these were just objective sides of an argument and that regional differences were merely coincidental would be to put one's head in the sand.

The war had a devastating economic effect on Southern churches, deepening and prolonging the regional bitterness. While the South suffered near financial ruin by the end of the war, the Northern economy largely prospered. Resentment simmered among congregations in the South as businesses collapsed, farms failed, and citizens went hungry.

Northern churches provided some relief to their Southern brothers and sisters, but not enough to make much of a difference. Besides, many Southern churches were not much interested in Northern handouts.

It was unthinkable for members of Southern Churches of Christ to return to missionary society meetings after what happened at these meetings during the war. The American Christian Missionary Society was forever tainted in the minds of the Christians who had lived in the Confederate States—because the society had taken sides during the war, because it essentially accused the Southern Christians of treason.

It was especially hard for Southern Churches of Christ to watch their Northern brothers and sisters erect what the Southerners believed were opulent new buildings with expensive stained-glass windows and big pipe organs, while many churches in the South were struggling just to maintain their run-down buildings and while many families were struggling to put food on the table.

Location was not everything, but it goes a long way in explaining how the ultimate division occurred. Even though its public recognition did not take place until 1906, when David Lipscomb was finally persuaded that the US Religious Census should list Churches of Christ and Christian Churches as separate groups, there had been essentially two increasingly distinct fellowships well before the end of the nineteenth century—one in the North, the other in the South, one that supported missionary societies and instrumental music, and one that did not.

At the very time that a commitment to unity was dying among churches in the South, the restoration of the ancient order had crystallized as their defining theme. The church conflicts had finally come to a head. The differences among the churches had gained clarity and precision. The primary grammar of these churches as a restoration movement rather than a unity movement gained weight. The vocabulary and principles of restoration were passed down from generation to generation. Perhaps most importantly, the restoration of conformity, not the restoration of freedom, was the impulse that prevailed.

Which is not to say that the restoration of freedom was dead. As editor of the most influential paper among Churches of Christ in the South, the *Gospel Advocate*, David Lipscomb modeled not just a marked gentleness of tone but also a certain level of openness to differences of opinion. As Campbell had done before him, Lipscomb published letters and articles reflecting positions different from his own, though Lipscomb's pen was far less pointed than Campbell's had been.

In 1888, for example, after Lipscomb wrote an article arguing that women should not have authority over men or teach men, he published Silena Holman's strongly worded rebuttal. Over several years, Holman and Lipscomb responded to each other through articles in the *Advocate*. While Lipscomb was never persuaded, he defended Holman's right to dissent and responded to her respectfully. Lipscomb published Holman's last article on the subject, entitled "The Woman Question Again," in 1913, two years before her death and four years before his, though his comments about her arguments were dismissive and somewhat patronizing.

In the closing years of the nineteenth century, several leaders among Churches of Christ occupied a moderating position between constraint and accommodation, including David Lipscomb and T. B. Larimore of Tennessee, James Harding of Kentucky, and F. D. Srygley, one of Larimore's boys from Alabama.

But as the twentieth century approached, their views and spirit began to decline in influence. A new style—more aggressive, more combative—began to emerge from out West.

Law and Ardor

His thick, black mustache covered his mouth like dark awning over a storefront window. His jaw was set hard, his gaze intense. His short-cropped hair and three-piece suit spoke of a certain respectability, but it barely masked the brawler he had once been and, to a significant degree, still was.

Austin McGary had grown up on the wild frontier of Texas. His father had fought in the Battle of San Jacinto, in the Texas War of Independence, and had guarded the defeated Mexican general Antonio López de Santa Anna the night he was captured. Throughout his life, the son carried his father's aggressiveness and bravado.

Three Church of Christ preachers, three brothers, were given responsibility for young McGary's education in Huntsville, about sixty miles north of Houston, though at the time he was a member of no church at all. Toward the end of the Civil War, McGary joined the Confederate Army along with two of his friends, Addison and Randolph Clark, brothers who later founded Add-Ran College, which would eventually become Texas Christian University.

McGary was a hard man living in a hard era. Shortly after the Civil War, McGary killed a man in Madison County and wounded another in a shooting incident whose circumstances were never quite clear. It may have been murder. Or maybe not. He was eventually acquitted on grounds of self-defense.

A few years later, McGary ran for sheriff of that very county, using underhanded means to keep citizens from voting. He ran as a Democrat during this era of Reconstruction, in which Republicans—what some Democrats still called "Black Republicans" because of their opposition to slavery—dominated the politics of the state. On election day, McGary confronted a White volunteer who was rounding up Black voters. McGary forced him at gunpoint to drink castor oil, then sent him home. Now without transportation, the Black voters were unable to get to the polls. Thus McGary secured for himself a narrow victory.

In 1881, at the age of thirty-five and still a religious skeptic, McGary set out to study Christian doctrine and practice. Influenced by the teachers of his childhood, he began by reading Alexander Campbell's 1829 debate with Scottish agnostic Robert Owen. Soon after, McGary was baptized.

Less than three years later, this rough-edged, racist, and often confrontational former lawman with virtually no theological education, or much education at all, launched a newspaper. He called it the *Firm Foundation*.

McGary began the paper for the specific purpose of opposing what he considered the liberalism of David Lipscomb and the *Gospel Advocate*, which was published in Nashville. McGary was frustrated with what Lipscomb was saying about baptism. And even though McGary was a relatively new Christian, he decided to do something about it.

Lipscomb was teaching that trust in God was a sufficient reason to be baptized, even if a person did not believe that baptism was for remission of sins. For this reason, Lipscomb argued, Baptists who wanted to become part of a Church of Christ should be able to do so without having to be rebaptized.

McGary was appalled. He called this position "shaking in the Baptists." In contrast, he said that the baptism of a person who did not know it was for remission of sins was illegitimate and that such a person needed to be baptized again, this time for the right reason. The alternative was eternal damnation.

McGary and Lipscomb carried on the debate for fifteen years. For the gentleman from Nashville, McGary's coarse style was almost more than he could bear, and he occasionally protested. Richard Hughes's description of McGary's response says a lot.

In the inaugural issue of the *Firm Foundation*, Austin McGary specified that the publication was being launched "to battle for the truth, ignoring the conventionalists of so-called 'polite society.'" And, indeed, when David Lipscomb complained that McGary had attacked him unfairly, McGary responded like a Texas sheriff dealing with a common criminal: "He richly deserves the castigation that is in store for him, and he should stand up bravely and take it. He plaited the whip with his own hands, and if he aimed it for a plaything, he should not have made it so *heavy*."[25]

During this time, McGary became the de facto leader of what John Mark Hicks and Bobby Valentine call the Texas Tradition, whose doctrinal positions included a sectarian understanding of baptism and the belief that the work of the Holy Spirit was only evident in the words of the Bible (in contrast to the Nashville Bible School Tradition, i.e., Lipscomb's view).[26]

McGary's smashmouth style won him enemies but also readers. In fact, many seemed especially attracted to his inflammatory language. Soon the *Firm Foundation* competed with the *Advocate* as the most influential paper among Churches of Christ.

By the time the paper's board of directors removed McGary as editor in 1902 because of his overly abrasive style, the tide had already turned. His doctrinal positions had become the prevailing view among Texas churches and soon would be throughout Churches of Christ in the United States. It would take most of the twentieth century for McGary's influence to diminish.

McGary's impact on Churches of Christ was particularly enhanced by the work of two men who were also part of the so-called Texas Tradition. One was an influential scholar. The other was the boy preacher.

Professor R. L. Whiteside had studied under Lipscomb and Harding in Nashville, but his theological positions diverged from theirs considerably. He disagreed with their belief in the indwelling of the Holy Spirit. He opposed their position on baptism. He said he believed in grace but taught that humans "could save themselves only by performing the conditions upon which salvation was so graciously offered."[27]

Whiteside did not share McGary's pugnacious spirit, but he did share most of his doctrinal positions, and his influence was considerable. He taught Bible at Abilene Christian College and served as the school's third president, from 1909 to 1911. His book *Sound Doctrine*, cowritten with C. R. Nichol, was widely used in Sunday School classes around the country, and his *New Commentary on Romans* cemented his views on grace and works as the standard position of mid-twentieth-century Churches of Christ.

And in Memphis in 1973.

It would be a few years before professors at Abilene Christian College would begin to articulate views that sharply contrasted with those of McGary and Whiteside, setting a dramatically different path for the decades to come. But in the early years the school was a stronghold of the McGary positions.

But McGary's hard-edged fighting spirit was best captured in the preaching and writing of Whiteside's young protégé Foy E. Wallace Jr. If people thought McGary was hard-hitting, they had never experienced anything like Wallace. Few people in Churches of Christ in the first two-thirds of the twentieth century could match Wallace's personal and political power.

In 1930, just a few months after he had served as a pallbearer at the Larimore funeral, Wallace was appointed editor of Lipscomb's paper the *Gospel Advocate*. The import of this appointment should not be missed.

Less than fifty years after the outspoken McGary had founded his paper in opposition to Lipscomb, McGary's positions became the orthodoxy championed by the new editor of Lipscomb's own paper. Through Wallace's articles in the *Advocate* and later in the *Bible Banner*, his editorial power, his tendency toward intimidation and control, and the overwhelming number of the gospel meetings he held in every region of the nation, Wallace solidified the doctrinal positions of McGary and Whiteside among Churches of Christ on both sides of the Mississippi.

And yet, throughout the middle years of the twentieth century, the language of freedom—that every doctrine is open for investigation and that all Christians have the right to determine for themselves what the Bible says—continued to have rhetorical power, if not substantial practice. At its best, this was what a commitment to restoration meant: men and women could study the Bible and arrive at conclusions different than those who had gone before them if they believed those positions reflected the biblical witness.

The origins of the Churches of Christ were rooted in freedom—freedom from creeds and confessions, freedom from denominational authorities, freedom from church leaders who told people what to believe. Christians in this movement were free to come to their own conclusions, to reexamine what they have long believed, and to disagree with one another in love.

But there is a difference between the language of freedom and its reality on the ground.

A Trace of Grace

I bought a copy of the 125-page transcript of the Memphis meeting on a bitter cold night in February 1974. A preacher had set up a display table in the old tent at the Abilene Christian College Bible Lectures. If people would just read the document, he was saying, they would see. The Herald of Truth was promoting heresy and Lynn Anderson and the others were false teachers.

I read the document and came to different conclusions. Then again, my personal context was different than that of the seller. I was a graduate student at the time, a product of a different generation and culture. I had a different set of church and educational experiences, and I knew a different set of players in the drama. Like him, I was affected by my setting, my experiences, my assumptions, and my relationships. But the differences were great and seemed impossible to bridge.

It is difficult, even today, to read the transcript of the 1973 Memphis meeting without sadness (though *transcript* may not be exactly the right word; I found out later that some strategic editing had taken place prior to publication by someone representing the accusers at the meeting).

The day was clearly unsettling for most who were there. I have visited with several of the attendees, on both sides of the discussion. Few of them find it easy to talk about it.

What happened was gut-wrenching. The tension was palpable, even on the written page. There were verbal scuffles, impassioned speeches, sharp exchanges, harsh accusations, and considerable word parsing. At times the give-and-take felt more like a courtroom than a gathering of Christian leaders. It certainly did not reflect the freedom, inherent in the movement's restoration language, that the church should be a community where every belief was open to reexamination and where people did not limit the faith and practice of church members.

There seemed to be little room for gray that day. Opinions about issues were either correct or incorrect. Preachers were either sound or false. For most of the questioners, anyone who believed in the present indwelling of the Holy Spirit was wrong and perhaps even hell-bent.

The four representatives of the Herald of Truth, especially the two young preachers who were the focus of most of the questioning, could not provide ample assurance, however hard they tried, that they believed substantially enough in the authority of Scripture or were sufficiently committed to restoration principles to appease the concerns of the accusers. One person who was present that day only as an observer said he witnessed Dr. Baxter during a break wiping tears from his eyes. As one of the objects of the relentless attacks, his sense of sadness and loss is easy to understand.

Despite the fireworks of that long day, despite the various charges and defenses, no one's mind seems to have been changed. It felt tragic. It feels tragic still.

It is possible, however, that something began to shift that day. In the months and years that followed, the nature of the dialogue within Churches of Christ seemed to change in small but significant ways. Many leaders figured that if discussions about differences resulted in this sort of arguing, they would rather not have the discussion at all. A great wariness settled in, as well as increased isolation between groups.

Many years later, a few apologies were eventually offered—some publicly and emotionally, some more quietly. But for the most part, folks stuck with their own group and went their own way.

This was not new. From its earliest days, churches in the movement have struggled to keep peace when opinions conflicted. Generation after generation, church leaders have expressed their desire to restore the church of the New Testament in their own time. But they have struggled to agree about what a restored church looks like. And so, they have gone their own way.

Most of the time.

Around the time of the Memphis meeting, a change on at least one doctrinal matter began to take place. Slowly but significantly. How much was a result of the meeting is difficult to know. Perhaps some. But a shift began to occur concerning the nature and work of the Holy Spirit. Since the early 1970s, believing in the Spirit's indwelling and present work has become the common view among Churches of Christ. Far fewer members today believe the work of the Spirit was completed in the writing of Scripture. Most now believe in the Spirit's ongoing and indwelling work.

But something else was at play, something new. For these churches, in spite of the fears and uncertainties of those years and the serious differences in temperament and doctrine evident in Memphis, a change took place about a difficult matter—in this case, the work of the Holy Spirit—that did not result in another division.

To be clear, not dividing is a pretty low bar. But considering the history of these people, it might also be a hopeful development. It may affirm that differences can sometimes be bridged, that conflicts do not inevitably lead to schism, and that even long-held beliefs may be open to reexamination after all.

Book, Head, Water, and Fire

Barton Stone has not appeared much in our examination of restoration ideals but not because he did not care about restoration. He did. Like Campbell, Stone connected restoration with unity and unity with the expected thousand-year reign of Christ, though he was not as confident as Campbell that human progress had a role in ushering in the kingdom.

But over time, Stone's influence in the movement began to decrease. In 1834 he moved to Illinois, removing himself from the center of movement politics. He was getting older. He lived quietly while continuing to write in his paper, the *Christian Messenger*, until his death in 1844. Soon after his move to Illinois, others had begun to take his place at the center of the growing movement.

The identity of these churches became more sharply defined during the critical years before the Civil War, at a time when Stone's influence was increasingly overshadowed by the younger, more aggressive Campbell. During those formative years, Campbell became the dominant gene and Stone the recessive gene in the DNA of the movement. Stone's views did not die, but like the man himself they receded from the center stage.

Campbell's influence seemed to increase with each debate he participated in, but Stone was not very interested in debates. He believed they made division more likely. Nor was Stone altogether comfortable with Campbell's "tart and severe" style. Like Campbell, Stone was concerned about heresy in the church, but he thought it was less about believing false doctrines than it was about exhibiting a divisive spirit and a lack of genuine love toward others.

Less than two years after he stood with Raccoon John Smith, grasping his hand and calling the gathered worshipers to unite in Christ, Stone wrote an article on the nature of true unity. During his years of ministry, he said, he had witnessed four types of unity.[28]

The first he called *book union*, which relied on the authority of "certain articles of faith, called a creed, confession of faith, or a discipline." But creeds, he said, have been the cause of disunion, not union. He believed that "as light and liberty progress, they will be banished from the christian community."

Stone called the second type of unity *head union*. Its goal is to follow the Bible alone, surely a noble desire. The problem, Stone believed, is that the end result of head union is the same as book union. The only difference is that creeds are written down while opinions about the Bible are not, making them perhaps more insidious. He wrote,

> Each one believes his opinion of certain texts to be the very spirit and meaning of the texts—and that this opinion was absolutely essential to salvation. . . . This plan of uniting on opinions, whether contained in a book, or in the head, is not worth a straw, and never can effect christian union, or the union of primitive Christianity.

Stone believed that a person should follow the Bible, of course. But claiming to just follow the Bible will not bring about unity because people will always disagree about what the Bible means.

The third type of unity is *water union*, "founded on immersion into water." It assumes that Christians will be united because of their common baptism. Again, Stone was committed to believer baptism, but he didn't think that everyone who has been baptized would be united. Such a union, he said, was "easily dissolved. . . . [I]mmersion will not keep those who are immersed, united."

Stone believed there was only one path to Christian unity. He called it *fire union*, a unity forged by the Holy Spirit.

Here is the heart of Stone's faith. Human action will not bring about unity. The kingdom belongs to God, not us. Only God can unite his children. Humans need to get out of the way and let God do what only God can do.

"No union but this will stand," Stone said. "No other union is worth the name." Only the fire of the Holy Spirit can break down walls and soften human hearts enough to cause them to love others. Only the Spirit can unite them in Christ. Only the Spirit can cure the sin sicknesses of the human condition.

One of the great virtues of a church shaped by a desire for restoration is the recognition that the way things are now is not the way they are supposed to be. The world is broken. The church is broken. And only God can fix it.

If our only vision for the restoration of the church is for everyone to agree on what the Bible says on every matter, our efforts will fail. If we assume that our own understanding of certain passages of Scripture captures "the very spirit and meaning of the texts—and that this opinion [is] absolutely essential to salvation," then we are seeking Head Union. It won't work. We are too broken, too blind, too willful, and too human to pull it off. The history of Christianity is littered with movements of people who believed they arrived at the very spirit and meaning of the texts.

To abandon the church's commitment to the authority of Scripture and its diligent study would be folly. We must continue to look back at the church of the New Testament, not out of nostalgia for a golden age in the past—first-century churches were as broken as our own—but out of a desire to connect to the fountainhead of our faith, to Jesus whom Scripture reveals and glorifies. But in so doing, we should be clear how transformation ultimately takes place, how the church can be restored, how our congregations can get better, how God's people can be united.

Only with fire.

Takeaways from Chapter 4: True Restoration

It is no small irony that a church movement so earnestly seeking restoration would end up so fractured. In other areas of life, such an effort might be deemed woefully unsuccessful.

My wife and I recently found a crack on a precious, old vase. We took it to a store that specializes in the restoration of antiques. If we had returned in a few weeks and discovered that the vase, after its restoration, was now a pile of pottery shards, we would have been devastated. The restoration master, however hard he may have tried or however sincere his efforts, should have second thoughts about whether he is much good at this sort of work.

Over the last century, restoration churches have demonstrated a tragic fondness for fracture. There are other, more positive, characteristics of these churches, of course, but for a movement so dedicated to restoration, the human and institutional debris left behind is awfully large. Perhaps we are not very good at it.

Not counting the nineteenth-century divisions, Churches of Christ in America have divided over pacifism, premillennialism, and whether local churches should hire professional preachers. They have split over whether the Bible authorizes multiple communion cups, individual Bible classes, the sharing of congregational resources to support parachurch efforts, or using church finances to build kitchens or gymnasiums. The International Churches of Christ became a separate fellowship, now experiencing its own fragmentation. And as a sad testament to the pervasive impact of the Civil War and institutional racism on church life, a largely separate fellowship of predominately African American Churches of Christ continues to this day.

But painful divisions have also taken place at the local level. More than a few congregations have divided about issues both profound and petty. Frankly, at least some of the new church plants that have sprung up in recent decades might more accurately be viewed as de facto church splits rather than strategic evangelistic efforts.

Even if there has been no split, most congregations go through smaller and subtler disruptions. People leave their congregation because they are unhappy. They leave because they don't like the sermons or because they disagree with the elders, because of something their Bible teacher said or because they hate the hymn selections. They leave because the church is changing too fast or because it's not changing fast enough.

Some of these responses simply reflect life in contemporary America. The gods of choice and mobility make changing churches simple and desirable. That's true of all religious groups. And occasionally, moving to another congregation is wise or even necessary. But embedded in the particular DNA of restoration churches is an impulse to split, one way or another: if my church does something I don't like or I don't think is right, then somebody better fix it or I will have to leave.

Could things be different? Does a commitment to restoration have to turn out this way? If a movement dedicated to restoration ends up broken into pieces, how should such restoration be assessed? If attempts at restoring the New Testament church nurtures attitudes and behaviors that do not reflect the gospel, if they do not exhibit the heart of Jesus, what kind of restoration could it be? And if we believe restoration is vital, then what kind of restoration should we be seeking?

The developmental psychologist Alison Gopnik has written an enlightening book about parenting called *The Gardener and the Carpenter*.[29] She presents an apt metaphor for the kind of Christian restoration that churches might consider.

When parents act like carpenters, Gopnik says, they see their task as shaping children to fit a model they had in mind to begin with. Childrearing, from this perspective, is like cutting, sanding, lathing, gluing, and nailing wood so that the final result looks like the original blueprint. Crucial to good carpentry are control and precision.

But making humans from blueprints rarely turns out as planned. Life is too messy, and children are too unpredictable.

If church leaders are like carpenters, their primary task is to follow a blueprint in order to shape the church into a predesigned product. But this type of leadership doesn't particularly fare well. Humans have this pesky tendency to think for themselves. They are not easily squeezed into molds. They don't seem to sit still for all the messy cutting and nailing. Leadership of this sort rarely produces healthy, mature churches.

Creating a garden is different. A good gardener makes space for plants to flourish. Gardening—like being a parent, like leading a church—is hard work. It requires digging, weeding, seeding, and nurturing. And it usually ends up with the gardener's hands and clothes covered in a lot of manure.

While the gardener has an idea what she wants the garden to look like, many things are unpredictable. Flowers may emerge a different color than what was expected. Some plants are scrawnier or taller or grow at a different angle or at a different rate than anticipated. But that's okay. Precision is not the goal but, rather, creating opportunities for abundance and celebrating diverse and unexpected beauty.

Designing a precise blueprint for one's garden would never work. Plants—like children, church members, and other wildlife—are always changing and astonishingly free. The church leader as gardener requires adaptability and patience, not control. The result is dynamic, variable, risky, sometimes heartbreaking, but usually meaningful and often lovely.

For Campbell and many restoration churches, the restoration ideal was like a blueprint from which a carpenter, not a gardener, might work. The result was not a focus on the adaptability, growth, and freedom of its members but a systemic expectation of precision, accuracy, and conformity.

Within the design of Campbell's original articles on restoration and the churches that grew out of them were at least two fatal flaws.

Flaws in the Argument

1. *The Restoration of Externals*. In his thirty-two articles on "A Restoration of the Ancient Order of Things," Campbell's primary focus was on church forms. Campbell attempted to "demonstrate by rational principles" what a modern church should look like. The impact of these articles on Churches of Christ were—and are—deep and profound.

Campbell examined, for example, which "social acts of Christian worship" should be done at every service. He demonstrated why Christians should meet on the first day of the week, why the Lord's Supper should be taken every week, why there should be a contribution every week. He argued that neither foot washing nor the kiss of charity were required of Christians today but that baptism was necessary and that it must be done by immersion. He laid out the qualifications and responsibilities of bishops and deacons and why these church officers should not have responsibilities over multiple congregations. He discussed church discipline and church governance, why Christians should not sing hymns in worship that were secular or that reflected bad doctrine, why prayers should not address the Holy Spirit, and why congregations should function independently.

It is hard to read these foundational articles and not feel that something is missing. The questions Campbell seemed to be addressing, like a good blueprint, were primarily focused on externals: what should a church look like and how does a person get into it? These are different questions than, say, Who is God? What is church for? and How should we live?

It is not that I disagree with many of Campbell's conclusions. I want to be part of a church that baptizes believers by immersion and takes the Lord's Supper every week, for example. But what was missing was substantial, and its absence had a massive impact on the future of the movement.

If Scripture serves as an authoritative resource for restoration, where is the heart of the gospel? Where is the good news? Where is Jesus? Where is Scripture's emphasis on grace? Where is discipleship? Where in Campbell's articles are faith and hope and love? How can we live without succumbing to greed or idolatry, which Scripture so often condemns? What does it mean to be aliens and exiles? How should we live when society ostracizes us because of our Christian commitments? What do we do when we see poverty, oppression, or injustice in the world?

Where are the soaring affirmations of the nature of God found throughout Scripture? What would it look like to live like Jesus? Where is the cross? What would it mean for us to take up a cross daily? What would the church look like if it were cross-formed? What would the church look like if we took the Sermon on the Mount seriously? What does it mean to be a peacemaker, to be meek, to love our enemies, to not be angry, to live wisely? How is the Holy Spirit transforming our hearts and lives, our behaviors and commitments, into the image of Jesus? And for what purpose?

When Jesus encountered the religious leaders of his day who insisted on tithing even their garden herbs, he challenged them: you have neglected the weightier matters of the law—justice, mercy, and faithfulness. You should have practiced these without neglecting the others. In other words, it is possible to get the externals right and still miss the point.

It is not as if Campbell was not aware of these gospel matters. In other places he talked about justice, mercy, and faithfulness, the nature of God, and the purpose of the cross, among other doctrines. In later articles, books, and sermons, Campbell wrote extensively about these gospel concerns and fought fiercely against the divisive spirit that began to emerge in the movement.

But these theological issues were mostly absent in his seminal articles on restoration. And these are the very writings that became almost immediately a cornerstone of the churches in the new movement, especially those that became, over time, what are known today as Churches of Christ. The language of many contemporary Churches of Christ concerning restoration comes directly from these thirty-two articles. But Campbell's focus in them was on the externals. Many churches have taken these principles and created out of them not a garden but a blueprint, which they have attempted to follow with precision and control. The end result hasn't always been pretty.

Perhaps the time is right for these matters to be rethought. If a church restores the externals but does not restore the gospel itself, it loses its heart. It loses its mission. It loses its way.

2. *Confidence in Humans.* Campbell and other early leaders had great confidence that any reasonable person can read and sufficiently understand the Bible. If a person just picked up a Bible and read it with honesty and sincerity, he or she should emerge with a view of church that looks virtually identical to a modern American Church of Christ because humans are capable of understanding the Bible clearly and, therefore, will understand the Bible alike. Or, if they simply followed a clear, scientific method for gleaning from Scripture its precise meaning, then they could become obedient, faithful Christians.

The problem is, there is no evidence that humans will all arrive at the same or similar answers to their questions, however hard they may work, or that sincere and reasonable humans will see Scripture and church alike. Such confidence in humans seems misplaced.

And it has consequences. Such a view of humans does not lend itself to humility. It is prone to overconfidence in one's own conclusions. It is likely to appear argumentative. It is not particularly open to constructive dialogue with other groups. One may assert that Christians should be open to examining long-held beliefs and changing their minds if presented with evidence, but that sort of behavior has been relatively rare within the history of the movement, in spite of its rhetoric to the contrary.

A high view of human ability to get things right has contributed to the reputation of arrogance and exclusion that Churches of Christ have now spent decades trying to undo. It may be time to examine the underlying causes of that reputation. More importantly, it may be time to reassess what kind of restoration these churches should desire.

True Restoration

If there will be a commitment to restoration, let it be genuinely restorative. Let it be restorative of relationships, restorative of gentleness, restorative of peace-making. Let it be restorative of respect for human dignity and divine worth, of patience and integrity. Let it be restorative of the gospel.

If we will be committed to restoration, let us treat others as God has treated us—with sacrifice, with mercy, by emptying ourselves first, by seeking others' interests ahead of our own. Before anything else, let our commitment to restoration be restorative of grace. Let it restore justice, joy, faith, longsuffering, and hope.

It is not that the restoration of externals has no merit. But church forms have no value if hearts have not first been transformed into the heart of Jesus. And this we cannot do on our own. No amount of human effort can bring it about. Some restorations only God can accomplish. Some miracles happen only by fire.

Grasping, or being grasped by, restorative grace may be a good beginning point for church leaders, especially when they recognize that the garden they till and cultivate belongs to God, not themselves. It turns out, most church members don't take well to being sawed, sanded, hammered, and nailed. Churches rarely measure up to the blueprint, to the mental image an elder or minister may have of them.

Humans are more like lavender than lumber. They don't always grow where we want them. They don't fit very well into a form or template. They do not usually respond well to control. Nevertheless, humans, like the God who created and planted them, can be surprisingly, painfully, delightfully, excruciatingly, gloriously beautiful.

Resources from the Blue Hole:
There Is Life beneath Us Still

The mind that is not baffled is not employed.
The impeded stream is the one that sings.

—Wendell Berry

Fieldnotes from the Blue Hole

Our journey to this point has been long and not always easy. We'd better stop, take a look around, and see where our travel has taken us.

On our first leg, we looked at the state of contemporary Churches of Christ. The hard truth is, they are in trouble. They are broken. All of them. Some more acutely than others. One way or another they're going to die. Whether they die out of self-interest or in self-denial is not yet clear. But this we know: we cannot fix them. Not on our own.

This stark reality led us to the second stretch of our journey. We have choices to make, and choices have consequences. Our future is not inevitable. While our past affects us profoundly, it does not have to determine what we do now. Moreover, we can choose which parts of our past we cast aside and which parts we take with us. God has provided the resources we need, but we will have to choose whether we use them.

From there we went to the beginning, to the root story, to a gathering of Christians where unity was embraced. Churches of Christ were shaped early on by a startling commitment to peace and peacemaking. This defining narrative is about people of profound differences not insisting on their own way, a people willing to give up things—even cherished things—for the sake of others, for the sake of unity, for the sake of the kingdom. That's where we came from. That's our Blue Hole.

Fourth, we saw that our desire to be a restoration people—to return to a once golden age, to be like the early church—had noble motives. But the difficulties with such a pursuit are many. The early churches were themselves broken. And some things are not replicable. Besides, Scripture is notoriously resistant to everyone interpreting the Bible the same. Moreover, when restoration itself becomes the object of our passions, when restoration is the end rather than the means, it loses its purpose. When freedom, which was restoration's aim, turns into conformity, restoration loses its power.

That's where our journey has taken us thus far. But the challenges of our present circumstance should not leave us in despair. In fact, precisely because our situation seems dire, we have cause for hope. It should be clear to us now that we are too broken to fix things for ourselves.

We thought we were smart enough and good enough to restore the church on our own. But we finally have had to face the limitations of our human striving. We have placed too much confidence in our own abilities. We have chosen for ourselves the responsibilities that belonged only to God.

Scripture has a word for that. It's called idolatry. It has been a hard lesson to learn. And it has taken a long time. We are not capable of restoring ourselves. Or our church. With that insight, now maybe we can allow ourselves a measure of hope. There is a way that our desire for restoration can be transformed into something genuinely restorative.

But how? That's our quest in chapter 5. The answers will not be easy. If we were facing technical challenges, we could simply draw up a list of things to do and fix them. But our problems are adaptive, not technical. They are complex. They seem unsolvable. In fact, in the face of our problems we may feel lost at times. It's hard to know which direction we should take.

If we look, however, we might find we have some tools already in our pockets—a compass, a knife, a box of matches, perhaps even a crude map. We have useful resources in our own story. Unity and restoration are the obvious ones, though we need to figure out how to use them constructively. But if we dig deeper we will find others—reason, harmony, generosity, and a sort of holiness that compels us to live today with God's end in mind. And then there's the turn toward death, reflected in our defining sacraments, which we have often claimed but too rarely utilized.

These gifts we already possess. They are already in our story, in our DNA. But before we can use them, there is a turn we must make—a turning away, a turning around, a turning toward. Turns out, such a turning may be our most difficult and most rewarding challenge.

Parting of the Waters

In a marshy, wooded wilderness south of Lake Yellowstone, about twenty miles as the crow flies or twenty hours by foot, lies a divergence of two streams. Technically, it's called a distributary—a fork in the creek, as it were, leading to two vastly different destinations.

On August 1, 1836, a fur trapper and mountain man named Osborne Russell, who later helped form the first state government of Oregon, came across the place and called it a dividing spring. Today, it is known as Parting of the Waters.

Above it, along a grassy plateau, a small creek trickles, slowly gathering water from nearby springs until it reaches a gentle slope of earth and a stand of trees. Here is the creek's dividing point. From here, one stream flows west, the other east.

Upstream, above the division, a person can drop two woodchips into the creek, side by side. Odds are, one chip would be pulled down the western stream, and if circumstances were right, it would flow to the Snake River, then into the Columbia River, past the city of Portland, and into the Pacific Ocean, a journey of 1,353 miles. The other woodchip, being pulled into the eastern stream, would make its way to the Yellowstone River, then into the Missouri and Mississippi Rivers, past the city of New Orleans into the Gulf of Mexico, 3,488 miles from its beginning.

In the state of Wyoming, within the Teton Wilderness, in a place called Two Ocean Pass, two creeks, the Pacific Creek and the Atlantic Creek, peel away from each other at Parting of the Waters. The creeks share the same source but end up oceans apart.

Churches have choices to make. Churches have to make decisions about what they do, what they believe, and how they practice. Some choices are mundane. Some are momentous. Like a puff of wind that pushes a woodchip headed toward

Parting of the Waters, some choices push churches toward a stream that carries them to an ocean far away from where they intended to be. The little breeze may have felt inconsequential at the time—a small choice, a seemingly ordinary decision. But choices have consequences, and not all of the outcomes are intended.

Churches of Christ buried one of their most loved preachers on a windy March day in Santa Ana, California, 1929. T. B. Larimore's peacemaking spirit, his generous heart, his refusal to divide churches over issues that were not gospel, could have been the path these churches chose for their future. It could have been how Churches of Christ in the succeeding decades would act and how they would be known. Peacemaking was, after all, in their DNA. Larimore's character and commitments went all the way back to the Blue Hole, to the original stream from which the movement emerged.

But in the vacuum created by Larimore's loss, a different impulse emerged. A hard-edged and often contentious spirit was soon exhibited by the young pallbearer at Larimore's funeral. His subsequent rise to power represented a crucial turning point in the movement. A stormier path was chosen than the one Larimore had been on.

It would be unfair, of course, to say that Foy Wallace was the sole cause of the change of direction in these churches. Causation is not always easy to determine. Wallace was uniquely influential in the middle third of the twentieth century, but he was not alone. Nor would it be fair to say that the peace-loving spirit so vividly seen in Larimore was totally extinguished upon his death. There were always peacemaking souls among these churches, though their voices were often muted in the decades following Larimore's funeral. The fear of being written up, labeled, branded, or disfellowshipped was a lived reality.

And to be clear, the combative style of Wallace and many of his contemporaries had been seen long before. Campbell himself, after all, was "tart and severe," a description that could apply to more than a few leaders in the first few generations of the movement. But the movement itself was born out of a desire to unite, not divide.

In the twentieth century, however, unity among people with substantial disagreements became unimaginable among Churches of Christ. Unity for most of the churches came to mean agreement on every issue rather than peace in the midst of disagreement.

These churches thought they were traveling on the same road they had always been on. But now, unexpectedly, they found themselves east of Eden. They had missed the cutoff. They had gotten off course. The choice between this road and the other one slipped past them without their even noticing. But the choice was always there. Things could have been different.

I know a once-thriving congregation of several hundred members with extensive ministries in its community that dwindled over several decades to less than twenty-five members, aging and afraid, because a preacher, powerful and controlling, condemned any idea and practice that he did not believe was sufficiently conservative.

I know another flourishing congregation of several hundred members whose preacher made sudden and substantial changes in worship, with little explanation or communication. It didn't work out well. Half the congregation left, and soon so did the preacher.

You may think you know which churches I am describing, but you do not. Frankly, there are many. And it misses the point. The issue at hand is not whose attendance is up nor whether a church considers itself conservative or liberal. It's about a church's values and behaviors, about its heart. How a church conducts itself—whether shepherds tend or control the flock, whether ministers serve or command the congregation, whether members look out for the interests of others or mostly take care of themselves—will have a massive impact on its future. Choices have consequences, and some choices are difficult to reverse.

There are many situations, of course, where the consequences don't matter all that much. If the journey is a lark, it won't matter whether you end up in the Pacific Ocean or the Gulf of Mexico. If the matter at hand is trivial, a church can just learn to live with the new purple carpet or overlook the unusually large purchase of overhead transparencies for the older adult Bible class. If the problem is a technical challenge, then answers are at hand, and wrong answers can be corrected.

But if the church is facing an adaptive challenge where answers are unknown, when the problem itself is unclear, when fixing a problem for one group of members creates problems for another group, where the congregation is under stress no matter what direction it takes, then the focus turns to the character of the congregation, to its maturity, its resilience, its generosity and patience, its ability to listen and forgive, its discipleship and Christlikeness.

These qualities take time to develop. They take teaching and modeling. They take prayer and pastoral care. A church doesn't come to maturity, to the measure of the full stature of Christ, overnight. Or easily. A church can't wait until the crisis strikes before it decides to grow up.

And ready or not, the crisis has come.

I'm not referring merely to the normal and expected crises that every congregation faces. These crises are not insignificant, by any means. They can create havoc in a church. Budgets are not met. Mission efforts fail. Programs fall apart. Conflicts occur. It's not that such matters are not difficult. They are. They may, in fact, be deadly serious. Attention must be paid.

But there's another matter of critical urgency that churches today must face, a reflection of our times, a substantial external pressure that is accelerating the decline and death of many contemporary churches: the world in which we live is changing dramatically and rapidly, and it is impacting the church in profound ways.

Life as we know it—in our churches, our homes, our society, our world—is in the midst of monumental change. This cultural transformation has been taking place for at least the last hundred years, picking up speed and power with every decade.

Since the turn of the twentieth century, we have experienced devastating world wars, the collapse of empires, the reordering of nation-states, a staggering revolution in science, the reshaping of global economics, the expansion of both wealth and poverty, a massive migration from farms to cities, the reformulation of gender norms, exploding religious conflicts, growing worldwide ethnic displacement, extreme political and cultural polarization, and enormous shifts in social values and customs. And that's just the outer layer of the onion.

Phyllis Tickle describes these times as the "Great Emergence," a period of cataclysmic change that happens every five hundred years or so.[1] The last time such a transformation occurred in the West was in the fifteenth and sixteenth centuries, the momentous years of the Renaissance and Protestant Reformation after which the world as it had once been could never be again.

The cultural changes we are now experiencing are just as substantial, as are the anxieties they are producing. The world as it once was will not endure. In fact, in many ways that world is already gone. Churches today face conversations and conflicts they could not have imagined a generation ago when the questions were more orderly and the answers more certain.

Millennials and their younger siblings will not be easily squeezed into the existing molds. They won't likely stay in churches that insist on doing things the way they have always done it. And they won't have patience for churches that cannot differentiate gospel from preference. Many of them struggle with churches that equate certain narrow political causes or party affiliations with the cause of Christ. They are willing to walk away from churches that do. And they are.

They won't tolerate—and shouldn't—the de facto segregation of races and ethnicities common in our churches. They won't tolerate hypocrisy. They won't tolerate churches that think it's their job to condemn others. They won't tolerate intolerance. Many of these young men and women are already gone, and churches are feeling their loss.

But the crisis that churches are experiencing isn't simply the result of young people turning away. Every generation is affected, every community has its pressure points, every congregation is facing, or will face, disruption and crisis. As the impact of a massively changing culture takes its toll, as conflicts—or apathy—increase, as too many church members look elsewhere for meaning and belonging, as we begin to open our eyes and see, at last, the terrible drought and look around for life-giving resources, we may find ourselves distressed that the old resources seem to be diminishing, that the old answers don't seem to work as they once did, that the spring is running dry.

If this picture does not describe our own congregation, then either God should be praised or our eyes are still closed. But if it seems true, then we need to take serious stock. What do we do now?

Two responses are common. The first is the most familiar. We look inward. We retrench. We work harder. We preach louder. We stoke the fear. We repair the fortress. We deepen the mote and pull up the drawbridge. We talk only to churches like our own and criticize or condemn those who are not. We convince ourselves that if we would only do things as we once did them, back in a golden age made brighter and more wonderful in the safety of our memories, then things surely will be better. They won't.

The other response is to look outward, to seek life-resuscitating resources in someone else's stream, someone else's story. Why, those churches over there seem to be growing. Maybe we should try that. Church on a beach? Church in a bar? Church in a gym? Perhaps a "Spin Class with the Spirit" would spark some interest because, you know, "Jogging with Jesus" seems trite. Better yet, let's try a little dose of liturgy. Maybe candles would be good. Millennials seem to go for candles. Or let's head to the latest how-to-be-a-cutting-edge-church conference at the events center in the posh new hotel downtown to find out what might be working out there.

We find ourselves adopting the style and language of others whose histories and influences, whose resources, are substantially different from our own, confused about why this borrowed vision of church doesn't seem to work for us. Still, we try the new style on for size. It almost fits. We reconfigure our seating. We slick up our websites. We accessorize our worship. Is our attendance up yet?

Over time the new language, awkward at first, begins to feel a little more comfortable. We begin to claim the label evangelical as our own, because that's where the action seems to be these days, largely unaware of evangelicalism's deep roots in the Reformed churches of Europe, whose original theological soil, rich in the nutrients of God's sovereignty, has already been remixed in many American churches with high-yield, individualistic, success-driven, human-centered, synthetic fertilizer to make bigger, more beautiful, genetically modified churches. We then pluck American evangelicalism's grammar and style out of that soil, shake off what little has remained of its original spiritual nutrients and transplant it into our own earth—rich in restoration but depleted in unity and deprived of water because of the long drought—and then seem surprised when the mutant plant does not grow.

Churches are facing a massive adaptive challenge. There are no easy answers. Building a fortress and hunkering down behind the walls is tempting, but it will only make things worse. Borrowing someone else's answers may energize us for a while, but it too will likely fail. The problems are complex. They feel intractable. It's hard to know what to do.

But if we stop and look. If we search beneath the vines and trees long overgrown because we have not walked there for a season, we may find that the Blue Hole has not yet run dry. There is life beneath us still. They are not the only waters, mind you. There are other streams feeding the great river. We should know them, learn from them, drink from them, and be grateful for them.

But the Blue Hole that serves as the headwaters of our stream has resources still untapped, still fresh, still useful. Deep in the underground caverns are lifegiving resources—cool, clear, God-given, Christ-touched Spirit Waters—that could open up for us, if we are ready, new streams and renewed hope.

One Size Never Fits All

The French call it *prêt à porter*—ready-to-wear clothes. Not made-to-order clothes but items sold in stores in standard sizes. Those are the only kind of clothes I know, really. I don't know what made-to-order even feels like. I've always just bought my clothes right off the rack. I don't even have to try a sport coat on. Just find a 42 long I like and take it to the cashier.

It would be great if churches could order the solutions to their problems like that: *prêt à porter*, ready-to-wear remedies right off the rack. Our youth program is falling apart. Is there a fix for that in an XL? Do you have anything that might help our elders get along, maybe in taupe? Our preacher is too tolerant of other groups. We need someone who's willing to tell us what's wrong with Baptists and Presbyterians. Could we get that in a narrow?

I often hear that sort of thing, though not quite so baldly, when I serve as a consultant to congregations. Church leaders often assume that the job of an outside consultant is to give them the solutions to their problems. You know, an extra-bright future, ready to wear. But churches don't get better that way.

The solutions are generally found in the church itself—in its people, in their story, among their gifts and passions. The task is to ask the questions and listen in such a way that a congregation comes to discover the resources God has already given them.

Each congregation is different. Each church's resources are different. Each church's future is different. God has supplied each one with a unique set of gifts— the people themselves, the particular configuration of God-graced experiences and talents, of wisdom and insight, of work skills, home neighborhoods and life circumstances that make it unique, and the distinct opportunities within the larger community that this congregation can address because God is already at work there.

As missional church leader Patrick Keifert often says, God has a preferred and promised future for each congregation.[2] A congregation's task is to discover among its people and in the surrounding community what God is already doing and join God in that work. That's our challenge and our opportunity.

There are no standard sizes for churches. There are no one-size-fits-all solutions. I certainly won't try to provide them here. The best answers for your church are going to be found within your church. But you have to have your eyes open. You have to ask questions without assuming you already know the answers. You have to talk to people who are not like you. You especially have to talk to people who don't like you. You will need to talk to folks who live or work in your community, who know nothing about your church, or who do know something and couldn't imagine being part of your congregation. They can tell you some things you need to know.

And you will have to listen—to their stories, to their complaints, to their pain. You will need to learn the story behind their story. You will need to listen long enough to discern the *why* before you can begin to map out a *what* or certainly a *how*.

Moreover, you will need a sense of your congregation's story. When and how was it started and out of what circumstances, out of what needs, by what impulses, led by which people who displayed what attitudes and concerns? Like character traits that are passed down from parent to child to grandchildren, the strengths and weaknesses, the personality and pathologies of a church's original *why* live among its members for generations, even if the members weren't there at the beginning.

Finally, you will need a sense of their larger history, the story of their people. In that story are clues about what's going on and resources for the difficult days.

What follows are some of those resources that flow from the wellspring of the Stone-Campbell stream. They will not be your only resources, of course, but they may be especially effective for particular ailments because they are already in the system. Like the COVID-19 vaccinations that many of us received, the antibodies are still inside us. They are still potent.

Two of the resources you already know: unity and restoration, the two driving forces behind the launch of the movement. The other four resources are also in the stream that feeds this heritage. Some of them are perhaps less obvious, but all of them are characteristic of the movement and may be especially valuable for churches teetering at the edge.

Resource #1: Unity as the Wellspring of Grace

Years ago, I found myself sitting in a most amazing worship service. It was a house church in Durban, South Africa, filled with the most joyous Christians I had ever seen. The smell of the evening's dinner drifted into my nostrils accompanied by the clatter of dishes and the chatter of cooks. The love in the place was thick. The house seemed almost electrically charged by the smiles and hugs. And songs. Loud songs. Enthusiastic songs. Unexpected songs, at least to my ear.

Most of what we sang that night came from the albums of the popular American Christian singing group Acappella—"Rescue," "Water from the Well." It was an all-out, joy-soaked, hand-clapping celebration.

The worshipers were Indian South Africans. They were of Indian descent but had been South African citizens for generations. I use the word *citizen* loosely. Under the policy of apartheid, they were among the non-White ethnic groups whose rights and properties had largely been stripped away from them.

I heard stories that evening of what had happened to their families. Beginning in the early 1960s, over three million non-White South Africans throughout the country were forcibly evicted from their homes and moved to assigned neighborhoods. Many of these worshipers had come from the city's professional class—doctors, lawyers, teachers. They barely had time to pack their belongings. As they moved into poorer homes in a Durban ghetto, homes that had just been vacated by other ethnic groups who were forcibly moved to still other areas, new White families began to move into their old homes, the homes they had built and had spent their lives in.

My evening with these Indian Christians took place only a couple of years after apartheid had been lifted. Though they had been totally disenfranchised, though they could not return to the homes or lives that had been stolen from them, though they had lost money and property and dignity and, in some cases, family and friends, these Christians were not bitter. Amazing. The dissonance I was feeling was not that these Indian South Africans were singing songs from the American group Acappella but that, after all they had gone through, after all that had been taken from them, they were singing with such joy. I was sobered and moved.

I found the same spirit among the family at Metro Christ's Church near Dallas, the predominately Black congregation that welcomed me into their fellowship for more than five years. This church's spiritual lineage can be traced back to Annie C. Tuggle, who fought against the oppression of her own community, and further back to Samuel Cassius, who was born in slavery, whose influence among Black Churches of Christ was profound but who was marginalized and humiliated by White church leaders much of his life.

The worshipers in our church in Dallas had painful stories to tell about their own marginalization and abuse—by churches and in their community. But no church I have ever known worships with such joy and offers their neighbors such hospitality.

How can people who have been so mistreated and oppressed find such a reservoir of delight? How could they have found the grace to forgive? What resources of faith could create such a heart for peace?

We have looked here at stories of Christian union from the past, of peace and peacemaking, of sacrifice and reconciliation. I continue to be moved by Barton Stone and Raccoon John Smith whose handshake and embrace marked a significant reconciliation among peoples of profound differences. They believed Christian unity was at the heart of the gospel, that it was the wellspring from which everything else flowed. They took Jesus's prayer for the unity of his disciples seriously and literally. They believed that Christ's reconciling work to break down the dividing wall, to remove the hostility between Jew and Gentile, to create in himself one new humanity in place of two and thus make peace, was actually meant for their churches as well.

Stone's own words stand at the mouth of the movement's Blue Hole, at the source of the stream of Christians that morphed into the Churches of Christ we know today: "We will that this body die, be dissolved, and sink into union with the Body of Christ at large." "We will that preachers and people cultivate a spirit of mutual forbearance; pray more and dispute less. . . ."

These remarkable words created a movement of Christians. Our early spiritual ancestors saw themselves as peacemakers, as a unified and unifying community of believers, despite their differences.

It should not be surprising, then, that the first child of the movement to become a US president focused his inaugural address on the unity of the nation. Less than twenty years after the Civil War and the liberation of slaves, James Garfield proclaimed that "sections and races should be forgotten and partisanship should be unknown." He predicted that within fifty years "our children will not be divided concerning our controversies," that they would "bless their fathers and their fathers' God . . . that slavery was overthrown," and that the descendants of slaves "will soon control the destinies of the Republic."

This yearning for peace, which had been planted in Garfield's heart by his church family, was reflected in this powerful first speech as the nation's President, calling his country toward a "final reconciliation."

Over the decades, however, for many of the children of this unity movement, Stone's words and Garfield's heart were forgotten. And so, the urge toward unity waned. The consequences have been tragic.

But the gift has not been lost. We just need to know where to look. Recovering it will not be easy.

It's not particularly difficult to be united with friends, of course. It's relatively painless to live in peace with people who think like you do. But what if they don't?

What if you disagree with them? What if the actions of others have been wrong? What if they ignored you? What if you don't like what they do and don't believe what they believe? What if they hurt you? What if the wounds run deep? Do you have to find peace with them, too?

In the years after apartheid in South Africa was abolished, a Truth and Reconciliation Commission was established, led by Desmond Tutu among others. It was a venue for justice—not retributive justice, not justice to punish, but restorative justice, justice that restores dignity, justice that restores relationships and hope. All over the country, public hearings took place where abusers stood in front of those they had abused. They told the truth about themselves, who they were, what they had done. They asked for forgiveness, and forgiveness was granted.

Peace is possible when truth is spoken and reconciliation is sought. But it requires both. And the road is hard. In 1960, at a time when Abilene Christian College was racially segregated—like most schools in the South, like most colleges in Churches of Christ—a White professor spoke truth. "We fear the mythical character named Jim Crow more than we reverence Jesus Christ," Carl Spain said, chastening his own school for rejecting student applicants whose only disqualifying characteristic was the color of their skin.

But truth is not enough. Though students of color began to be enrolled at the school within a few years, the scars were deep and the nature of the wound not fully recognized. It's easy to justify one's own behavior and to miss the consequences of one's own actions. It took almost forty years after the truth was confessed before reconciliation could begin, when the school's president, Royce Money, publicly confessed his school's racist past and asked forgiveness for the school's wrongdoing.

In 1940, an African American preparatory school, the Nashville Christian Institute (NCI), was founded by White Church of Christ donors. The establishment of the school, led for almost two decades by Black preacher Marshall Keeble, enabled and strengthened the ongoing segregation of these churches. When David Lipscomb College finally began to be integrated in 1967, NCI was closed, and most of the school's assets went to the mostly White college. The resentment about the financial maneuver, on top of the long history of racism, smoldered within the Black community. Understandably so. Forty-five years later, Lipscomb University president Randy Lowry apologized for what had happened, leading the school in an act of institutional repentance.

The road to peace is hard. In each case, the wounds from the long transgressions still fester. But peace is possible when the truth about oneself is finally spoken. We admit our failings and accept, without judgment, the failings of others. We confess we are wrong. We ask and offer forgiveness.

Even then, there is peacemaking work that must be done. Reconciliation does not end with a few well-chosen words, however heartfelt they may be. Reconciliation demands action. Peace requires the restoration of relationships, especially when the rift is great and certainly when an entire people has been aggrieved.

Speaking the truth should never lead to cheap reconciliation where the past may be swept under the rug and the wounds left to abscess. Confession must never result in self-satisfaction for finally coming clean. It should lead, rather, to the hard and humble work of restitution, of empowerment, and of justice.

If Churches of Christ are ever to become spiritually healthy, there are confessions to make. We were wrong about some things.

What White Churches of Christ did over the years to marginalize and disempower Black people and Black churches was wrong. White church leaders were wrong. I was wrong. No excuses. No evasion.

White church leaders created and maintained a distinct fellowship of Black churches, a sort of religious redlining fashioned out of Jim Crow values, separate and in no sense equal. Even after the Civil Rights era, White churches, reflecting the larger American culture, have too often treated ethnic minorities with subtler forms of racism. They have not fully grasped the ways White privilege disadvantages non-Whites in this country. As a result, people have been hurt, families disadvantaged, neighborhoods neglected, congregations devalued.

Something must be said. Something must be done.

And, I believe, another confession is called for. What Churches of Christ said and did that led to the great division within the Stone-Campbell unity movement was wrong. However strongly we may have believed in our doctrinal positions, our divisive spirit was wrong. Our exclusiveness was wrong. Our harsh judgment of others was wrong. Our neglect, even disdain, of Christian unity was wrong.

I'm sure there were faults on all sides in the tragic split with Christian Churches at the turn of the twentieth century. But it didn't have to happen. Churches of Christ were the ones who walked away. We could have chosen a different path. We could have chosen unity rather than division. We didn't. We were wrong.

While Churches of Christ bring many wonderful gifts to the larger Christian world, we will need to admit the ways our words and behaviors have hurt others. To become well, we must tell the truth about ourselves. And seek to become a peacemaking people again. It will be hard work.

Even within the mundane daily life of individual congregations, loving one another in spite of our differences will be hard. Occasional moments of superficial greeting are not enough. Sunday morning handshakes and hellos are not sufficient to create meaningful community. Peacemaking is forged out of urgency, sweat, tenacity, and sacrifice. It requires eyes open enough to see when others are broken, hearts soft enough to ease their anguish or bridge their alienation, and a spirit strong enough to make a difference in someone else's life.

When all is said and done, peacemaking is gospeled work. God creates it. The Prince of Peace died for it. God's Spirit empowers it. But we have decisions to make as to what we do about it today. We choose to become peacemakers because it is in God's nature and we are God's children, because we are partners in God's ongoing peace work. But God will have to bring about its ultimate end. God heals broken spirits and fractured churches, if we are willing to receive it. Christ reconciles races, factions, relationships, and sinners. He makes from two, one. From division, unity. From oppression and injustice, a home and a future.

The long night may bring many tears, but there is joy in the morning. No wonder the Indian Christians love to sing.

Resource #2: Restoration and Life

The drive to restore the ancient church first entered the bloodstream of Churches of Christ through the Alexander Campbell articles of the 1830s. Campbell's desire for restoration, as we have seen, was never intended as an end but only a means. His primary commitment was to the kingdom of God.

Christian unity was the means by which the kingdom of God would break in, and restoration was the means to bring about unity. When restoration is separated from unity, when peacemaking and reconciliation cease to be the goals of restoration, restoration by itself becomes self-absorbed and self-consuming. That's what began to happen to some of Campbell's churches early on.

The drive to recreate the golden age, a common theme in America and Europe, had serious flaws. Among other problems, the golden age wasn't always golden—not in classical Greece and Rome, and not in the churches we read about in the Bible. I am not suggesting that the Bible itself should not be the source of life and faith. It should. But the churches of the first century are hardly models to replicate. They were terribly broken, which is to say, they were like our own. The letters and gospels were written to them in order to address what was broken.

Part of the problem was that the early restoration leaders, like others in their day, largely missed the situational nature of Scripture. The Bible was written to address specific situations, so it requires modern believers to discern how to apply Scripture to our own situations. The original context was crucial to Scripture's original meaning. Understanding Scripture requires modern believers to discern Scripture's own settings and, from that, make sense of our own world. But restoration leaders tended to ignore the historical context. They often ended up strip-mining the biblical witness, extracting what they were looking for, smelting some laws and principles from the ore, then discarding the rest. Churches in our day too often perpetuate the same practices.

When we view the Bible as laws or principles that need to be excavated from the text, when we overlook the real-life situations into which Scripture was poured, we lose something critical. When we ignore the original situation, we miss the original point.

Similarly, when we overlook the literary forms in which the Bible was written—like history, law, poetry, apocalyptic, prophecy, and wisdom—we are likely to misunderstand and misapply the message. Poetry doesn't work the same as history. Law has a different function than wisdom. When apocalyptic is confused with prophecy, a person might think the last chapters of Daniel or the dramatic narrative of Revelation were predicting twenty-first-century world events, allowing modern readers to calculate with imagined precision the day and time the world will come to an end. Like anyone would try to do that.

When the original context and the literary form are boiled away from Scripture's meaning like overcooked tea, what's left are only the bitter, soppy tea leaves at the bottom of the pot. Tea was what we needed, but the residue sludge is what we got, and that simply won't nourish a church.

But perhaps the most crucial problem with the early restoration attempts at understanding Scripture was that they focused so extensively on externals. That was certainly Campbell's emphasis in his defining articles on restoring the ancient order. Though Campbell himself had a well-thought-out theology, the type of restoration embraced by many in the subsequent generations was largely disconnected from theology or even the gospel itself. Ironically, the older Campbell got, the less important restoration was for him, while for many of his followers restoration had become the primary if not exclusive lens through which they viewed the church.

To be clear, things like church organization and polity are not unimportant, but by themselves they are not gospel. Restoration of this sort focuses on form apart from grace, structure apart from discipleship.

Several years ago, the missionary and teacher Paul Hiebert provided a framework for helping churches understand these issues.[3] Hiebert distinguished between "bounded set" and "centered set" thinking.

Bounded-set concerns are about where lines are drawn, about the boundaries, about who is in and who is out, who is right and who is wrong. A focus on restoring external forms is a bounded-set concern.

If, for example, you get the order of salvation right, if you correctly determine the right church organization and name and mode of baptism and frequency of communion, if you determine correctly whether churches can cooperate with other churches or whether it's okay to believe in a literal millennial reign of Christ or conduct Bible classes at the building or believe Christians shouldn't vote or whether a woman can pray in the presence of a man or can teach baptized boys or must wear a hat to church or is forbidden from braiding her hair or whether praising God with a guitar will cause a person to be separated from God for eternity—if you get all of the answers right, then you are inside the fence. If not, well, you better figure out how to get everything right.

A friend of mine recently compiled a list of twenty doctrinal issues that Churches of Christ have fought over—from instrumental music to women in leadership, from observing Christmas to whether communion should be open to non-Christians. He created a matrix categorizing possible answers. The various combinations of possible opinions numbered more than sixty million. That's with twenty doctrinal issues. Add just two more issues with all the variables and the possible combination of opinions numbers over a half billion.

Is that what God expects of us, getting all the answers right on all the important questions? If church is about everyone agreeing on every issue, we're in big trouble.

Bounded-set thinking is about fences—building fences, guarding fences, repairing fences. *Centered-set thinking*, on the other hand, is not about the boundaries but about the core. Its focus is not what divides us but what holds us together.

A centered-set people seek the heart of things where life may be found. It's the difference between a corral and an oasis. The purpose of a corral is to keep the right things inside the fence and the wrong things outside. An oasis, on the other hand, is about the life-giving resources in the center. A church can focus on guarding the fence or it can gather at the oasis. Those are very different kinds of churches.

A centered-set church doesn't spend its time trying to calculate who is in and who is out. That's God's job. Christians have different responsibilities. They are looking not toward the boundary but toward Jesus.

Campbell's original articles about restoration, which substantially shaped these people, were mostly about externals, about the boundaries. That sort of restoration is incomplete. It stops short. It misses the goal. To be clear, the restoration of forms and structures has value, but only if they are connected to the center, only if the *how* grows out of the *why*. True restoration is not about building fences but restoring relationships. It's about focusing on what's at the heart of things—about loving God and loving others, about Christ's death and resurrection, about faith and mercy and justice.

Stone himself gave the most eloquent response to the notion of restoring a church on the basis of boundaries. Building a fence can't make us a community. The church will never be united if it assumes people will come to agreement on the basis of a creed, whether written or unwritten, nor in believing that somehow everyone will understand the Bible alike, or that they even can. And it won't happen through water union, as if baptism itself will unite us. History undercuts that notion.

There is only one way that peace will occur, one way that the church will be restored. God will have to do it. Only through the Holy Spirit. Only by fire. This is the renewal we are looking for, not at the fence line but at the center where Jesus is.

Resource #3: Reasoned Inquiry

On a brisk, windy February morning in 1970, wearing a dark suit with cartoonishly wide lapels, considered stylish in that dark period in men's sartorial fashion, I walked in solemn procession along with fellow class officers just behind the faculty, gloriously costumed in their academic plumage, into Moody Coliseum for the inauguration of Dr. John C. Stevens, Abilene Christian University's eighth president.

Stevens was not just a distinguished professor of history and longsuffering administrator, he had been a lifelong family friend. I still occasionally look with tears at the iconic World War II photo of the American 28th Infantry troops marching down the Champs-Élysées, leading the parade celebrating the liberation of Paris in 1944. At the very front, right in the middle, the tallest soldier in the row, framed by the Arc de Triomphe behind him, is Captain John Stevens, a medic in Patton's Third Army, less than two months after the invasion of Normandy. Dr. John often quipped about that photo, "Never were so many led by one so unaware of where we were going!"

Stevens's presidential inaugural address that February morning is perhaps the most remembered in the university's history. Stevens told the crowd, "I hope . . . that we can always be a liberal arts institution in the finest traditions of higher education." In other words, the students at this university, like most other schools of higher education in the history of Churches of Christ, will be broadly educated. They will know history, philosophy, literature, languages, the sciences, and the arts, no matter what career they pursue.

And then came the line most often quoted from the speech: "There are no subjects on this earth, or in outer space, or in the metaphysical realm, which we cannot study on the campus of a Christian institution of higher learning." Christians do not need to be afraid of thoughtful inquiry. They should be open to rethinking any belief and examining any topic.

"Everyone can know our basic commitment," he said, "but I hope that people will also realize that there are no closed minds and no off-limits subjects on this campus. . . . We can study—and I hope with a fair and reasonable approach—even those viewpoints which might not be in agreement with our basic presuppositions."[4]

This commitment to reason—to critical inquiry, to reasoned engagement with others concerning disputable matters, to openness in seeking truth wherever it may be found and a willingness to change one's mind when new evidence is brought to bear—is one of the greatest virtues of the Stone-Campbell heritage, passed down from generation to generation among Churches of Christ. Of all the cultural and intellectual springs that have fed this movement, few have had as much impact.

There can be a downside to this impulse toward reason, of course. Just because people think their opinions are reasonable doesn't make them so. Among other concerns, humans often use reason to see or interpret information in a way that confirms what they already believe, what social scientists call confirmation bias. Hugo Mercier and Dan Sperber call this tendency "myside bias."[5] We are good at spotting the weaknesses of others but tend to be blind about our own. At the very least, reasonable people can come to vastly different conclusions about things.

Nevertheless, the impulse toward reason can be helpful during times of conflict or stress. Facts still matter. Not every opinion has equal merit. Every conclusion is open to question. Reasonable people acting in good faith are able to change their minds when presented with alternative evidence or reasoned arguments.

The application of reason to their Christian walk lies close to the heart of the churches fed by this intellectual stream. And reason's resources may still provide a means, though not the only means, by which Churches of Christ may address their most stubborn adaptive challenges.

Much of this impulse toward reason and a commitment to education entered the bloodstream of Churches of Christ directly from Scotland. At the beginning of the nineteenth century, Scotland's universities were considered among the best in the world. The impact of the Scottish intellectual climate on the creation of the American system of government, the establishment of American colleges and schools, and the drive to educate all children in America was immense.

This same impulse profoundly shaped the Stone-Campbell Movement. Walter Scott and both Campbells studied at the finest Scottish universities. Barton Stone and others were trained in America as Presbyterians, in the community of Christians shaped by Scottish values about reason and education. From their beginning, Churches of Christ were driven by this passion for knowledge. They nurtured the assumption, drawn straight from the Scots, that all Christians—male and female, wealthy or poor, minister or member—were capable of studying and thinking for themselves.

These churches began launching schools and colleges, beginning, not surprisingly, in Georgetown, Kentucky. In 1836, Bacon College was established there, in honor of the seventeenth-century scientist and philosopher Francis Bacon, symbolically affirming that the Christian faith should be guided by reason. Walter Scott was appointed the school's first president. Within a few decades, directly out of Bacon College, came the schools we now know as Lexington Theological Seminary, Transylvania University, and the University of Kentucky.

In many ways, it was James Garfield who embodied the movement's drive to think and educate. As a young professor at Western Reserve Eclectic Institute, later named Hiram College, Garfield dazzled his students with his commanding intellect, occasionally writing on the chalk board with both hands simultaneously, one hand writing in Greek and the other hand in Latin. A few years later, as the Hiram College president, Garfield defended the right of students and professors to study the works of controversial figures such as Charles Darwin, because there is no subject a Christian should be forbidden to read or study.

Similarly, Bethany College, which Alexander Campbell established, insisted that higher education should be non-sectarian, that is, not supporting or advocating only one Christian denomination or group. There were always members of that faculty who did not come from churches in the movement. All knowledge is God's knowledge, and knowledge should not be feared, whatever its source.

This legacy of reason and education was passed down, unevenly but surely, from church to church, generation to generation, to today. In light of that extraordinary commitment to reason and inquiry, it would be a shock to the system if a church or a school were to discourage disagreement, if dissent were not allowed, if certain subjects were forbidden to be studied or discussed.

All Christians, but certainly Christians from this heritage, should be expected to read and to think, to be willing to change their minds, to embrace learning and not fear it. Churches of Christ should be places of freedom, not conformity. Everyone doesn't have to agree, but everyone should be willing to listen to others. And respect them.

Resource #4: An Ear for Harmony

A distinguished president of an evangelical college was once invited to the campus where I taught. He was a fine scholar and a highly respected administrator in one of the nation's best-known evangelical schools. He didn't know a lot about Churches of Christ, which was one of the reasons he was invited. It would be good for him but also for us.

After three days of lectures and conversations, he was invited to visit with some of the theology faculty. One of them asked him, "So, what are your impressions of Churches of Christ?" He told the group how much he had enjoyed coming to the campus and how impressed he was with the faculty and students. He confessed that he had not known many Church of Christ people before but that his most distinct impression had to do with the a cappella singing. "It is your greatest drawback," he said. "Every time you sing without instruments you pronounce judgment against every other church, every other group. As long as you insist on singing a cappella, you will always be an outsider to the rest of us."

His words were unsettling. They were not what we were expecting. It was hard not to feel, well, judged. We felt a little defensive. But we listened. We were respectful. If there was something to learn, we were willing to learn it.

It took me a while to get past his comments. He was right that he didn't know us well. He probably should have been less critical. His words were perhaps too harsh. But we also knew that he was trying to be honest and helpful, and that he carried a measure of truth.

My new San Antonio neighbors, who recoiled a little when my wife and I told them we went to a Church of Christ, were expressing something similar. They weren't trying to be critical, but it was important to them to go to a church that "had music." We knew what they meant. They, too, had felt judged. Over the years, some of that judgment has been direct—I still flinch when I think about some of the sermons I have heard—but it is often indirect. Did we intend to judge everyone else? In my heart, I hadn't. But I shouldn't have been surprised to hear it.

Whatever our intentions, many churches do feel judged and over matters that many and perhaps most Church of Christ members now agree are not related to one's salvation. But does that mean a cappella singing is useless, that it is foolish? Was nothing gained by a cappella singing, no matter why our ancestors chose it?

My friend Pat Keifert, the theologian and missional church expert, has spent years researching Churches of Christ, helping many of them become viable congregations in the midst of the changing cultural landscape. Pat loves Churches of Christ. He especially loves to sing with them. He loves a cappella music. I worshiped once with Pat at his Lutheran Church in St. Paul, Minnesota. For this service, the choir was not on stage but was scattered throughout the sanctuary. Most verses of each hymn were sung a cappella. A cappella singing, Pat said, encouraged full congregational participation. The whole church singing together was an important value for his church.

Then he said something that stopped me in my tracks. Churches of Christ regularly and intently practice the discipline of listening, he told me. Every congregation, every service, engages in an exercise of congregational spiritual discipline. You have to listen to one another. To get the pitch, you have to listen to each other. To find your part, you have to listen. To know how loud or how fast to sing, to know when to come in and when to stop, you have to listen. That's a spiritual discipline. Churches of Christ, he said, of all people should be equipped to listen to others because you do it every week.

It was a stunning revelation to me. The very practice of a cappella singing should make a church a listening people. We sing in harmony. We ought to be harmonious. But for that to happen, our congregational spiritual discipline must have purpose. If the only reason we sing a cappella is because early Christians did, then it's little more than an act of mimicry. We were trying to conform to the example, but is there not more?

What if the goal of a cappella singing was not conformity but formation? What if these churches saw themselves as being formed into the image of Jesus in and through their singing—not just what they sing but how they sing it? What if singing, with or without instruments, were a congregational discipline enacted with purpose and care, involving the whole church in the discipline of listening and sharing?

What if singing were a means to a larger goal, like encouraging full congregation participation, since worship in the assembly is not a collection of isolated individual acts but a collective response to the working of God? If full participation were the larger goal, then it might say something about how even a cappella churches use worship teams or how they choose hymns—to encourage not inhibit congregational participation, to nurture with care and purpose the spiritual discipline of harmony. It is possible, frankly, for a congregation to use no musical instruments in worship and still find itself with few people singing together. Surely, that misses the point.

And as more and more Churches of Christ introduce musical instruments, whether in Sunday assemblies or youth groups or other occasions, do the lessons of a cappella singing have to be totally discarded? Can our singing, with or without instruments, form the church into a more Christlike community? If a cappella singing is a means to an end, not the end itself, might it be possible to still listen to one another even if instruments are used? Could such congregations not still encourage full participation? Could singing still be a spiritual discipline for the whole church?

Of all groups, Churches of Christ should be equipped to serve as peacemakers, as people who not only sing in harmony but who live harmoniously, whether or not they sing with instruments. That's a discipline worth seeking.

Not long after the visiting college president told the faculty members that our a cappella singing in Churches of Christ acted as a judgment on all other Christian groups, he spoke in graduate chapel. The chapel facility is a wonderful place for worship. The aesthetics are pleasing; the acoustics are lively. The room was filled to overflowing that morning. I had been asked to lead the singing.

I should probably confess that I selected songs that allowed us to show off a little. Perhaps I should feel bad about that. I don't. We sang hymns like "O Praise the Lord," "O Lord, Our Lord," "Christ, We Do All Adore Thee," and "O Sacred Head," songs with beautiful harmonies, songs we knew and sang well. After he spoke, we all stood and sang "The Lord Bless You and Keep You." I watched tears flow down his cheeks.

When the last of the seven amens was sung, he headed straight to me. "I've never heard anything like this. Ever. You must never lose this," he said. He told me that this gift of singing should be considered God's gift to the larger Christian world, that we must not neglect this gift. He said, "Maybe if you used a guitar from time to time in your services, you wouldn't come across as judging others. I don't know what you should do. But no matter what, *you must not lose this!*"

I have thought about his comments a lot. I have wondered often what the "this" is that we must not lose. It was more than just the blending of voices, surely. The a cappella singing that day was great but it was merely a means, not the end.

No, it was something else, something more. It was the energy. It was the Spirit. It was the mysterious bond of fellow worshipers singing their hearts out to God. It was the community, bound together, sharing a common commitment, a common faith. We listened to one another. We had been equipped over many years not just to sing but to listen, because to sing well you have to listen first. It came from discipline, from practice, from spiritual memory, from unspeakable power beyond human ability or understanding. There was harmony in the room and urgency. And there was peace. We were being equipped through our singing to be people of peace, not people of judgment.

I saw it happen right in the moment. I witnessed a transformation. A change of mind, a change of heart, a softening. What a great gift. We must not lose it.

Resource #5: Living Generously

Love in the Time of Cholera. It's a long way from the compelling novel by Colombian Nobel Prize–winner Gabriel García Márquez to the story I want to tell— actually a continent and a little more than a hundred years distant—but the title is still apt. Our story is about cholera, and it's about love.

In the summer of 1873, a cholera epidemic broke out in Nashville. The disease was cruel and deadly. Of the 25,000 residents who lived in the city, more than a thousand died. As is usually the case, the poor suffered most.

The preacher and editor David Lipscomb lived about ten miles south of Nashville, but as residents poured out of the city to escape the ravages, Lipscomb drove his buggy straight into it. Roman Catholic nuns, the Sisters of Mercy, were on the frontlines of care. Lipscomb joined them. He carried the nuns in his cart from house to house. And even though the disease was contagious and lethal, Lipscomb ministered day by day to the sick and their families, including, it should be noted, African Americans, whose death count was almost double that of the city's White population.

Lipscomb's criticism of those who stayed away while their fellow citizens were suffering and dying was withering. And so was their criticism of him: he had his priorities wrong; he should have taken care of himself; he was a fool; the gospel is about saving souls, not saving lives.

I've heard these sorts of comments before: Giving to the poor is a waste of resources. They are responsible for their own condition. They're just looking for handouts. Why should we have to take care of them? Jesus told us to seek and save the lost, not rid the world of poverty. And on and on. I know Christians who argue against church money being budgeted for any ministry to the poor. I've heard tirades against any notion of social justice because, well, you see, social justice is a liberal cause and I read on the internet that it's a form of socialism. Any excuse will do, I suppose.

A ministry of mercy is not what Churches of Christ have been most known for, but it's there, in the tributary from whence we came. The instinct to generosity may be a small stream, a trickle at times, but it is there if we look. And walking beside it is old Brother Lipscomb, stooping down and drinking from the little spring, working side by side with the nuns, helping the poor, burying the dead, ministering to the families, sacrificing his own health for the sake of others, not in order to convert them but to be Jesus to them.

"The religion of our Savior," Lipscomb said, "was intended to make us like Christ, not only in our labor of love—of our self sacrifice for the good of others, but also in raising us above a timid, quaking fear of death. If it does not make us willing to brave death and spend our time and money for the good of our suffering fellow-creatures, offcast and sinners though they be, it does not raise us above a mere empty profession that leaves us scarcely less than hypocrites."[6]

Maybe this is the restoration we need. Maybe this is the strong medicine our churches require in order to get well. A lot of churches are focused on their own needs, their own problems, which may be substantial, but they are rarely life-threatening.

My wife and I remind each other from time to time that most of our problems are first-world problems. Our car recently had a flat. We had to drive on the run-flat tires for twenty-five miles or so. Then the tire shop didn't have a lug lock key for our lug nuts, and there was not one in our car. I had not even heard of lug locks for wheels before. So, we had to go to the dealership, and they had to order a new lug lock key and a new tire. It was six days before we got the new tire on. It was frustrating. I found myself whining a little because of how inconvenient it was.

Really? For that? We had another car in the garage. We have a garage. We have a home. We have plenty of food to eat. We have everything we need. So, we were without our second car for a week. First-world problem.

Our churches struggle to keep the contributions up and find Bible class teachers and fuss about the praise team and wish the services were shorter and make sure the teenagers have transportation to Six Flags. Frustrating at times, but first-world problems. Surely, we can find some perspective.

People are living under bridges and scavenging for food and going bankrupt trying to pay the medical bills and working three jobs to pay for the apartment, they are bullied by classmates and discriminated against by businesses, they are stopped for driving through a White neighborhood simply because they are Black or they send most of their paychecks back home to their large extended family that depends on their income. If, in Lipscomb's words, the dire circumstances of others do "not make us willing to spend our time and money for the good of our suffering fellow-creatures," then, perhaps, the insistent declaration of our Christian values in the face of the miseries and misfortunes around us "leaves us scarcely less than hypocrites."

For several years I was blessed to head a foundation in Dallas that partnered with economically distressed neighborhoods to find economic stability and human worth. The founder and my boss was J. McDonald (Don) Williams, who for many years led one of the most influential international commercial real estate companies in the world. But his heart was always turned to the economically disadvantaged residents of Dallas.

The system was, and is, methodically killing the poorest neighborhoods in the city, robbing them of their dignity and their future. Don was willing to fight anyone—the city council, the mayor, businesses, banks, the Department of Transportation, the State Fair of Texas, the powers and principalities of the universe, Satan himself, anyone who marginalized these neighbors whom Christ loved, for whom Christ died.

I partnered at times with Larry James and John Siburt of CitySquare as they addressed the root causes of poverty in Dallas in one of the most astonishingly effective works on behalf of the economically disadvantaged I have ever seen. In all the years I was involved in that work, immersed daily in the homes and lives of blighted neighborhoods, I never saw a poor person who just wanted a handout or was not willing to work. I'm sure there were some, but I never met them.

I wish I could say I helped these neighbors a lot. Truth be told, they had more to offer me than I could offer them. It's what Larry calls the wealth of the poor.[7] A number of years ago, I heard Larry tell the Matthew 25 story about Jesus and his disciples. You know how the text goes. I was hungry and you gave me food, Jesus told them. I was thirsty and a stranger and naked and sick and in prison and you cared for me. When we act in Jesus's name, Larry said, then we are Jesus to the world. But the people we serve are also Jesus—when you did it to the least of these, you did it to me. So, when we serve the poor, it's as if the eyes of Jesus are looking into his own eyes, Jesus in the servant and Jesus in the served.

Talk about an incarnational moment. How could we not, then, spend our time and money for the good of our suffering fellow-creatures? Christ to Christ, face to face. I suspect Don and Larry and John, all three of whose personal stories have been shaped by Churches of Christ, know something of what Lipscomb felt.

If we could get over ourselves, if we could find perspective about our problems, if we stopped worrying about protecting our own stuff and started feeding and clothing and visiting and caring for the marginalized and oppressed, if we helped find a way out for the victims of racial violence and a way forward for the victims of economic discrimination, if we saw in the strangers and aliens in our midst the eyes and heart of Jesus, if we were willing to brave death and spend our time and money for the good of our suffering fellow-creatures, if we loved the cholera patients more than ourselves, then maybe we would have the spiritual resources we need to deal with our own issues or decide that some of the things we fret about don't matter that much after all.

Lipscomb went on to say, "The religion that does not induce us to do this essential work of a true Christian cannot save us. The rich often think that they cannot condescend to do the work of nursing or caring for the poor. It is degrading. It is hard, I know, just precisely as hard as it is to enter the kingdom of heaven, not a whit more difficult to do the one than the other."

Perhaps this is our salvation: to be willing to do the heartbreaking, difficult, degrading, glorious work of the kingdom of heaven.

Resource #6: Apocalypse Now

When we use the word *apocalypse* today, what we usually mean is some sort of massive destruction, the flaming end of the world. That's really a shame because it misses the point. Apocalypse doesn't mean destruction but an unveiling of something that had been hidden, in other words a revelation.

Greek-speaking Christians called the last book of the New Testament the Apocalypse. That's how it opens: "The revelation of Jesus Christ, which God gave him to show his servants . . ." We think of apocalypse as destruction only because parts of this book describe—symbolically, like all ancient apocalyptic literature—the end of days.

But we have something else in mind here than global destruction, something more akin to the message of Revelation itself. To live apocalyptically is to live today from the vantage point of the end times.

There was a time in the history of Churches of Christ that an apocalyptic vision was a primary impulse of this people. It's how we saw ourselves. It's what we taught and how we lived. But over time, this apocalyptic perspective was pushed underground. It has almost been forgotten. The time is right for its awakening.

We have discussed some of the differences between Stone and Campbell, not just in doctrine but in temperament. As Campbell rose in power and influence within the young movement, he brought to the movement his optimism about human capacity. He had great confidence in his own ability, to be sure, but he believed that all humans were capable of understanding Scripture, obeying God, and getting things right. And ultimately, he believed, human progress would spark the onset of the millennium.

Stone, on the other hand, was not all that confident in humans. His trust was in God's sovereignty, God's power, God's reign, not human ability. It didn't make sense to Stone that humans had the capacity to bring about the inbreaking of the kingdom. If there was to be a millennial reign, Christ would have to do it. But, frankly, Stone wasn't focused much on the thousand-year reign, certainly not speculations about how and when it would come about. He was interested in how humans lived here and now. For Stone, discipleship was about living today with the end times in mind.

Because of his misgivings about human ability, Stone ultimately came to believe that no ruler or governing institution could fix what was broken in the human condition. Earlier in his life, Stone had placed considerable confidence in the US Congress, believing the government would abolish slavery. But the older he got, the clearer it became that Congress was not going to pass legislation to end this abominable practice. This failure of the government to do justice for these enslaved peoples amplified and fueled Stone's apocalyptic vision. No authority on earth could fix what's broken. Only God can.

From that perspective, the task of Christians is to live here and now in contrast to the world. Humans can't build God's kingdom. God has to do that. Our role is to receive it and announce it. We have different values and commitments than the culture around us. That's what it means to live apocalyptically—to live as God intends us to live, in this world but in ways that only God can bring about.

There's a certain separateness that is characteristic of such churches. Not isolation from others. Not fortress-building. Not self-protection. And certainly not an unwillingness to recognize or work side by side with other Christian groups, even ones we may disagree with. Stone's countercultural vision was focused on holiness, not exclusion; on trusting God, not human institutions; on living as part of the world but not characterized by the values the world most celebrates.

For Stone, being a Christian was not the same as being an American. Not even close. He had little confidence that American people or American leaders, or any humans anywhere, could usher in the kingdom of God. Stone and Campbell never came to agreement on this matter. In Stone's view, the kingdom of God is God's prerogative, not ours. Our responsibility is to relinquish control. God's role is to make us holy.

Stone's understanding of church and culture became the prevailing view of the churches in the upper South, at least for a while. By the end of the Civil War, twenty years after Stone's death, David Lipscomb of Nashville picked up the apocalyptic mantle. Throughout his life, Lipscomb expressed pessimism about the ability of any human, certainly any government, to fix what's broken here. His loyalty was to the kingdom of God. His views both influenced and reflected Churches of Christ in Tennessee and the South.

But over time, this view of church as Christian counterculture waned, in part because the confidence of these people in human ability to get things right grew. As the Northern Christians lost their emphasis on restoration, focusing on unity, Southern Churches of Christ lost their emphasis on unity, focusing on restoration.

But here's the switch, and it had tragic consequences. Stone's and Lipscomb's lack of confidence in human ability, which had been a key characteristic of Churches of Christ, was gradually overtaken by Campbell's optimism. For Churches of Christ, this new optimism meant confidence in human progress—not toward Christian unity or the onset of the millennium, as Campbell had originally hoped, but toward the total restoration of the church of the New Testament. These churches became confident that humans could understand all that God wanted and could get everything right.

By the late 1920s, around the time of Larimore's death, Churches of Christ had come to a crossroads. They were taking a new direction. The countercultural vision was largely lost. The post–World War II generation within Churches of Christ began building great schools and church edifices, great mission efforts and innovative programs. Confident they had gotten salvation and worship and church organization right, they were taking the world by storm, and the movement grew, at least for a few decades.

But there's always a problem with spiritual kingdoms built primarily with human hands. And now, in the current long decline, the price is being paid.

I don't mean to be overly bleak about twentieth-century Churches of Christ. I am a product of them. Many of us have been positively impacted by what happened then. But Churches of Christ in America now stand at the edge. They are at the edge of a new future, of new cultural pressures, of aging and shrinking membership, of substantial congregational stresses and conflicts.

What seemed like the strengths of the twentieth-century church are not likely to make things better now. Extensive confidence in our ability to figure things out and fix what's broken will not help much. That confidence, at least in part, largely got us into this mess. It won't get us out.

But we don't have to start from scratch. We are not reinventing the wheel. Tucked back in the recesses of our faith is a memory, almost faded, about a different way of doing church, a different way of seeing our situation. This would be a good time to find our way back to the Blue Hole. There, still cool and fresh, is a stream that could renew us. But this time, renewal will need to start not with us but with God.

The beginning place is God's sovereignty, God's power and will. Our response to God's work in our midst is not confidence in ourselves but humility. This is a time not for self-exertion but self-surrender. It's time we looked at our situation from the vantage point of the apocalypse.

At the turn of the first century, the Christian community was battered and on the defensive. Many Christians felt they were at risk of being wiped out altogether. In the last decade of the first century, a great persecution of Christians had begun, unlike anything they had experienced before. The church was reeling. Numbers were down. Churches were folding. Spirits were low. Sort of like today.

Into that dire situation, the vision of Christ in the book of Revelation breaks in. Here, mighty Rome is brought low. Here, the battle is waged and the Christians triumph. But Christians themselves would not accomplish it. God would.

I once heard Randy Harris summarize the book of Revelation in four sentences: God has a team. Satan has a team. God's team wins. Pick a team. Now, that's an apocalyptic vision. The powers of this world will not win. The mighty will fall. The weak will take their place at God's right hand. The end has already been accomplished. The story has already been written. So, get up and be Christian. Live today out of the victory that has already been won for you. Live as God intends you to live. You won't do it perfectly. Stop worrying about that. God has empowered you. You are God's people. God will give you a future. Live like it.

It's too easy to see ourselves today as a community of believers beaten down by the powers of this world. The sky has grown dark. Massive thunderstorms are in the forecast. There could be hail and perhaps tornados. As the storm envelops us, what should we do? Centers of cultural power are no longer advantaging Christians. In significant ways, Christians are being pushed to the margins. Religion is becoming less important. Congregations are dwindling. Church attendance is in decline everywhere.

But if we have eyes to see it, this could be good news: the church is struggling, hallelujah! Like Christians at the end of the first century, our plight is not cause for alarm but confidence—not confidence in ourselves, surely, because we know now that we can't pull it off, but confidence in a sovereign God who alone can make things right.

Out at the margins, we have home field advantage. We thought we needed to be aligned with centers of power, that we needed to push or legislate a certain

Christian agenda in order to live Christianly. But it turns out our advantage comes when we are no longer playing the power game.

On the surface it appears Christians are on the run, but God always works in hidden ways. Don't be fooled. God's wisdom is different than human wisdom. Christ was crucified in weakness, remember? When I am weak, then I am strong. That's good news, because I now know how weak I am. We all know, or should, that we don't have the power or capacity to bring about the change we need. God is up to something. God is already at work. Maybe it's time to stop working it all out ourselves. The battle has already been fought. God has already won. Pick a team.

That's the view from the perspective of the end times. But that perspective is not foreign to us. It's already part of our story. It's our long-buried instinct to be a community living in contrast to the world around us. It hasn't died. It can still be recovered. We're on a journey. We're not in our home country. Not yet. Not here. We can't place our confidence here.

No king or president, no government or human authority, can usher in the kingdom of God. That's God's job. Humans will always disappoint us. Humans will always fail. We are awfully blind, awfully broken. We are aliens here, refugees. We are not home. It's our homeland we are seeking. So we better travel light. We better be careful not to plant our roots too deep. There's kingdom work ahead.

But we should be clear. Having an apocalyptic vision for our churches doesn't happen simply by our walking in the right direction or making sure we travel without too much baggage. As if it's about what we do, where we go, how we live. The assumption that we can figure things out and do things right is what got us into this pickle in the first place. Doing more of it will not lead to the renewal we seek. Some things only God's Spirit can do.

An apocalyptic vision of the church and a robust view of the Holy Spirit go hand in hand. One is not possible without the other. To live apocalyptically is to be committed to a life of holiness, and holiness is not possible apart from the gifts of God's Holy Spirit. The problem is, many of us have too little spiritual energy or discernment to draw upon, too little experience with the things of the Spirit.

No wonder. The history of Churches of Christ is littered with stories of the diminishment of the work of the Holy Spirit. Even though the movement erupted in the early nineteenth century at places like Cane Ridge in Spirit-fueled revival, many of the later leaders found all that Holy Spirit stuff a little embarrassing. Stone never denied or downplayed the spiritual rebirth that took place at Cane

Ridge or the way God's Spirit had been present throughout his life, but his views on the Spirit were not fully embraced by others in the movement. As the end of his life approached, Stone's mind turned more and more toward Christian unity. He insisted that true unity could never take place apart from the fire of the Holy Spirit. But his words were not heeded, and, consequently, the decades that followed were strewn with division upon division.

Throughout much of the twentieth century, many if not most Churches of Christ denied the present indwelling of the Holy Spirit. Even with the spiritual renewal that began to occur in the late sixties and seventies, the Holy Spirit was rarely a topic of conversations or sermons. And now, after all these years of spiritual drought, as the movement in America faces serious decline, the one resource these churches most need seems remote, almost foreign. We have little memory of the Blue Hole, the Spirit Waters that nourished and sustained us early in our history.

Tragically, this marginalization of the Holy Spirit was a choice we made and often continue to make. And choices have consequences. It's not that we haven't believed in the Holy Spirit. We have, sort of. But the Spirit remains distant in our teaching, our worship, our homes, our relationships, our prayers, our work, our imaginations. We thought we had gotten the Spirit tamed. We put the Holy Spirit in a safe place, off in a retirement home somewhere, out of town, barely accessible, like a beloved aunt too senile to have around the house. Still a family member but really old and no longer able to do much. Remembered but only vaguely. A little embarrassing to talk about. If we ever let her out, no telling what she might say or do. Better to keep her locked up.

But in reality, God's Spirit was never locked away, never contained, however much we thought we had done so. The Spirit has always been present, always with us and in us, even when we denied it or relegated it to a mostly forgotten past.

To be clear, our task now is not to somehow unleash the Spirit, as if the Spirit were somehow bound and gagged. The task before us is not liberation—the Holy Spirit is already free—but surrender. What's needed now is a profoundly, aggressively passive act, an act of relinquishment. We relinquish our sense that we have to control God's Spirit, or channel it or contain it. As Jesus told Nicodemus, "The wind blows wherever it pleases. You hear its sound, but you cannot tell where it comes from or where it is going. So it is with everyone born of the Spirit" (John 3:8).

We are Spirit-born people. Only when we claim that spiritual birthright can we embrace God's preferred and promised future for ourselves and our churches. Only then will we be open to the renewal that only the Spirit can give.

If there's anything we can learn from the apocalyptic vision of Stone and other early leaders, if there is anything the book of Revelation might teach us in these troubled days, it is this: God has not abandoned us. We may feel encircled by enemies and frightened by what the future seems to hold for churches like ours. But the future belongs to God. The battle has been won. The enemy has been defeated. Wait. Listen. Pray. Hope. Trust. Surrender. God is here. God is still among us. And God's Spirit is leading us home.

Takeaways from Chapter 5: Our Greatest Resource

It was the only time I remember being angry at a funeral. I know I shouldn't have felt that way. I felt bad about it. It was surely inappropriate, especially since I was delivering the funeral sermon.

But the death seemed so senseless. The deceased was so young. When you're young, you think you can live forever. He had had symptoms of something serious but ignored them. When he could no longer ignore them, he went to a doctor. The prognosis was grim, but there was treatment that might make him better. He refused it.

Don't worry, he kept saying. I'll be all right.

I sat beside his hospital bed and held his hand and heard him take his last breath.

I spoke words of praise for the young man on the day of his funeral. Those good words were deserved, to be sure. But I looked at his grieving parents and distraught friends and kept thinking, this didn't have to happen. He didn't have to die. Didn't he want to get well?

Churches of Christ are dying. Certain facts have to be faced. Denying it won't change the prognosis. Healing is possible if they want it, but some things have to be done before it's too late.

Will these churches grasp their condition? Will they prepare for the looming crisis—as congregations decline, as the polarization becomes more pronounced, as the long thread of certainty about who these churches are and what they believe continues to unravel? Will they seek treatment? Will they get well?

I don't know. It depends. Every congregation is different. Treatments will vary. I wish this weren't the case. I wish there was a vaccine we could all take. Or perhaps a good "how-to" book somewhere about how to fix my church. But it doesn't exist. And if it did, it wouldn't be worth much.

But we are not left helpless. There are things we can know. There are things we can do. We have already seen six resources that could make a difference, all of which come from our own past, our own story.

1. We can instill in our churches a thirst for unity, even when folks disagree—especially when they disagree.
2. We can embrace restoration by focusing on the right things, by joining God in restoring the things that matter.
3. We can discuss anything reasonably, welcoming dissent and encouraging Christians to think.
4. We can engage in the spiritual discipline of harmony, listening and adjusting our ideas and behavior for the sake of others.
5. We can be a generous people, even to those who are profoundly different from us, with mercy and gratitude.
6. We can be an apocalyptic people, a holy people, a Christian counterculture formed and nourished by God's Spirit, serving the world with grace and pointing the way to Jesus, living today with God's end in mind.

To be honest, however, most of these resources don't make a lot of sense to many of us. I mean, they're interesting and they're good, but they don't seem familiar. They don't feel like ours. We just have too little memory of them.

I have been a part of Churches of Christ for seven decades. I can trace my spiritual ancestry among these people almost back to the beginning of the movement. My grandparents' grandparents became members of a Church of Christ when Alexander Campbell was still holding gospel meetings. My own grandparents overlapped T. B. Larimore's ministry by more than thirty years. My roots run deep. But through most of my life I could not have named more than two of these six resources. Probably only one.

I would have claimed restoration, of course, though its emphasis would have been mostly on externals. But unity? Not a chance. I have no memory of our striving to be a peacemaking people. Harmony? In singing, obviously, but not as a spiritual discipline for getting along with others. Generosity? I've known many generous church members, but our group was never known for having a particular emphasis on helping the poor or healing the sick.

A focus on reason? I have sometimes lamented the rationalism of our past. But I have never thought of Churches of Christ as encouraging members to think for themselves rather than following prescribed doctrines or as a people who cherished the life of the mind. Living apocalyptically by the power of the Holy Spirit? I can't remember a single sermon, including any I have preached, where the word *apocalyptically* was ever used. And our churches speak about the Holy Spirit about as often as we study the book of Revelation, which is to say, hardly at all.

But that's the point, really. Our best resources are largely unfamiliar to us. Yet, these gifts have been a part of us all along. Churches of Christ, down deep in the marrow of our shared story, were given resources that could help us be better. Here, now, today. If we had known. If we could have remembered. If we can grasp what they are and what they are for.

That's our most difficult task, I think. Understanding what our God-given resources are for. Because resources are not skills. They are not solutions. They don't fix things. They don't provide easy answers.

Resources are more like a capacity. Our churches have the capacity to be better, to be healthier, to be more gospeled. We have the capacity to be more like Jesus. God has given us the resources we need. God's preferred and promised future for our congregations has already been funded. The assets we need are in our bank account.

But just because we have the capital for our transformation doesn't mean we will actually be changed. Capacity is about possibility, not inevitability. It's about what God has equipped us to be, about what is already ours even if it's not fully realized. But for too many churches, such a future is remote, unclaimed, and therefore unusable.

The problem also lies within our own story. Alongside our remarkable, transformative, heaven-blessed resources resides a fundamental disability. An incapacity, if you will. We have convinced ourselves that what we need in order to get well, what we must do in order to be saved, can be achieved. It can be accomplished. We have the ability. We can do it.

We just need to follow the right steps. In the right order. In the right way. For the right reasons.

This, I believe, may be our greatest shortcoming, the enormous obstructing boulder in the river. The longstanding and enduring confidence in our own ability to see what's right and to do it has robbed us of the resources we most need. It has placed a hold on our inheritance. It has stolen our birthright. It has so constricted the flow of the river that we have forgotten there once was a gushing spring.

Over time, we have gotten used to the drought. The trickling stream has come to feel normal. We have lost all memory of the Spirit Waters rushing from the earth, lifegiving and abundant. Of what use are these bountiful resources if we cannot access them? They certainly won't help us much if we don't know how to use them or if we can't remember they were ever ours in the first place.

But here is the good news. We have within our story another resource, a two-pronged, interconnected, sacramental promise and power—our seventh resource here, the one that can unlock all the rest. The difficult part is that before we can grasp it, we will have to embrace the very thing we have been putting off till now. We will have to face our own death.

Nevertheless, it's right here, right in front of us, our greatest resource. It has been in our traveling kit all along. Since the Blue Hole. And long before.

The words are familiar. Most of us can quote the defining verses without even opening a Bible. "They were pricked in their hearts and said to Peter and the other apostles, 'Brothers, what shall we do?'"

Ah, the sermons I have heard where those words were spoken. They number into the hundreds, surely. The Pentecost after Christ ascended to heaven. Thousands of pilgrims gathered in Jerusalem, hearing the apostles in their own tongues.

"Repent and be baptized every one of you," Peter told them, "in the name of Jesus Christ for the forgiveness of sins. And you will receive the gift of the Holy Spirit."

Or these words from Paul to the Romans, "What shall we say then? Shall we continue in sin that grace may abound? By no means. How can we who died to sin go on living in it? Do you not know that those of us who were baptized into Christ Jesus were baptized into his death?"

Or this: "On the night he was betrayed, Jesus took bread, and when he had given thanks, he broke it and said, 'Take, eat, this is my body, which is broken for you.' In the same manner, he also took the cup after supper, saying, 'This cup is the new covenant of my blood. This do, as often as you drink it, in remembrance of me.'"

For many of us over a certain age, hearing these words is comfort food for our souls. We feel grounded, centered. It's like climbing up a ladder into our attic and spotting an old, dusty cedar chest in the corner. You have a vague recollection, a flicker of a memory. You carefully open the lid, and there on top are your own child's baby clothes. You can still smell the talcum powder. The memories are vivid, powerful. You know where you are. And who you are.

Whatever else might be said about Churches of Christ—rightly or wrongly, for good and for ill—these churches have believed in baptism and the Lord's Supper. These events are nothing short of God's miraculous inbreaking, our life-changing encounter with God. Baptism and table are who we are. They are key to our story.

We can hardly understand salvation or church apart from stories about water and a table. We are not unique in this understanding, even though we have sometimes claimed we were. But few groups have insisted on baptism and Supper with quite the same tenacity or resolve.

The word we have often used to describe the importance of baptism and Supper is that they are essential. And they are. Not as a work or a step or a duty but because they are elemental and indispensable, crucial threads in the fabric of the gospel. They are essential in the way that death is essential to life.

Here is our compass. Here is our center. Until we grasp—no, that's not right—until we are grasped by the power and vision of baptism and Supper, the other resources we have been given won't help us much. But for baptism and Supper to matter, what we mean by them will have to change.

Churches of Christ have always claimed that baptism and weekly communion are important pieces of our life in Christ. But we have too often missed the power of our own teaching—not because we have emphasized them too much but, rather, too little. By focusing on the *requirement* of baptism and Supper rather than their *essence*, we have undershot our target. We have aimed too low.

When churches focus primarily or exclusively on the externals of baptism and Supper—the how-and-when, the what-age, how-often, what-elements, what-order, and who-is-eligible questions—something vital is missing, something connected to the gospel itself. It is not enough to say the Bible tells us to do it so we better do it. Obedience is no small thing, of course. It is necessary, but by itself it misses the larger point. Scripture simply does not teach a God-said-it-I-believe-it-that-settles-it theology. The what and how are always rooted in the divine why.

And the why of baptism and Supper is rooted in death and resurrection, in self-emptying and self-sacrifice, in subsuming our will under the will of God, in relinquishing our own power so that Christ's power might reign in us. Baptism and Supper are crucial not simply because they are commanded but because they are transformative. They change us. They empower us to serve others ahead of ourselves. Baptism and Supper form us into a people who look like and act like Jesus. They defy death, not because death is avoided but because death is embraced.

Baptism and Supper compel us to see the world differently, to see our neighbors differently. If Christ has taken our brokenness and, through his own death, healed us, we have little choice but to see and touch the broken souls around us—not by working to teach them properly so that they may understand things rightly but out of compassion for their woundedness, which we, of all people, should know something about.

For that reason, baptism and Supper should forever change how we view evangelism. At its most basic, evangelism is not about persuading but good-news-ing, not about instructing but healing, not about correctness but surrender. Baptism is not so much the goal of evangelism but its starting place—its catalyst, its urgency, and its heart. Our death and resurrection, inaugurated in baptism and renewed in the Supper, make us inevitably a people of good news, which makes evangelism not an occasional teaching activity by a handful of eager members but the lived experience of the whole church.

In baptism, we die to our own little worlds, die to what we want, to being in control, to getting our way. We are born again, to be sure, but we are also born into something new—more sacrificial, more caring, more forgiving, more aware, more hopeful, more humble, more Christlike.

The Lord's Supper, likewise, is an unrelenting renewal of our death and new life. Each time we take the bread and the cup, our baptismal commitment is reembraced, our surrender is reaffirmed, our eyes are reopened. At the table we not only proclaim Christ's death until he comes; we proclaim our own. Christ's death and ours become one. We don't take communion simply because the disciples did it a long time ago. We do it because of what happens there, of who we become there, because the same power that rolled the stone away from Christ's tomb rolls the stone away from our hearts, here and now.

And if God can roll the stone away, God can resurrect a dead church.

God can take a people divided by their beliefs or desires, by their selfishness and pettiness and willfulness, by their pride and passions, and in the name of Jesus make that people one. God can restore our longings and our hope. God can make us generous and holy. God can. Not because we understood everything correctly or did everything right. We didn't. We can't. But because God, by God's very nature, is a roll-back-the-stone-and-open-the-whole-universe-to-the-glory-of-his-resurrected-son kind of God. The kind of God who takes dead faith and resurrects it. Who breathes a holy gust into the lifeless lungs of dead churches.

In the face of that kind of God, we can receive with joy the resources God has provided, the gifts God has given us. We can be peacemakers. We can be partners in God's restorative work. We can read and think and change our minds. We can be harmonious. We can serve others with Christ's own mercy. We can live by the power of the Spirit, fully aware that we are strangers here, that no government, no nation, no political party, no church can save the world. God gave us only one Savior, God's own Son who died for us so that we might die for others.

Those are the resources God gave us, drawn from the Spirit Waters of the Blue Hole. We may have forgotten them, but they were never lost. They were just buried awhile. Turns out, so were we. And God has a good track record with buried things.

At the beginning of our journey, I asked a question about whether Churches of Christ are going to die. At the time I said, I don't know. I'd like to take another run at that.

Yes. Yes, they are. One way or the other these churches are going to die.

They will figure out how to live together and love one another despite their differences; they will learn to distinguish the heart of the gospel from the things they like or want; they will join in Christ's death, embrace Christ's sacrifice, and give themselves up for the sake of others; or they will weaken and diminish, year by year, issue by issue, fight by fight, until all that remains is a casket and a funeral.

Either way, death will be required. But that shouldn't come as a surprise. It's what baptism and Supper have been teaching us all along. What's needed is courage, because what churches are facing now is the crisis of our lifetimes.

Stop for a moment. Set aside the demands and busyness of church. Still your heart long enough to listen. Can you hear it? Out in the distance. Barely audible. The sound of lament. A requiem for the dead. Powerful words of mourning and remembrance. An elegy for your church. For you.

Let the words of this funeral sermon—spoken over you, about you—rest on your heart for a little while. Welcome the words if you can, though they may be painful. But do not grieve for long, because God resurrects dead churches, no matter the cause, even when we are the ones responsible for our own destruction. We should have done things differently. We should have listened better and loved more. We should have chosen death by discipleship rather than death by self-immolation. The demise of our own church because of our own bad choices is hard to bear. But the road to humility has many on-ramps. God has a way of getting us to our knees even when we chose poorly, even when we didn't know we needed it.

Our churches are facing death. Your church. My church. But here's the good news. "Facing death," Michael Jinkins has said, "does hold the possibility . . . that the church may face up to its identity, its vocation, and its responsibility, may own its baptism and offer up its existence in the Spirit of Christ."[8]

But how? How do we own our own baptism? How do we claim our identity? What does offering up our existence in the Spirit of Christ look like? Where do we start? What will it take?

Let me tell you a story.

At the pool known as Bethesda, Jesus came across a lame man who stayed all day by the water. Not in the water, mind you, just near it. Over to the side. Several steps away from danger. Or from needing to do anything. Or risking anything. He was just observing. Waiting. Hour by hour. Every day.

"Do you want to be healed?" Jesus asked him.

"Well, sir, I have no one to put me in the pool," the man said. "And when I start to go, someone comes and steps in front of me." Someone else always seems to be getting in my way. Something is always stopping me. I know things are not great, but I'm not to blame, you see. It's not my fault that I can't get well.

Sure, I want my church to be better. But what can I do to make that happen? Someone is always stepping in front of me, messing things up, making church frustrating. Why can't the elders do something? Why can't the preacher make things better? I'm tired of being unhappy with church. Do I have to feel upset all the time? I like things the way they used to be. Isn't it okay to just want to sing some songs I like for once? How much more do I have to give up? What are our options here? Is there not a consultant we could bring in? A book we could read? Couldn't some great preacher come in and inspire us to do better?

Jesus saw.

The lame man.

Sitting.

All day.

By the water.

He asked him,

"Do you want to be healed?"

Cloudburst of Grace

To be honest, none of us were all that excited about seeing another church.

It was the mid-1990s. I was a young faculty member. About a dozen graduate students were with me and two fellow professors. We had spent several weeks in England and Scotland studying church history and Christian worship. Our sojourn together was nearing its end.[1]

Over the previous weeks, we had been inside a lot of churches. All of them were interesting in the way old churches often are. But we had seen about enough. These great edifices felt distant, removed from our world. They were artifacts of another age, more like museums than vibrant communities of faith.

But the church on this day's itinerary, just north of downtown Edinburgh, was relatively new. New in the European sense. Only a couple hundred years old or so.

The church, in its day, had been one of the independent churches in Scotland that had so significantly influenced Thomas and Alexander Campbell. You may remember glancing at this group earlier in our story. This meetinghouse was part of the Glasite community, an independent congregation begun by John Glas who influenced the Campbells who, well, you know the rest.

Our coach turned the corner onto Barony Street and stopped in front of a fairly ordinary building, constructed from sturdy gray stones, nestled in between some old offices and homes. It wasn't until we entered the sanctuary that everything became clear.

After having walked through countless ancient churches and monasteries, with high arched ceilings and underground burial vaults for kings and nobility, this Glasite meetinghouse felt different. It seemed strangely familiar. The room was filled with row after row of plain wooden pews facing a small stage and a prominent pulpit. If there had been a baptistery with a painting of the Jordan River on the back wall, I would have sworn I had entered my grandparents' old church in Sweetwater, Texas.

We looked around the room, taking it in. This felt like home. The old churches we had toured felt distant, but these people we recognized. They had been our spiritual ancestors. We had come from people like this.

We sat quietly in the pews for a while, thinking, remembering. We sang a hymn. A few of us wiped tears from our eyes.

What a sweet, touching story. Except for one thing. At the time we stopped by this church on our tour of Edinburgh, there were only three members of the Glasite congregation left. Three elderly women. Worship at the meetinghouse had shut down several years earlier. By the time our group visited the place, the women were too frail to attend.

For decades, this church had hung on for dear life, with declining membership and increasing isolation from others. By the late twentieth century, it was in spiritual hospice care. All these good, sweet members didn't want anything to change. They didn't want to do anything different than what their people had always done. They liked the way things were. How they did things seemed good and right. It seemed like the gospel. It's who they were.

They tenaciously preserved the status quo until the church finally died. But there was no funeral. No pallbearers. No one stood at the cemetery singing "In the Sweet By and By" next to a freshly dug grave.

Today, more than two decades later, the three women are themselves dead and gone. The building has been sold and renovated. The old meetinghouse is now the proud home of the Ingleby Gallery. You can go there today and admire many wonderful artists and exhibitions.

But there is no church there. Not anymore.

Will Churches of Christ have a future? It's hard to tell. This once-vibrant movement is on the decline, at least on the surface, at least in America. The evidence is pretty clear. Membership numbers are dropping. Polarization is increasing. Congregations are having to make hard decisions about who they are and what they do, about what is gospel and what is not. The future of these churches will depend on what each congregation decides is important. There are choices to make, and choices always have consequences.

There will be many who will insist on keeping things the way they are. Or the way they remember them being back in a once-golden age. They don't want things to change. Church as they have done it seems like gospel to them. They're not going to give that up. And so, before too long, they will die.

But don't be overly harsh about such churches. These are good Christian brothers and sisters. They don't need or deserve to be judged. We should love and honor them. They and their churches should be able to die in God's care and with our gratitude.

But I'm not ready for my church to be turned into an art gallery. Not yet. God is still in the kingdom business and will continue to be—with or without me, with or without the church I'm a member of. God is not waiting on Churches of Christ to figure things out. God is already at work in the world. We have to decide whether we will join God there. It will be a hard decision. The cost will be high. Much is at stake. But this I know—before all is said and done, a great turning will be required.

One of the first Greek words most ministry students learn is *metanoia*. Repentance. The word literally means to think differently, to change one's mind or one's mindset. In other words, to turn. To repent means to turn around, to turn back.

Dying churches, which is to say all our churches, need a hefty dose of *metanoia*. In humility we need to turn back. In submission we need to repent. Without it, we will not become the person or the church God has called us to be.

My concern is that when we think about repentance, if we think about it at all, we tend to see it as something *we* do. Or that we once did a long time ago. As if repentance were a human work, a step we must take on the way to our salvation. Then, when we have completed our work, the purpose of our repentance has been accomplished. Done. Behind us.

But that misses the point. That's not what repentance is. There's no gospel in that. No grace. No place for the working of God.

Repentance is not simply an act of mobilizing our own will to do things better. It's not about finding the inner strength to make a 180-degree turn so that we can work our way back to God, so that we might somehow deserve the resurrection we have been promised. Repentance requires a different sort of move.

Recently, I heard the singer John Michael Talbot suggest what I think is a more gospeled understanding of *metanoia*. The sinner—the church, I—is standing under a great downpour of God's blessings. All the time. Every day. We are thirsty. Our needs are great. We stretch out our arms to the heavens. But our cup is turned downward, toward earth, toward ourselves. We need water, but we cannot drink. We need God's mercy, but our cup remains empty.

Repent! Turn your cup over!

That's the turning we need. God is not sitting somewhere in a distant heaven waiting for us to solve our own problems. God is here, now, among us, lavishing us in a torrent of grace. God is in our neighborhoods, in our cities and communities, even when we are largely absent. God does not abandon us when we turn our churches into businesses and manage ourselves to death. Rather, God still sees us, still pursues us. God is still raising us from the dead. And when it comes to the resurrection we need, God is not stingy. That's good news, because our needs are great.

We are tired. We don't know what to do now. Our future is unsure. We are seeking our homeland, but we are not home yet. We will need sustenance for the journey.

We are thirsty. The drought has already lasted too long. We walk down an old path, trying to recall the way, stopping, looking for forgotten landmarks, wandering off the trail then retracing our steps, pushing forward in search of the spring. At last we come to an old stone well, almost hidden beneath a tangle of trees and vines. A small stream flows out one side, spilling through a chute beneath the stones.

We stand cautiously at water's edge, listening, waiting.

At last we step into the stream and dip our hands in the cool waters. Then, perhaps, we will remember.

There was a day, not all that long ago, when God opened up the earth at a handshake and a song, when people of profound disagreement chose peace over division, mercy over judgment. On a cold New Year's weekend, the gathered Christians who had come from different traditions, whose church lives had centered around different practices and beliefs, claimed their baptism. If Christ had died for them, they would choose to die for one another, even in the midst of their differences.

Then the next day, the first day of the New Year, the first day of the week, they sat down at table. Together. Brothers and sisters. That Christ might bless their union. That in the sharing of the bread and the drinking of the cup they might claim Christ's death. That Christ might place the power and character of his own resurrection within their hearts.

Here is where it happened. It is here that clear, fresh water from a massive underground reservoir of grace poured from the earth, offering life and peace, creating a people and a future. Here, at the Blue Hole.

This is our story. We are still that people. We know the way home.

Now, today, even in our brokenness, in our fears and discouragement, in our squabbles and disputes, in the confidence we have placed in our own ability to figure things out and do things right, when we aren't seeking it or even know we need it, God is raining down upon us a roaring, restoring, extravagant, glorious, lifegiving, peace-pursuing, future-changing, blood-drenched, Spirit-soaked cloudburst of grace.

For Christ's sake, turn your cup over.

Acknowledgments

The idea for this book began in 2012 with two conversations that took place just a few days apart. The occasions were very different—one was in a meeting, the other was a chance encounter in a hallway. But the conversations were close enough in time and topic that they generated a spark of imagination that resulted, nine years later, in this book.

First, Royce Money, the chancellor of Abilene Christian University, asked if I would consider writing a book that highlighted what's best about Churches of Christ. We had had many conversations over the years about the highest values and greatest strengths of the heritage we share. What I began to write in response to Royce's prompting ultimately resulted in the resources discussed in chapter 5.

A few days later, Doug Foster and I bumped into each other just outside his office door. Doug is one of the leading Stone-Campbell Movement scholars in the country. His recent biography of Alexander Campbell (Eerdmans, 2020) continues to receive wide acclaim. More important to me, Doug is one of my closest friends. The conversation that day, like so many of our discussions over the years, was about the history of our people and the state of our churches.

Was there a turning point, I asked him, when Churches of Christ, which had originally been devoted to unity, became something very different? Obviously, this shift did not happen at a single point in time. And the transition away from unity had begun to take place almost from the beginning, at least for a segment of the movement. But Doug told me a story that day out in the hallway that I had never heard before and could not stop thinking about. One of the pallbearers at T. B. Larimore's funeral in 1929 had been Foy E. Wallace Jr. My head almost exploded. Two divergent arcs of history intersected on that solemn occasion—a symbolic passing of the mantle of leadership from the peacemaker to the polemicist, anticipating what would happen to Churches of Christ in the decades that followed. What Doug told me that day would become the hinge story of the book. It was the first of many insights I would receive from him by the time the book was finished. So, while there are many people whose ideas and support made this book possible, Royce and Doug played key roles in its existence in the first place. I'm grateful for their encouragement and their friendship.

The entire nature of the book changed when I moved to Dallas in 2013 and began to work for the Foundation for Community Empowerment, addressing issues of poverty and race in severely disadvantaged neighborhoods. Social justice suddenly became a lived reality for me rather than a theological construct. Don Williams, who was both my boss and my friend, was like a bolt of lightning in my life, exhibiting a passion for justice and mercy I had never experienced before. It dawned on me only gradually that Don's commitments to the blighted neighborhoods of South Dallas, which continue to be victimized by the moneyed and the powerful, were actually in continuity with Church of Christ instincts rather than in contrast to them. That revelation significantly shaped my discussion of generosity in chapter 5. Don's encouragement to write and his penetrating suggestions on an earlier draft of the manuscript had no small impact on the final outcome.

During my years in Dallas, few relationships impacted me like those at my church home. Metro Christ's Church in Cedar Hill, far south Dallas County, became my spiritual family unlike any I had experienced before. Dr. Kenneth Greene, the church's founder and senior pastor, and First Lady Mary Greene had been my friends for years. Because of them, I committed myself to this congregation as my church home before I even moved to Dallas. But I was not prepared for what would take place within my heart. I began to experience from the inside out what my White culture and my church heritage had done to Black families and churches. I saw firsthand the enduring impact of slavery and racism in America. And yet, somehow, these Black Christians embraced this White stranger in their midst. And loved him. And changed him.

How could people so oppressed, so marginalized, so hurt by people, well, like me, be so gracious, so welcoming, so joyful? Because of them, I became a different person, a different kind of Christian. I have no words strong enough to sufficiently express my gratitude to my Metro family. During the years I lived and worshiped there, I wrote almost nothing on the book. Everything in my life was being changed. By the time I left, five years after first walking through the church doors, my writing project was no longer a book about history but something more personal. Writing it was now not a choice but a matter of urgency.

Upon my arrival in San Antonio in 2017, the book began to take on a new shape and thrust. After my sojourn in Dallas, my many years of conversations with leaders in the global missional church movement now seemed especially relevant. For more than twenty years, Patrick Keifert, the long-time professor of theology at Luther Seminary and executive director of Church Innovations, had challenged pretty much everything I knew about church systems and congregational change. More importantly, through those years Pat had become my pastor, my confidant, my friend.

Mostly because of Pat, I found myself having exhilarating conversations about the future of the church with folks like Pat Taylor Ellison, Al Roxburgh, Lois Barrett, George Hunsberger, Craig Van Gelder, and other missional leaders. The annual retreats of the "Ichtheology" group, a gathering of national church leaders at Yellowstone National Park initiated by Pat, where a dozen or more of us flyfished for cutthroat trout half the time and talked about the future of the church the other half, were transformational for me. Among the regulars were Wes Granberg-Michaelson, Brian McLaren, Jim Johnson, Becca Stelle, Dick Welscott, Kathy Brown, Bruce Stevens, Nigel Rooms, Ben Ries, Aaron Metcalf, Mark Wiebe, Kent Bogle, Danielle Keifert, and Elaine Heath. All of these ministers and friends greatly influenced how I thought about ministry, theology, and church. The insights I gained from those conversations began to shape the book toward something larger than a discussion about the history and future of my tribe of Christians, to something that might be of benefit to any Christian community.

From the time Lesa and I first arrived in San Antonio, Lynn and Carolyn Anderson have taken care of us like an older brother and sister. Mere thanks for their love and friendship is not adequate. Carolyn's transparent walk of faith and her thoughtful care for the two of us have been lifegiving. Lynn for more than fifty years has been an inspiration and encouragement to me, as he has to literally hundreds of other ministers. I doubt there is another person in Churches of Christ this past half century who has had a greater positive impact on these churches. If they are spiraling toward their own demise, it is not because of Lynn. Since retiring to San Antonio many years ago, Lynn has met with a group of local ministers every month, encouraging and mentoring them. Not too long after I arrived, I was welcomed to this gathering of preachers, whose insights and ministries have contributed greatly to my understanding of what vibrant communities of faith might look like. So, thanks to my fellow travelers David Allen, Mark Abshier, John Harp, Marvin Bryant, Mic Biesboer, Chris Palmer, Bob Grigg, Tommy Le-Fan, and Jimmy Sportsman.

In early 2018, the Northside Church of Christ in San Antonio became not only a spiritual home but a fertile resource for ideas that greatly informed the writing of this book. I am grateful for the elders, who invited me to serve as the executive minister for the congregation in mid-2020 and who shepherd this Christian family with purpose and care, for my fellow ministers—Tina Wharton, David Allen, John Hodges, Nicole Largent, Bruce Utley, Jenni Jones, Ben and Rachel Crain, and David Ingram—who have inspired me by their discipleship and have given me joy and encouragement most every day, and for the community of believers with whom I am honored to work and worship.

Few people have influenced my thinking about the history of the Stone-Campbell Movement—or, frankly, most any topic—as much as Leonard Allen has. Since being graduate students together and co-ministers during our doctoral years at the University of Iowa, and through decades of friendship, my conversations with Leonard have shaped my understanding of theology, history, and ministry immeasurably. There were times in the writing of this book that I thought I would walk away from it. I simply couldn't find the connections I was looking for. Leonard's insights provided important pieces to the puzzle, and his encouragement motivated me to stay at it.

During the years of writing, several friends made particularly helpful comments or critiques, all of which made the book better. These include Sean Palmer, Dan Bouchelle, Jim and Mignon Martin, Mark Tucker, Grady King, John Frias, Ken Preslar, Philip Slate, John Mark Hicks, Richard Hughes, Newell Williams, Ross Thomson, John York, Gary Holloway, Rick Atchley, Chris Seidman, and David Fleer. The research of Stan Granberg and Tim Woodroof about the state of Churches of Christ in America has contributed greatly to my understanding of the nature of the crises these churches face.

I particularly want to thank Bob Randolph, the long-time chaplain of the institute at MIT, whose church in Brookline has given me more insights than Bob ever knew about what a healthy community of faith might look like, whose stories of the Santa Ana church made this body of Christians whom I knew little about come alive in my imagination, and whose wisdom, kindness, support, and friendship have made him one of the most important and most influential people in my life. I'm also grateful for my old professor and friend Tom Olbricht, whose perceptive critiques of the book, whose generous words of encouragement, and whose vivid stories of earlier days we shared together were made all the more poignant by his death shortly after our last correspondence.

My three children are not only sources of joy to me; they also provide me critical perspective on our times and culture, insights into language and literature, and an understanding of what church and discipleship look like for their generation and the ones that follow. My thanks to them and their families—Jessica with Jonathan, Simone, Gabriella, and Etta; Jocelyn with Mark, Margot, Isla, and Benjamin; and Jay with Mary Kate.

Eerdmans Publishing has been a joy to work with. Thanks to editor-in-chief James Ernest for his early and strong support of the manuscript, to Jenny Hoffman (along with freelance copyeditor Christopher Reese), Amy Kent, Michael Debowski, Laura Bardolph Hubers, Alexis Cutler, and especially Trevor Thompson, who believed in this project and in me from the beginning. I am grateful.

Finally, no one impacted the writing of this book or its author more than my wife Lesa. Lesa was touched and changed, as I had been, by our experiences in the ravaged neighborhoods of South Dallas, among the homeless who lived in the parks and under the bridges downtown near our home, and especially among our dear family at the Metro church who welcomed and loved her without restraint. When we moved to San Antonio, Lesa provided the primary support for our household while I wrote. She listened with patience as I read long passages to her, responding always with kindness and always with candor.

Lesa's academic disciplines are education and communication disorders, so her scholarly expertise did not overlap much with theology, history, or ministry, allowing her to read the things I was writing like a church member would. She wouldn't let me get away with being high-minded or vague. She cut through the pretense. She reminded me that not everyone loves history and that I needed to make my stories more accessible, more vivid, more personal. Most importantly, Lesa loves Jesus and cares about the church. Her comments pushed me to be more practical, to write not primarily to scholars but to the friends and neighbors we know and love. I am grateful to her for walking the Blue Hole with me, for loving this city and this church with me, for her love and partnership in the gospel and in life.

I am indebted to these friends and family who, in various ways and over many years, helped shape what I have written. I pray that this book may find resonance within communities of faith who are willing to embrace their own death in search of the resurrection only Christ can give.

Notes

Chapter 1

1. All of these statistics are from Stanley E. Granberg, "A Case Study of Growth and Decline: The Churches of Christ, 2006–2016," *Great Commission Research Journal* 10, no. 1 (Fall 2018): 88–110.

2. Tim Woodroof and Stanley Granberg, "Churches of Christ in 2050," *Interim Ministry Partners*, https://interimministrypartners.com/resources, 2019.

3. Michael Jinkins, *The Church Faces Death: Ecclesiology in a Post-Modern Context* (Oxford: Oxford University Press, 1999), 14.

4. David H. Freedman, *Wrong: Why Experts Keep Failing Us and How to Know When Not to Trust Them* (New York: Little, Brown, 2010).

5. Ronald Heifetz, *The Practice of Adaptive Leadership: Tools and Tactics for Changing Your Organization and World* (Boston: Harvard Business Press, 2009). For other resources by Heifetz, see https://cambridge-leadership.com.

6. 1 Corinthians 1:18–25.

Chapter 2

1. F. D. Srygley, *Smiles and Tears, or Larimore and His Boys* (Nashville: Gospel Advocate, 1889), 58.

2. Srygley, *Smiles and Tears*, 93.

3. "Brother Larimore's Tribute to Mrs. Silena Moore Holman," *Gospel Advocate* 57 (October 14, 1915): 1027–28.

4. O. P. Spiegel, "An Open Letter to T. B. Larimore," *Christian Standard* 33 (July 10, 1897): 891.

5. T. B. Larimore, "Reply to O. P. Spiegel's Open Letter," *Christian Standard* 33 (July 24, 1897): 965.

6. T. B. Larimore, "Suggestions and Selections," *Gospel Advocate*, February 29, 1888, 3. Emphasis in original.

7. Larimore, "Suggestions," 3.

8. "Two Christian Leaders Go On," editorial, *Christian Standard*, March 30, 1929, 297.

9. Michael Shermer, *How We Believe: The Search for God in the Age of Science* (New York: W. H. Freeman/Henry Holt, 2000), xv.

Chapter 3

1. "Georgetown / Scott County History," https://georgetownky.com/about-us.

2. Minutes of the West Lexington (Kentucky) Presbytery, January 1801, quoted in Robert Davidson, *History of the Presbyterian Church in the State of Kentucky: With a Preliminary Sketch of the Church in the Valley of Virginia* (New York: Robert Carter, 1847), 337.

3. Robert Richardson, *Memoirs of Alexander Campbell* (Philadelphia: J. B. Lippincott & Co, 1868), 96.

4. A contemporary singing of this hymn might substitute "family" for "brethren." This hymn can be sung to several tunes: NETTLETON ("Come, Thou Fount of Every Blessing"), HOLY MANNA ("Brethren, We Have Met to Worship"), BEACH SPRING ("Come, Ye Sinners, Poor and Wretched"), AUSTRIAN HYMN ("Glorious Things of Thee Are Spoken"), Beecher ("Love Divine, All Loves Excelling"), or ODE TO JOY ("Joyful, Joyful, We Adore Thee").

Chapter 4

1. Ovid, *Metamorphoses* 1.126–154, trans. Charles Martin (New York: W. W. Norton, 2004).

2. Cornelius Plantinga, *Not the Way It's Supposed to Be: A Breviary of Sin* (Grand Rapids: Eerdmans, 1995).

3. Foy E. Wallace Jr., "The Gospel Guardian," *The Gospel Guardian*, October 1935, 2.

4. Edward J. Robinson, *I Was Under a Heavy Burden: The Life of Annie C. Tuggle* (Abilene: ACU Press, 2011), 11.

5. Robinson, *Heavy Burden*, 51–52.

6. Robinson, *Heavy Burden*, 42.

7. Foy E. Wallace Jr., "Negro Meetings for White People," *Bible Banner*, March 1941, 7.

8. Kathryn Schulz, *Being Wrong: Adventures in the Margin of Error* (New York: Harper-Collins, 2010). Also see Kathryn Schulz's TED talk "On Being Wrong," March 2011: https://www.ted.com/talks/kathryn_schulz_on_being_wrong?language=en.

9. Lawrence Wright, *God Save Texas: A Journey into the Soul of the Lone Star State* (New York: Alfred A. Knopf, 2018), 5.

10. W. Hirst et al., "A Ten-Year Follow-Up of a Study of Memory for the Attack of September 11, 2001: Flashbulb Memories and Memories for Flashbulb Events," *Journal of Experimental Psychology: General* 144, no. 3 (June 2015): 604–23.

11. For a fuller discussion of freedom and conformity in primitivist churches, see the groundbreaking work of Richard T. Hughes and C. Leonard Allen, *Illusions of Innocence: Protestant Primitivism in America, 1630–1875* (Chicago: University of Chicago Press, 1988).

12. Hughes and Allen, *Illusions of Innocence*, 80, 81.

13. G. H. Orchard, *A Concise History of Foreign Baptists* (London: George Wightman, Paternoster Row, 1838), v.

14. Cited in Leroy Garrett, "Alexander Campbell," in *The Encyclopedia of the Stone-Campbell Movement*, ed. Douglas A. Foster et al. (Grand Rapids: Eerdmans, 2004), 121.

15. Alexander Campbell, "A Restoration of the Ancient Order of Things, No. I," *The Christian Baptist*, February 7, 1825, 136.

16. Alexander Campbell, "A Restoration of the Ancient Order of Things—No. II," *The Christian Baptist*, March 7, 1825, 133.

17. *Christian Baptist*, August 7, 1826, 26. Cited in Leroy Garrett, "Alexander Campbell," in Foster et al., *Encyclopedia of the Stone-Campbell Movement*, 121.

18. "Replication No. II. to Spencer Clack," *Christian Baptist*, September 3, 1827, 369–70.

19. See, for example, Ronald Inglehart and Wayne E. Baker, "Modernization, Cultural Change, and the Persistence of Traditional Values," *American Sociological Review* 65, no. 1 (February 2000): 19–51; Roy Sudderby and Royston Greenwood, "Rhetorical Strategies of Legitimacy," *Administrative Science Quarterly* 50, no. 1 (March 2005): 35–67; Lynne G. Zucker, "The Role of Institutionalization in Cultural Persistence," *American Sociological Review* 42, no. 5 (October 1977): 726–43; Michael J. Chandler and Travis Proulx, "Personal Persistence and Persistent Peoples: Continuities in the Lives of Individual and Whole Cultural Communities," in *Self Continuity: Individual and Collective Perspectives*, ed. Fabio Sani (New York: Psychology Press, 2008).

20. Richard T. Hughes, *Reviving the Ancient Faith: The Story of Churches of Christ in America* (Grand Rapids: Eerdmans, 1996), 56.

21. Henry Errett, "On Baptism," cited in Foster et al., *Encyclopedia of the Stone-Campbell Movement*, s.v. "Scott, Walter."

22. See the seminal work of James L. Gorman, *Among the Early Evangelicals: The Transatlantic Origins of the Stone-Campbell Movement* (Abilene: ACU Press, 2017).

23. Leroy Garrett, *The Stone-Campbell Movement: The Story of the American Restoration Movement* (Joplin, MO: College Press, 1981), 343.

24. David Lipscomb, "I Did Wrong," *Gospel Advocate*, March 13, 1866, 170–71.

25. Hughes, *Reviving the Ancient Faith*, 180; italics in original.

26. John Mark Hicks and Bobby Valentine, *Kingdom Come: Embracing the Spiritual Legacy of David Lipscomb and James Harding* (Abilene: Leafwood, 2006), 18.

27. C. R. Nichol and R. L. Whiteside, *Sound Doctrine*, vol. 1 (Clifton, TX: Nichol Publishing, 1920), 153.

28. Barton W. Stone, "The Retrospect," *Christian Messenger* 7 (October 1833): 314–16.

29. Alison Gopnik, *The Gardener and the Carpenter: What the New Science of Child Development Tells Us about the Relationship Between Parents and Children* (New York: Farrar, Straus and Giroux, 2016).

Chapter 5

1. Phyllis Tickle, *The Great Emergence: How Christianity Is Changing and Why* (Grand Rapids: Baker, 2008).

2. www.churchinnovations.org. See also Patrick Keifert and Wesley Granberg-Michaelson, *How Change Comes to Your Church* (Grand Rapids: Eerdmans, 2019).

3. Paul G. Hiebert, *Anthropological Reflections on Missiological Issues* (Grand Rapids: Baker, 1994).

4. John C. Stevens, *No Ordinary University: The Story of a City Set on a Hill* (Abilene: ACU Press, 1998), 328.

5. Hugo Mercier and Dan Sperber, *The Enigma of Reason* (Cambridge: Harvard University Press, 2017).

6. David Lipscomb, "The Cholera and the Christian Religion," *Gospel Advocate* 15, no. 28 (17 July 1873): 649–53.

7. Larry M. James, *The Wealth of the Poor: How Valuing Every Neighbor Restores Hope in Our Cities* (Abilene: ACU Press, 2013).

8. Jinkins, *The Church Faces Death*, 29.

Epilogue

1. I shared a briefer version of this story in *The Crux of the Matter: Crisis, Tradition, and the Future of Churches of Christ*, coauthored with Jeff W. Childers and Douglas A. Foster (Abilene: ACU Press, 2002), 259.

Key Resources

Ackerman, Kenneth D. *Dark Horse: The Surprise Election and Political Murder of President James A. Garfield*. Falls Church, VA: Viral History Press, 2011.

Allen, C. Leonard. *Distant Voices: Discovering a Forgotten Past for a Changing Church*. Abilene: ACU Press, 1993.

———. *Things Unseen: Churches of Christ In (and After) the Modern Age*. Abilene: Leafwood, 2004.

Allen, C. Leonard, and Danny Gray Swick. *Participating in God's Life: Two Crossroads for Churches of Christ*. Orange, CA: New Leaf Books, 2001.

Allen, C. Leonard, and Richard T. Hughes. *Discovering Our Roots: The Ancestry of Churches of Christ*. Abilene: ACU Press, 1988.

Baker, William R., ed. *Evangelicalism and the Stone-Campbell Movement*. Vol. 1. Downers Grove: IVP, 2002.

———. *Evangelicalism and the Stone-Campbell Movement*. Vol. 2, *Engaging Basic Christian Doctrine*. Abilene: ACU Press, 2006.

Carson, Glenn Thomas, Douglas A. Foster, and Clinton J. Holloway. *One Church: A Bicentennial Celebration of Thomas Campbell's Declaration and Address*. Abilene: Leafwood, 2008.

Casey, Michael W. *Saddlebags, City Streets, and Cyberspace: A History of Preaching in the Churches of Christ*. Abilene: ACU Press, 1995.

Casey, Michael W., and Douglas A. Foster. *The Stone-Campbell Movement: An International Religious Tradition*. Knoxville: University of Tennessee Press, 2002.

Childers, Jeff W., Douglas A. Foster, and Jack R. Reese. *The Crux of the Matter: Cri-

sis, Tradition, and the Future of Churches of Christ. Heart of the Restoration Series 1. Abilene: ACU Press, 2002.

Childers, Jeff W., and Frederick D. Aquino. *Unveiling Glory: Visions of Christ's Transforming Presence.* Heart of the Restoration Series 3. Abilene: ACU Press, 2003.

Crawford, Wes. *Shattering the Illusion: How African American Churches of Christ Moved from Segregation to Independence.* Abilene: ACU Press, 2013.

Cukrowski, Kenneth L., Mark W. Hamilton, and James W. Thompson. *God's Holy Fire: The Nature and Function of Scripture.* Heart of the Restoration Series 2. Abilene: ACU Press, 2002.

Cummins, D. Duane. *The Disciples: A Struggle for Reformation.* St. Louis: Chalice Press, 2009.

———. *The Disciples Colleges: A History.* St. Louis: CBP Press, 1987.

Daughrity, Dyron B. "Alexander Campbell's View of Baptists." In *Revelation and Leadership in the Kingdom of God: Studies in Honor of Ian Arthur Fair*, edited by Andrei A. Orlov, 47–64. Piscataway, NJ: Gorgias Press, 2020.

Dunnavant, Anthony L., Richard T. Hughes, and Paul M. Blowers. *Founding Vocation and Future Vision: The Self-Understanding of the Disciples of Christ and the Churches of Christ.* St. Louis: Chalice Press, 1999.

Eckstein, Stephen D., Jr. *History of the Churches of Christ in Texas: 1824–1950.* Austin: Firm Foundation, 1963.

Ferguson, Everett. *A Cappella Music in the Public Worship of the Church.* 3rd ed. Abilene: ACU Press, 1999.

Foster, Douglas A. *As Good as the Best: A Sketch of the Life of Theophilus Brown Larimore.* Nashville: Learning Skills, 1984.

———. *A Life of Alexander Campbell.* Grand Rapids: Eerdmans, 2020.

———. *The Story of Churches of Christ.* Abilene: ACU Press, 2013.

———. "The Struggle for Unity During the Period of Division of the Restoration Movement, 1875–1900." PhD diss., Vanderbilt University, 1986.

———. *Will the Cycle Be Unbroken? Churches of Christ Face the 21st Century.* Abilene: ACU Press, 1994.

Foster, Douglas A., Paul M. Blowers, Anthony L. Dunnavant, and D. Newell Williams, eds. *The Encyclopedia of the Stone-Campbell Movement.* Grand Rapids: Eerdmans, 2004.

Garrett, Leroy. *A Lover's Quarrel: An Autobiography—My Pilgrimage of Freedom in Churches of Christ.* Abilene: ACU Press, 2003.

———. *The Stone-Campbell Movement: The Story of the American Restoration Movement*. Joplin, MO: College Press, 1981.

Gorman, James. *Among the Early Evangelicals: The Transatlantic Origins of the Stone-Campbell Movement*. Abilene: ACU Press, 2016.

Harrell, David Edwin, Jr. *The Churches of Christ in the 20th Century: Homer Hailey's Personal Journey of Faith*. Tuscaloosa: University of Alabama Press, 2000.

———. *Quest for a Christian America, 1800–1865: A Social History of the Disciples of Christ*. 2 vols. Tuscaloosa: University of Alabama Press, 1966–73.

Helsabeck, Dennis W., Jr., Gary Holloway, and Douglas A. Foster. *Renewal for Mission: A Concise History of Christian Churches and Churches of Christ*. Abilene: ACU Press, 2009.

Henry, Douglas V., and Michael D. Beaty, eds. *Christianity and the Soul of the University: Faith as a Foundation for Intellectual Community*. Grand Rapids: Baker Academic, 2006.

Herman, Arthur. *How the Scots Invented the Modern World: The True Story of How Western Europe's Poorest Nation Created Our World and Everything in It*. New York: Broadway Books, 2001.

Hicks, John Mark, and Bobby Valentine. *Kingdom Come: Embracing the Spiritual Legacy of David Lipscomb and James Harding*. Abilene: Leafwood, 2006.

Hicks, John Mark, and Gregg Taylor. *Down in the River to Pray: Revisioning Baptism as God's Transforming Work*. Abilene: Leafwood, 2004.

Holloway, Gary, and Douglas A. Foster. *Renewing God's People: A Concise History of Churches of Christ*. Abilene: ACU Press, 2001.

———. *Renewing the World: A Concise Global History of the Stone-Campbell Movement*. Abilene: ACU Press 2015.

Hooper, Robert E. *Crying in the Wilderness: The Life and Influence of David Lipscomb*. Nashville: Lipscomb University, 2001.

———. *A Distinct People: A History of the Churches of Christ in the 20th Century*. West Monroe, LA: Howard Publishing, 1993.

Hughes, Richard T. *The Apocalyptic Origins of Churches of Christ and the Triumph of Modernism*. Abilene: ACU Press, 1993.

———. *Reclaiming a Heritage: Reflections on the Heart, Soul, and Future of Churches of Christ*. Abilene: ACU Press 2001.

———. *Reviving the Ancient Faith: The Story of Churches of Christ in America*. Grand Rapids: Eerdmans, 1996.

Hughes, Richard T., and William B. Adrian. *Models for Christian Higher Education:*

Strategies for Success in the Twenty-First Century. Grand Rapids: Eerdmans, 1997.

Hughes, Richard T., and C. Leonard Allen. *Illusions of Innocence: Protestant Primitivism in America, 1630–1875*. Chicago: University of Chicago Press, 1988.

Hughes, Richard T., Nathan O. Hatch, and David Edwin Harrell Jr. *American Origins of Churches of Christ*. Abilene: ACU Press, 2000.

Hughes, Richard T., and R. L. Roberts. *The Churches of Christ*. Denominations in America 10. Westport, CT: Greenwood Press, 2001.

Jinkins, Michael. *The Church Faces Death: Ecclesiology in a Post-Modern Context*. Oxford: Oxford University Press, 1999.

Love, Mark, Douglas A. Foster, and Randall Harris. *Seeking a Lasting City: The Church's Journey into the Story of God*. Heart of the Restoration Series 4. Abilene: ACU Press, 2005.

Millard, Candice. *Destiny of the Republic: A Tale of Madness, Medicine, and the Murder of a President*. New York: Doubleday, 2011.

Olbricht, Thomas H. *Reflections on My Life in the Kingdom and the Academy*. Eugene, OR: Wipf & Stock, 2012.

Peskin, Allan. *Garfield*. Kent, OH: Kent State University Press, 1978.

Reese, Jack R. *The Body Broken: Embracing the Peace of Christ in a Fragmented Church*. Abilene: Leafwood, 2005.

Robinson, Edward J. *The Fight Is On in Texas: A History of African American Churches of Christ in the Lone Star State, 1865–2000*. Abilene: ACU Press, 2008.

———. *I Was Under a Heavy Burden: The Life of Annie C. Tuggle*. Abilene: ACU Press, 2011.

———. *Show Us How You Do It: Marshall Keeble and the Rise of Black Churches of Christ in the United States, 1914–1968*. Tuscaloosa: University of Alabama Press, 2008.

———. *To Save My Race from Abuse: The Life of Samuel Robert Cassius*. Tuscaloosa: University of Alabama Press, 2007.

Rushford, Jerry. "The Apollos of the West: The Life of John Allen Gano." Master's thesis, Abilene Christian University, 1972.

———. "The Relationship Between James A. Garfield and the Disciples of Christ." PhD diss., University of California Santa Barbara, 1977.

Shaw, John. *Lucretia*. Presidential Wives Series. New York: Nova History Publications. 2004.

Stevens, John C. *No Ordinary University: The History of a City Set on a Hill.* Abilene: ACU Press, 1998.

Tippens, Darryl. *That's Why We Sing: Reclaiming the Wonder of Congregational Singing.* Abilene: Leafwood, 2007.

Toulouse, Mark G. *Walter Scott: A Nineteenth-Century Evangelical.* St. Louis: Chalice Press, 1999.

Toulouse, Mark G., Gary Holloway, and Douglas A. Foster. *Renewing Christian Unity: A Concise History of the Christian Church (Disciples of Christ).* Abilene: ACU Press, 2011.

Tristano, Richard M. *The Origins of the Restoration Movement: An Intellectual History.* Atlanta: Glenmary Research Center, 1988.

Webb, Henry E. *In Search of Christian Unity: A History of the Restoration Movement.* Rev. ed. Abilene: ACU Press, 2003.

Williams, D. Newell. *Barton Stone: A Spiritual Biography.* St. Louis: Chalice Press, 2000.

Williams, D. Newell, ed. *A Case Study of Mainstream Protestantism: The Disciples' Relation to American Culture, 1880–1989.* Grand Rapids: Eerdmans, 1991.

Williams, D. Newell, Douglas A. Foster, and Paul M. Blowers, eds. *The Stone-Campbell Movement: A Global History.* St. Louis: Chalice Press, 2013.

Index

Anderson, Lynn, 78, 112, 125–29, 165
apocalyptic living, 14–15, 203–9, 210, 211, 215

Bacon College, 195
Baptists
  and Churches of Christ, 74, 76, 97, 105, 135, 137, 138, 163
  "Reforming" Baptists, 81, 93, 95, 96
  "Regular" Baptists, 81, 95, 96, 136
Baxter, Batsell Barrett, 112, 128, 166
Bethany College, 148, 156, 196
Blacks
  African American churches, 44, 117, 159, 170, 186, 188
  in America, 40, 43, 117, 122, 200, 201
  and Whites, 24, 54, 55, 78, 107, 118–20, 189
  See also racism
bounded set and centered set, 192–93
Bowser, G. P., 119
Burnet, David S., 156, 158

Campbell, Alexander
  churches, 8, 12, 47, 48, 50, 69, 71, 101, 102, 111, 135–37, 143, 146, 147, 149, 151
  confidence in human ability, 139, 167, 203–5
  divisiveness, 78, 95–96, 99–100, 140, 161, 168, 179, 190
  Holy Spirit, 78, 103, 113–14, 128, 172
  in Ireland and Scotland, 81, 90–92, 195
  restoration, 92, 112, 129, 134, 137–44, 172–74, 190–93
  teaching and leadership, 9, 93, 97–98, 155, 156, 158, 159, 162, 196, 218
  unity, 92, 93, 96, 100, 105–6, 111–12, 134, 138–41, 143, 156, 167, 190
Campbell, Thomas, 71, 83–92, 97–98, 105, 135, 147, 148, 156, 218
Cassius, A. L., 44, 116
Cassius, Samuel Robert, 44, 80, 186
Christian Church (Disciples of Christ), 10, 48, 52, 53, 54, 56, 60, 65, 69, 96, 97, 98, 129, 161, 156, 189
Christian Churches and Churches of Christ (Independent Christian

Churches), 10, 48, 52, 53, 54, 56, 60, 65, 69, 98, 129, 143, 148, 156, 161, 189

Churches of Christ

and the Civil War, 51–55, 65, 141, 155–61

confidence in human ability, 47, 64–65, 174, 205

criticism of, 13–14

decline, 5, 6, 15–17, 29, 37, 181, 209, 219

divisiveness, 52, 65–68, 69, 70–73, 81–82, 88–90, 97–98, 105, 106, 111, 112, 114, 117, 118, 158–61, 170–71, 179, 186, 188–90, 196

doctrine, 153–54, 162–67, 212–15

education, importance of, 39–40, 50, 52, 53, 94, 148, 156, 193–96

Holy Spirit, 78, 128, 207–8

name, 10, 47–48, 96, 97

origins, 36, 47, 75, 83, 111, 129, 135, 139, 142–44, 146, 152, 156, 165, 176–77, 187, 203

restoration, 49, 106, 129, 134, 141–44, 152, 161, 165–67, 172–74, 183, 185, 190, 192, 204, 205

unity, 18, 49, 52, 59, 79–80, 86, 87, 105, 111, 159, 161, 176–77, 179, 183, 185–90, 197–99, 204, 210, 215

death, facing

baptism and Lord's Supper, 49, 212–16

as church, 6, 19–22, 35, 94–95, 111, 176, 180–83, 209, 212, 219

as discipleship, 18, 22–23, 32–35, 66, 177–78, 202, 214–15

and resurrection, 20, 22, 33, 109, 214, 216, 221

Declaration and Address (Thomas Campbell), 85–87, 92

Fanning, Tolbert, 56, 156–57

freedom and conformity, 112, 135–41, 146, 153, 165, 166, 171–72, 177, 196, 198

Gano, John Allen, 8, 9, 98

Gano, Richard Montgomery, 52, 53, 80

Garfield, James

Civil War, 52–53, 155–56, 158

education, 39–40, 52, 93–94, 195–96

family, 40, 50

preaching, 40, 80

unity, 187

generosity, 199–203, 210, 211, 215

Georgetown, Kentucky, 8, 9, 52, 71–74, 81, 98, 99, 100, 195

Gray, Fred, 120

harmony (peacemaking), 12, 18, 72, 100, 177, 196–99, 210, 215

Hazelip, Harold, 112, 127

Herald of Truth, 126–29, 165, 166

Holman, Silena, 57, 80, 161

Holy Spirit, 34, 81, 98, 129, 163, 164, 173, 193, 211, 212, 215. *See also* Campbell, Alexander; Churches of Christ; Scott, Walter; Stone, Barton

International Churches of Christ, 10, 69, 89, 170

James, Larry, 202

Jinkins, Michael, 22, 216

Johnson, John T., 8–9, 98, 99, 152

Larimore, T. B.
childhood, 49–51
Civil War, 53
controversies, 57–59
death, 60, 62–63, 73, 111, 205
ministry, 55–57, 210
restoration, 68
unity, 56, 65–67, 68, 70, 72, 80, 161, 179
Last Will and Testament of the Spring-field Presbytery (Barton Stone), 79–81, 86, 87, 105, 187
Lexington meeting, 4–6, 8–10, 12, 15, 18, 39, 44, 70–74, 81, 99, 100–104, 111, 112, 187, 221
Lipscomb, David
apocalyptic living, 204–5
Civil War, 159
generosity, 200–203
pacifism, 88
unity, 112, 161, 163
Lowry, Randy, 188

McGary, Austin, 112, 162–65
Memphis meeting, 111–14, 125–29, 137, 146, 164, 165–67
millennial expectations
postmillennialism, 138–41, 143, 152, 203, 205
premillennialism, 67, 88–89, 118, 170
missional values, 28–29, 33, 71, 177, 180, 183–85, 197–98, 206–7, 220
missionary societies, 52, 56–58, 88, 107, 114, 146, 155–61

Money, Royce, 188
Mormons, 50, 149

pacificism, 67, 88, 118, 170
patterns, 64–68, 135, 143
persistence, cultural, 141–44, 146

racism, 11, 30, 116–17, 118–21, 122, 157, 158, 159, 170, 182, 186, 188–89, 200, 201
reason, 12, 40, 49, 51, 71, 78, 94, 97, 98, 174, 177, 193–96, 210, 211, 215
restoration
Campbell, Alexander, 92, 112, 129, 134, 137–44, 172–74, 190–93
Churches of Christ, 49, 106, 129, 134, 141–44, 152, 161, 165–67, 172–74, 183, 185, 190, 192, 204, 205
history, 48, 78
ideals, 33, 49, 54, 117–18, 124–25, 128–29, 138–41, 169, 170–77, 190–93, 201, 210, 215
Larimore, T. B., 68
Stone, Barton, 167, 169, 193
Wallace, Foy E., Jr., 68, 112
Rigdon, Sidney, 149
Rogers, John, 8, 9, 98

Saunders, Landon, 112, 127
Scott, Walter
Holy Spirit, 150–54
preaching, 147, 149–51, 155
restoration, 151–52
Scotland, 144–46
teaching, 147–48, 195
unity, 112, 152

Smith, Raccoon John, 9, 18, 98, 99, 101–3, 158, 168, 187. *See also* Lexington meeting
Stone, Barton
  anti-slavery, 77
  apocalyptic living, 203–5, 209
  Cane Ridge Revival, 75–76, 207
  churches, 8, 9, 47, 48, 50, 69, 74, 80, 96–97, 111, 135, 136, 137, 143, 151, 158
  doctrine, 80, 81, 97–98, 128, 159
  Holy Spirit, 78–79, 97–98, 102, 113–14, 166–69, 208
  hymn, 110, 152
  pacifism, 88
  Presbyterians, 75, 76–77, 79, 81, 195
  racism, 122
  restoration, 167, 169, 193
  unity, 71, 72, 79–81, 86, 87, 99–103, 105–6, 112, 167–69, 187, 205, 208
  See also Lexington meeting
Stone-Campbell Movement, 18, 40, 47, 50–56, 72, 73, 74, 86, 89, 96, 137, 148, 152, 159, 185, 189, 194

Tuggle, Annie C., 118–20, 186

unity
  Campbell, Alexander, 92, 93, 96, 100, 105–6, 111–12, 134, 138–41, 143, 156, 167, 190
  Campbell, Thomas, 71, 84, 86–87, 89–90
  Churches of Christ, 18, 49, 52, 59, 79–80, 86, 87, 105, 111, 159, 161, 176–77, 179, 183, 185–90, 197–99, 204, 210, 215
  history, 18, 37, 48, 49, 52–54, 69, 71

ideals, 26, 63, 73, 79, 103–9
Larimore, T. B., 56, 65–67, 68, 70, 72, 80, 161, 179
Lipscomb, David, 112, 161, 163
Scott, Walter, 112, 152
Smith, Raccoon John, 101–3
Stone, Barton, 71, 72, 79–81, 86, 87, 99–103, 105–6, 112, 167–69, 187, 205, 208

Wallace, Foy E., Jr.
  divisiveness, 66–68, 72–73, 118, 164–65, 179
  pallbearer, 62–63
  racism, 118, 119–20, 122
  restoration, 68, 112
Western Reserve Eclectic Institute (Hiram College), 39–40, 50, 52, 53, 94, 195, 196
Whiteside, R. L., 164
Williams, J. McDonald (Don), 201–2